SIAMESE WHITE

MAURICE COLLIS

Siamese White

faber and faber

This edition first published in 2008
by Faber and Faber Ltd
3 Queen Square, London WC1N 3AU

A CIP record for this book is available from the British Library

ISBN 978-0-571-24086-9

Dedicated
to
the Inhabitants of Mergui
English, Burmese, Indian and Chinese
in happy memory

PREFACE

The text of the present paper covered edition of *Siamese While* is the same as the text in the original edition after correction of a few errors and misprints. The present book also contains, printed as Appendix IV, an account of a long and important letter from Samuel White relating to his family affairs, which was found in the Bath Municipal Library by Mr. Reginald Wright after the publication of the original edition.

MAURICE COLLIS

Maidenhead 1965

NOTE ON THE 1951 UNIFORM EDITION

In preparing this new edition I have, besides making a few additions and corrections, devoted an appendix to the interesting letter written by White in 1683, which was discovered after the publication of the first edition of this book in the Victoria Municipal Library, Bath, by Mr. Reginald Wright, the Director.

MAURICE COLLIS

February 1951

CONTENTS

MAPS

PART ONE
INTRODUCTORY

I. WHITE GOES EAST

This book sets out to give an 'Accompt of the Passages at Mergen', as Samuel White, in the felicitous language of the seventeenth century, called his account of what happened at Mergui in 1687. For the last hundred years Mergui has been a British possession[*] situated in the extreme south of Burma, but at the time of James II it belonged to Siam, being that kingdom's port on the Bay of Bengal. It was then, as a rule, called Mergen by the English. I much prefer the name Mergen to Mergui; it is more euphonious, it carries with it the sound of that remote shore. But, except when I am quoting from the original authorities, I must discard it for the modern name.

I was at Mergui myself for nearly three years in charge of the administration. It is a town of some 20,000 inhabitants, situated on an island of the utmost fertility at the edge of a great archipelago. The inhabitants in general are dressed in Burmese clothes and use the language of that country, though they are of the mixed blood of Burma, Siam, Malaya, China and India, with strains of Portuguese and Arab. It is a place overshadowed by a various past.

While I was resident there, I heard a great deal about the now forgotten Englishmen, Samuel White, Francis Davenport and Captain Anthony Weltden, and of the strange drama of violence and fraud in which they were involved. I made it my business to examine on the spot everything which bore upon their history. On my return to London, I immersed myself in the original sources preserved in the India Office Library. The present narrative is built on these two foundations.

I have cast about in my mind for some method by which I might plunge straight into the deep of the story, but I have not found it. The reader of this book must be content to march at first with an easy step, making his observations as he goes

[*] From 1825 to 1948.

of the relevant facts, which I hope to put before him. In that way I seek to draw him on imperceptibly through enough informative detail to make the drama, when it opens in Part Two, fully intelligible. If he is not by then prepared to relish an exotic clash, wherein the great fundamentals of human conduct arc at issue, I shall have failed in my exposition, and ruined by incompetent writing what I feel to be a singular episode in our history.

Samuel White, the principal personality in this book, was born in England about the year 1650. His childhood was therefore passed in the strong air of the Commonwealth, the most vigorous air which had blown through England. The probability is that he belonged to a Bristol merchant family, which was no supporter of the restoration of the Stuarts in 1660. He was educated as a sailor and merchant. He had an elder brother called George, who in 1670 sailed east and took tip his residence in Madras, where as a free merchant, not on the establishment of the East India Company's factory at that place, he made trade voyages to coast ports and to the Persian Gulf, accompanied by a young assistant of his, aged twenty-two, called Constant Phaulkon, a Greek. Another young man, Francis Davenport, had also gone east on the same ship and found employment with the East India Company, We shall hear a great deal more about Phaulkon and Davenport.

Five years later, in 1675, Samuel White, having secured his mate's certificate, followed his brother to Madras on board the East India Company's ship *Loyal Subject* (Captain Good-lad). He was about twenty-five years of age. There is a curious irony in the association of these two names with him at the beginning of his Career, for at the end of it there was much debate whether he was a loyal subject or an 'ill man'.

On board the ship was a certain Mary Povey, who was going out with other women, all of whom were engaged to marry English residents at Madras. Mary Povey was destined for a Mr. Jearsey, who was probably the younger brother of

William Jearsey, a noted adventurer. White fell in love with her during the voyage. From what we know of him later, he had a vehement way. She returned his love, though nothing was settled on board ship. On landing, against her heart, she went to Jearsey's house. But the more she saw of Jearsey, the more she thought of White. Suddenly one day she returned Jearsey his presents, left his house and was married to White by the French Catholic priest, as the English minister refused to do it.

In this brisk and romantic style Samuel White began his career in the East. Before he met Mary Povey, it does not seem that he intended to stay in India. His voyage may have been undertaken in connection with the family business or for educative purposes. The Bristol merchants frequently sent their sons on such a cruise early in their career. It made them more useful in the office afterwards. But now that he was married, White decided to remain in Madras. To do this, he had to obtain the sanction of the President and council of the factory and pay the sum of £100. That was a large sum in those days, representing, at a moderate estimate, £500 in present values. The fact that he was able to find it confirms the view that he came of substantial family. The cash was actually paid by Captain Goodlad, guarantees being given that the captain would be repaid by White's family as soon as the *Loyal Subject* returned to England. When the formalities were complied with. White came on to the books of the East India Company as a pilot on the establishment of Fort St. George, Madras.

II. MADRAS-ON-SEA

In 1676 Madras was the headquarters of the East India Company's trading establishments on the Bay of Bengal. There were several of these, such as Masulipatam and Hugli, but Madras was far the largest and strongest. It consisted of the fort, called St. George, and the native town with its fields.

It was an attractive-looking place and there are some excellent contemporary descriptions. Dampier in his *New Voyage* gives an idea of its striking appearance:

'I was much pleased with the beautiful prospect this place makes off at sea. For it stands on a plain Sandy spot of ground close to the shore, the sea sometimes washing its Walls, which are of Stone and high, with Half Moons and Flankers and a great many guns mounted on the battlements; so that what with the Walls and Fine Buildings within the Fort, the large town of Maderas without it, the Pyramids of the English Tombs, Houses and Gardens adjacent, and the variety of fine trees scatter'd up and down, it makes as agreeable a Landskip as I have any where seen,'

We may be sure that, after eight months or so at sea on a 500-ton ship, Samuel White and Mary Povey, in their then state of mind, will have found it enchanting.

There was no harbour at Madras, no mole of any kind. Ships had to anchor in the open roadstead and landing was in boats on to the beach. A Doctor John Fryer, who was there two years before White, wrote of how his boar ran through the breakers and how he was carried ashore upon the shoulders of the Indians to the 'scalding sand', which was so dazzling that he hastened to enter the fort through the water-gate. Describing what he saw inside, he says: 'The streets are sweet and clean, ranked with fine Mansions . . . rows of Trees before their doors whose Italian Porticos make no ordinary conveyance into their Houses built of Brick and Stone.'

Continuing his promenade—and we may well suppose that

White saw the same when he landed—he noticed the garrison, a very few English soldiers with some 600 Portuguese of half blood or less, the remains of the Portuguese empire of the previous century, masterless men, who were neither Indians nor Europeans, but whose impulse was to throw in their lot with the white.

Doctor Fryer passed the President's house, those of his council, the mint and the courts. The state, in which lived the President, was remarkable; 'He never goes abroad without Fifes, Drums, Trumpets, and a Flag with two Balls on a Red Field; accompanied by his Council and Factors on Horseback, with their Ladies in Palenkeens . . .'

Leaving the fort by the north gate, a wide parade was crossed into the Black Town, which was no less interesting, with its market, wherein for the first time he saw jasmin and lotus, and where fruits in abundance—guavas, pomegranates, plantains—were for sale. There were 40,000 black Hindus, he estimated, and some few Mahomcdans, going about their business, contented to be safe under the flag of St. George.

Yet there was another side. Dampier's phrase 'the Pyramids of the English Tombs' gives pause. The English had not yet learnt the art of living safely in the tropics. The churchyard was full. The survivors made money, but they had to hurry. It was a great risk to stay out for more than ten years, for there were no hill stations, nor was there possibility of a change home. In January or February, when White landed, the climate was at its best. 'It has', says Thomas Bowrey, another traveller of the period, 'full benefit of all sea breezes . . . but in May and June . . . it is something sulphurous.'

White's brother, George, was not in Madras at the moment. He had gone on business to Ayudhya, the capital of Siam. But his wife was there and we may assume that Samuel stayed at her house, one of those mansions in the fort. But before carrying the narrative any further, I must invite the reader to consider the meaning of this fort, this organized community of Englishmen on the Indian coast. What did the East India Company amount to in 1676?

III. THE COMPANY

To understand White's subsequent history one must know what was the legal position of the East India Company at this date, it was this. By a series of charters Elizabeth and the Stuarts had set it up under their royal prerogative. It had no statutory existence, Its legality depended upon the inherent right of the king to make such a grant on his own motion. In the course of his charter granted in 1661, Charles II had said:

'We of our ample and abundant Grace have granted the Company of Merchants Trading in the East Indies that they and their Successors shall forever hereafter have the whole intire and only trade and the whole intire and only liberty, use and privilege of trading to the East Indies, And all other our Subjects we prohibit to visit or trade in the East Indies by virtue of our Prerogative Royal.'

This is plain enough. No one outside the Company could trade in India or the Far East. Those enormous areas of the world were reserved for one company. Nor was that company of the kind a merchant could join by paying an entrance fee and on satisfying its committee that he was a proper person. It was a joint-stock company; no one could be a member who did not hold a capital share. But its shares, as a rule, were not on the market. It was impossible for the ordinary merchant to take them up. They were all held by a limited clique, whose policy it was, with the assistance of the king's grace, to keep the profits of a wonderful monopoly for itself.

For the bestowal of his grace the king had substantial consideration. It has been calculated that the total value of loans and presents of cash received by Charles from the Company between 1660 and 1684 was £324,150, which represents a million and a half of our money at least. As he was impecunious, this amounted to a pleasant douceur. In addition, the Company gave him large presents of plate, and they knew how to make an impression at court. As Macaulay put it: 'Ministers, mistresses, priests were kept in good humour by presents of shawls and silks, bird's nests and attar of roses, bulses of diamonds and bags of guineas.'

The Company was an extreme example of a monopoly and a highly lucrative one, for over a long course of years its dividends averaged 22 per cent,

It was argued in its defence that no other system could have been successful. The dangerous state of the eastern seas, the greed and treachery of oriental governments, the brutality and strength of the Dutch, made individual trading impossible. A strong company, with the king behind it, organised in London under a court of directors and in the East under councils in settlements on land, sometimes fortified, was the only kind of organization able to cope with the difficulties and to make profits. 'A loose and general trade would be the Ruin of the whole,' as James II observed in his charter,

But the English have never been a docile race. They loathed royal monopolies. The rising mercantile class was not impressed by the arguments in favour of the Company. People were very poor in England at that time. They had seen with envy the enormous profits made overseas by the Spaniards, the Portuguese and the Dutch. When, thanks to the intrepidity of their explorers and seamen, their chance of riches seemed at hand, they were excluded by this monstrous

Company. Everything free and adventurous in that young community was outraged.

It maddened them to see a few favoured merchants making fortunes. In 1675 the East India Company's stock was valued at £1,700,000 and it was said that forty persons owned the majority of the shares. It was widely asserted that the king had no right to prevent his subjects trading where they willed, that his prerogative gave him no power to order the confiscation of a merchant's cargo on the ground that he was not a member of a particular company. The monopoly seemed a contradiction of Magna Carta, of the whole course of English constitutional history, of the struggle of the people to limit the king's prerogative by Parliament.

Well, in England there are the law courts, the judges, with their record of independence, the glory of the island. The question came before them in various forms. What was regarded as the final test case was brought in 1683, when the East India Company prosecuted a man called Sandys for poaching on their preserves. As luck would have it, Judge Jeffreys was then Lord Chief Justice of England, His Lordship, after a judgment in his usual provocative style, said in conclusion: 'Upon the whole matter I am of the same opinion as my brothers; and do conceive that that grant to the plaintiffs of the sole trade of the Indies, exclusive of others, is a good grant and that the action is well brought. And therefore let the plaintiff take his judgment.'

As Jeffreys had made himself notorious in his support of the Stuarts, whose popularity was waning, the free merchants felt that Ms finding for the prerogative was what might have been expected. Unfortunately Jeffreys was a very clever man, and the reasons he advanced in the body of his j udgment in support of the king's power to grant monopolies outside, as opposed to inside, the realm, were at the moment unanswerable.

But the English, in the days when they were setting out to found their world commerce, had not the same respect for law which they developed later. The courts might support the East India Company's charter, but that did not deter adventurous merchants from doing their utmost to break down the monopoly, From the early days of the seventeenth century there had always been men who traded privately in the East Indies, Under the later Stuarts they increased in numbers and importance. They called themselves free merchants, but the Company called them interlopers.

IV. CAPTAIN ALLEY AND CO.

Now I have already pointed out that George White, Samuel's elder brother, though not a member of the Madras establishment, was trading on that coast and as far as the Persian Gulf. He was therefore, strictly speaking, an interloper. But it is curious to observe that he was apparently on good terms with the Madras authorities, Under their charter they had the power of seizing interloping ships with their cargoes and of imprisoning their owners or taking surety from them in £1,000. As they had done none of these things to George White, It must be assumed that they had a private arrangement with him.

It is of importance to examine this question, in view of what follows. The kind of interloper, to whom there was the greatest objection, was the London merchant who fitted out a ship from England, bought in Indian markets the commodities in which the Company also traded, and who then returned to England, where he sold his cargo in competition with the Company's goods, and at a cut price. There was less objection to the merchant of George White's type, who did not sell in the English market but made his money by

exchange of commodities in the East itself. This was what they
called the coast trade. The London merchants of the Company did not go in for that kind of trade. As a Company, they
could not make it pay. The profits were normal trading profits, not the huge margins shown by exchange with England.
And they would have had to enter into competition with
Indian merchants, who managed the coast trade and who
would have squeezed them out by lowering their prices, had
they been annoyed by so serious a rival.

The Company, therefore, was indulgent to coast interlopers, if they behaved themselves in other ways. Such activity
kept them away from the main trade. But there was another
strong reason for complacence. The servants of the Company
in the East were allowed to engage in private commerce.
From the President of the council himself down to the last
joined apprentice, they all sought to make a fortune. It was in
the coast trade that this could most easily be managed. They
did not scruple to go into partnership with the interlopers.
The arrival of an interloping ship in, say, Madras was often a
happy moment. As private individuals the Company, represented by its servants in the East, was heart and soul with the
amenable interloper. The following extracts from William
Hedges's Diary show the type of the popular free merchant.
Captain Alley, evidently a great boy in the opinion of the
Hugli factors, was Samuel White's intimate friend.

'*Sept.* 26, 1683. Capt. Alley came up to Hugly in his Barge,
rowed with English Marines in costs with Badges, and 4
Musicians. He put himself into a great Equipage, like an
Agent, and took about 70 or 80 Peons to wait on him.'

When he went to call on the Mogul official in charge of the
locality, he was: 'habitted in scarlet richly laced. Ten Englishmen in Blue Capps and Coats edged with Red, all armed with
Blunderbusses, went before his pallankeen, 80 Peons before
them, and 4 Musicians playing on the Weights, with 2
Flaggs before him.'

Captain Alley knew that you are much more likely to get a concession If you are well dressed. He got his, whatever it was, and a few days later we find him being entertained to dinner on board one of the Company's ships, his host and some of the guests being servants of the Company: '*Nov.* 13. This day Capt. Alley dyned aboard Capt. Lake of the *Pru dent Mary*, with Honor, Clerke, and divers Interlopers, making great mirth and jollity by firing guns all the afternoon.'

No doubt they were congratulating him on a deal in which they all had some share. Lake went so far as to say that 'if he did not like the Company's employment that voyage, he would turn interloper the next'. Poor fellow, he came to a bad end, dying three years later in a Siamese prison,

But there were other kinds of interlopers, men who were so mean that not only did they give impecunious factors no share, but their way of business was such as to harm them. They thought nothing of winning the favour of oriental princes or governors by suggesting to them ways of squeezing the Company's servants, or they ran in competition with these, securing concessions by higher bribes. Such interlopers were exceedingly unpopular, officially and unofficially, and ranked with men who sailed from England, returning with cargoes to undersell the shareholders.

There was still another class. As eastern seas were unpoliced by any power, for none of the kings or princes possessed an effective fleet, rich merchantmen were a temptation. They all carried a few guns, it is true, but they were no match for a well-armed ship. Some interlopers saw their chance in this and turned pirate. Others of a like desperate sort, but disinclined for a fight with their own countrymen, became filibusters and sacked coast villages or the ports of island rajahs. A certain John Hand is often cited as an example of this type. in 1683 he cleared his ship, the *Bristol*, from London with papers for Lisbon and Brazil, On arrival at Madeira, he called the officers and crew aft and informed them that he was going to the East Indies, and not for trade only. His meaning was plain and some of his men protested, but as Hand was 'a mighty passionate man' their objections were drowned in his strong language. They all rounded the Cape, once in eastern waters he turned plain pirate, adding to his armed decks the original touch of a block, beside which lay conveniently the carpenter's axe. To this gear the attention of native pilots, seized to steer him into unfortified island ports, was invariably directed. Leaping ashore one day to plunder and burn a town in Sumatra, with a cocked pistol in his pocket, he blew his thigh to bits and died there. The Company disliked men like Hand. They gave the whites a bad name with the natives.

This was the world into which Samuel White had arrived. The most junior member of the Madras establishment of the East India Company, he saw his brother a successful interloper of the kind tolerated by his employers. He himself had been given the appointment of pilot. His pay was probably very small. On first arrival apprentices in the office only earned £5 a year. After five years that was raised to £10. Factors only received £20. Allowing that board-and-lodging was free and that these figures should be multiplied at least by five to give modern equivalents, it was still poor pay. We cannot suppose that White began on more than £10. Elihu Yale, afterwards to be President and White's greatest enemy, a man who made an enormous fortune in private trade and eventually founded Yale college, now Yale University, was then a senior Madras apprentice on £10. But there was no question of exiling one-self for that income. Some line of trade had so be taken up at once. As pilot, steering Company ships into the various ports in the bay, where they collected their cargo before sailing for home, no doubt there would be opportunities. But it seemed to White that his best course was to get his brother, George, to give him a start.

Shortly after his arrival in Madras, Mrs. George White received a letter from her husband, in which he asked her to join him in Ayudhya. She sailed for Siam on 20th May 1676. It may be taken as certain that Samuel sent his brother messages by her and a letter.

Before describing what resulted, there are some further points relating to the position of affairs in the East at this date, which I must inflict upon the reader.

V. TRADE AND SECURITY

Mention has been made of the fort at Madras. To the modern ear this suggests that the Company's was an armed trade, that it had designs upon India. Such is an anticipation. In the sixteen-seventies the Company was run as far as possible on commercial lines. The fort at Madras was like the few guns carried on the merchantmen—only for defence. Sir Josiah Childe, President of the court of directors at this period, has a sentence in one of his despatches to India which sums up the position:

'Our business is only trade and security, not conquest, which the Dutch aimed at, (but) we dare not trade boldly nor leave great stocks, where we have not the security of a fort.'

The sort of danger to which the Madras settlement was exposed may be illustrated by a quotation from Dominic Navarette, who introduces his description of Madras in 1670 with these words: 'When we came to this place, we found it beseig'd by the King of Golconda's army, but without his orders; their design was to exact something from the English, but they were disappointed.'

Madras was within the dominions of the second most important kingdom in India, namely Golconda, But the administration of that king, who was a Mahomedan, did not extend to the southern end, where Madras lay. That part was in the hands of Hindu feudal barons. The Company had permission from the king to fortify Madras, because he knew that the feudal barons, over whom he had imperfect control, were dangerous.

This suggests the precarious position of the Company at Madras. Licensed to trade by a Mahomedan ruler, it was exposed to the attack of his Hindu vassals.

Nearer the capital of Golconda there were English agencies at the ports of Masulipatam and Madapollam. These were out of reach of the feudal barons. Law and order were preserved by the Moslem administration. There was no need of fortification. But the officials were very corrupt and oppressive.

Finally, at the head of the Bay of Bengal, there was another agency at Hugli, in the region of the present city of Calcutta. This was in the empire of Aurangzebe the Mogul, the greatest prince in India, indeed at that time probably the greatest prince on earth, after the Emperor of China, K'ang Hsi of the Ta Ch'ing.

Both Golconda and the Mogul could have thrown the Company into the sea at any time, yet the shareholders in London were satisfied with this position. A proposal at a general meeting to increase the garrisons or send out warships had no chance of passing, The directors were adamant against overhead charges of the kind. Dividends were what they looked for, It was a private company, not a national venture. Even the moderate bills for keeping the fortifications in repair were subject to criticism and were passed with difficulty. Tactful attention to business was the Company's motto,

I mention these facts for a good reason. Had the Company at this date been a national venture backed by soldiers and ships, Samuel White could never have made himself master for a time of the Bay of Bengal, as he was fated to do.

The scene now shafts to the other side of the bay, to Siam, the coast of which lay opposite to Madras.

VI. ACROSS THE BAY

M rs. George White, reaching Siam safely later in this year 1676, joined her husband at Ayudhya, Some months later Samuel White received an invitation to stay with them.

To-day a traveller from Madras to the Siamese capital would go by ship via the Straits of Malacca, a journey of three thousand miles, equivalent to one from Liverpool to New York. But in the seventeenth century there was an alternative route, one by ship straight across the bay to Mergui on the west coast of Siam, a distance of twelve hundred miles, and thence by river and road to Ayudhya, This occupied about a month, three weeks to cross the bay and ten days or so for the land section. The route by the Straits of Malacca was also used, but it might take six months, if winds were unfavourable.

Travellers from India as a rule chose the shorter route. White, in accepting his brother's invitation, decided to go that way, and early in the following year, 1677, he crossed the bay on some ship with a cargo for Mergui, and proceeded overland to the capital. Before following Mm there, I propose to give some description of the approach to Mergui, of its significance as a port and of the nature of the overland journey.

There exists an old Admiralty chart of Mergui and the archipelago. It dates from the early years of the eighteenth century and represents the knowledge acquired during White's time. The coast of Siam is shown under the name of Tenasaty (now called Tenasserim), the name of the province. The town of Mergui is also called Tenasary on the chart, though the actual town of that name was situated forty-five miles up the river, the mouth of which is marked immediately south of Mergui.

The first island of the archipelago sighted by a ship beating across from Madras on the N. E. wind of the early part of the year was the Tenasany island shown in the chart. It is about eighty miles from Mergui. I have visited this island and, as it has importance later in the narrative, and is moreover characteristic of the archipelago, I will attempt a description.

On its western side it rises sharply from rocks to some eight hundred feet, thickly wooded down to high water mark. This is no pleasant wood of great trees and glades, but an impenetrable undergrowth from which forest trunks stand up white against the greenery. Under the pale blue sky and intense sun, which accompany the N. E. wind, the island has a certain forlorn beauty. The white breakers at its foot and the vivid green suggests a freshness which is not there, for the temperature hardly falls below 75°F.

A little west of the north point is a narrow bay, which sinkt into the island and is as sheltered from all winds as a loch. As the inner end of this cove is a white strand, with five fathoms of clear water close to the edge. By the side of it there flows down from the mountain a perennial stream. Between the sand and where the slope begins, stretches a small mangrove swarnp, in which crawl iguanas and mudfish. The forest is full of wild pig and monkeys. The place is tin inhabited and has always been so, though on its fertile soil fruits and hill rice could be grown.

This lonely spot, with its fresh water and sheltered anchorage, was a rendezvous for pirates. The Bay of Bengal is so huge a sea that its pirates—and there were pirates then on all seas—congregated only at points by which merchantmen had to pass when making port. As Tenasserim island lay on the main approach to Mer gui, the cove I have described was a favourite waiting place.

Besides occasional pirates, the Mergui archipelago was well known as the lair of certain professional freebooters called Saleeters, men of a race distinct from those who lived on the mainland. They seem to have been very formidable and were great seamen. Of them, Bowrey, in the book already quoted, writes in 1675:

'The Saleeters are absolute Piratts and are often cruiseinge about Janselone[1] and Pullo Sambelon Isles near this shore. They arc subject to no manner of Government and have many cunniuge places to hide themselves and theire men of warre Prows in upon the Maine of the Malay shore.'

The cove on Tenasserim island was such a cunning place, and I know two others. The Saleeters, in boats of a peculiar build, which could weather the roughest sea, had no settled abode. They moved from place to place like gypsies, encamping on the islands but never cultivating the soil. Piracy and fishing for pearls were their only means of support. They infested the routes through the archipelago, like outlaws on a heath over which pass roads to a capital.

Captain Hamilton, another writer of the day, says of them:

'Between Mer gee and Jonkcelaon there are several good harbours for shipping, but the sea coast is very thin of inhabitants, because there are great numbers of Freebooters, Called Saleiters, who inhabit islands along the sea coast and they both rob and take people for slaves and transport them for Atchen and there make sale of them and Jonkcelaon often feels the Weight of their Depredations.'

It is a very curious fact that these sea gypsies still exist in the archipelago, under the name of Salons, but with the suppression of piracy, which came in the nineteenth century, when the English dominated the bay, their warlike manner of life was interrupted. This loss of a traditional occupation broke their spirit, for they are now a timid, slinking race, very poor, making a precarious livelihood by diving for pearl-shell and collecting ambergris. Like other disheartened people, they have taken to drugs. Opium simulates for them in dream the energy which once drove them against Junkceylon.

[1] Equals Junkceylon, which, with the other islands mentioned, lie at the southern extremity of the archipelago.

The old chart already mentioned shows a course from Tenasary island due east to a channel between Iron island and King island, forty miles away. This piece of sea is more thickly covered with islands than the old map pretends. On all sides are gleaming beaches, wooded heights. King island itself has a range of peaks which rise to nearly three thousand feet. From the upper valleys waterfalls drop to the shore. Some sign of habitation begins. On passing through the channel, called Iron Passage, there now appears what has been concealed by the islands, for about thirty miles ahead is the mainland, a low coast fringed with mangrove, behind which range on range of mountains stand up to seven thousand feet.

The traveller is at last upon that inner water, which leads down to Mergui, still forty miles distant and difficult to find. That is the strangeness of the place. It is tucked in behind further islands on a piece of ground which rises from the mangrove swamp. For a person without a chart, it was easy to miss. in 1568 Cesare dei Fedrici pulled along the coast for eight days, looking for it in the maze of islands, and never found it. His men, rowing in that heat, were sustained by the report that there a wine of the finest quality was cheap.

The course now begins to bear S, E., avoiding the wide belt of shoal-water stretching from the shore. King island is left astern, with its deep bays fringed with the richest fruit gardens in Indo-China. That these existed in White's time is known. The old chart itself is evidence here, for the next island is marked Plantain-tree island, though now it bears another name—Kalagyun, the foreigner's island, and contains fine rubber estates. After another ten miles the ship makes Pataw island, rising some eight hundred feet, the lower part covered with fruit trees, especially duryans, mangosteens and jackfruit. The chart calls it Madramacon, after a strange shrine, named by the people Buddha-makhan, where all religions join on certain days to make offering to a spirit, who concerns himself with the safety of those at sea. This temple lies at the bar and entrance to Mergui harbour. Opposite the island is the town, the water between being the safest anchorage imaginable. 'The Port of Merguy, they say, is the most lovely in all India,' wrote de La Loubère in 1688. The Chevalier was well informed. It has an overwhelming power to delight.

VII. MERGUI

The ports of Indo-China and the islands have changed little with the centuries. Mergui to-day is much the same as in White's time. This is not only true of the scenery. The ridge, the woods of Pataw with their heavy greenery, the shimmering islands farther out—these are naturally the same. But the town itself has changed little. Its thatched and bamboo houses, winding streets, roadside bazaars and monastery stairways are still what they were in the seventeenth century.

The ridge round which the town is clustered is not high, hardly more than one hundred feet, but it rises nearly as steep as a cliff. On the highest point is a Buddhist pagoda, which by its design alone stamps the place as Indo-China, an art-integration distinct from India. In White's day the pagoda was there, and immediately to the south of it on a rather lower part of the ridge, was a large battery. The Deputy Commissioner's house now occupies that site. When I lived there, I found in the garden remains of brick ramparts and some cannon balls.

At the foot of the ridge was a single street. The houses nestled into the steep hillside and looked towards the water of the harbour, which at full tide washed underneath the piles on which they were perched. At low tide there was an expanse of mud and mangrove. Many of these houses had their own jetty, at which lay long, thin boats, the hull made from one piece of wood, a cabin roofed over with thatch occupying the centre. These boats carried sail, and with their racing cut were Capable of ten miles an hour with a good breeze aft.

As the street continued along the harbour face, it began to multiply, where the ground permitted, until at the southern end it had become a block of roads and houses creeping round the ridge and eventually enclosing it up to the northern extremity. The whole was protected by a stockade of earth and bamboo.

In these streets there moved a cosmopolitan crowd, Burmese, Siamese, Chinese, Indian, Malay and European, Though the town was within the kingdom of Siam, it seems that the middle and lower classes were chiefly Burmese. In this connection, the Jesuit, Nicolas Gervaise, a contemporary writer, is quite explicit. He says of the whole province of Tenasserim: 'Its inhabitants, who are fairly numerous, are almost all foreigners. The language of Burma and Ava is still much more in use than Siamese.'

The presence of this Burmese population is explained by infiltration down the coast from the Pegu dominions, and also by the fact that in the twelfth and thirteenth centuries Mergui belonged to Burma. But the official language was Siamese, as were most of the government officials. Yet neither the Burmese nor the Siamese counted for much in the port. As will be explained later on, it was the Mahomedans, chiefly from India, who dominated the commercial situation. If Indian enterprise was the life of the place, the Mongolian inhabitants gave it an air. The atmosphere was Indo-Chinese and Buddhist, animated but polite; the crowd was brightly dressed and clean; Burmese and Siamese men sauntered and idled; the women, stout, downright and handsome, managed the bazaars; Malays, lowering and touchy, flitted by fingering their snaky daggers; and the Chinese, careful and smiling, made their profit.

I have spoken of Europeans in the streets. As a great business centre, Mergui had attracted many white adventurers in the course of two centuries. The Portuguese were the first on the scene, and the church, which they founded, still stands on the side of the ridge facing the harbour. Close by it there live numerous Catholic families, now much intermarried with the Burmese, bearing such names as de Silva and de Castro, and tracing their descent to the explorers and navigators of the sixteenth century. After the Portuguese came Dutch, French and English. Some of these people were what we should call beachcombers to-day. 'There are abundance of S traglers of all nations in Mergee,' wrote one of the Madras establishment in 1686. As we know that there were about sixty English, it may be assumed that the total European population, including the Portuguese, ran into hundreds.

In this matter of intermarriage of Europeans with the indigenous inhabitants, contemporary writers have something interesting to say. Captain Hamilton, from whom we have already quoted, observes:

'The Europeans that trade to Siam accommodate themselves as they do in Pegu with temporary wives, almost on the same conditions too, and it is thought no disgrace to have many temporary Husbands, but rather an honour that they have been beloved by as many different Men.'

De La Loubère, the French ambassador to Siam in 1685, compares the attractions of Siamese and Burmese women, He says:

'There is nothing disreputable about free love in Siamese lower-class opinion, Such love is regarded as a marriage and inconstancy as a divorce. Moreover, Siamese women have naturally such a good opinion of themselves that they do not easily yield to strangers or, at least, do not solicit them. The Burmese women in Siam, as strangers themselves, suit strangers better. Some people are stupid enough to say that they are women of loose character, but the fact is that they want a husband, and when they take a European are faithful to him until he abandons them. If they hive children, far from their reputation suffering, their position is assured, and that their so-called husband is white, redounds further to their reputation. It is argued by sonic observers, who know, that they are more amorous than the Siamese; certainly they are more sprightly and animated. I have heard it generally said throughout the East Indies that the closer a people lives to Burma the more lively and intelligent it is.'

The character of a nation is strangely constant. La Loubère's remarks about Burmese womea might stand to-day.

But though the Burmese were the most attractive among the residents of Mergui, they had not, as I have said, a position comparable to that of the Mahomedans, who were not only rich merchants and shipowners, but who also held some of the high appointments of state, The explanation of this anomaly will bring out Mergui's international significance at this date.

VIII. AN EMPORIUM OF THE COAST TRADE

I pointed out further back that there were two kinds of trade in the East. The first was the exchange of commodities between it and Europe; the second was exchange within the East itself, which was called by Europeans the coast trade. The most important aspect of this was the commerce between India and China, which was managed in the following manner. The Chinese did not navigate direct to India, nor did Indian or Persian vessels go all the way to

China; Siam was the halfway house where they met and exchanged their Commodities. As Mergui was Siam's port on the Bay of Bengal, it was convenient for Indians to go there, rather than to round the Straits of Malacca. Mergui was connected with Ayudhya, the capital, by a land route via Tenasserim. In consequence, dealers lived at Ayudhya, Tenasserim and Mergui, who received from China and Japan goods in demand in India and Persia, or vice versa, and there effected the exchange.

It is true that some Indians navigated the Straits of Malacca to reach Ayudhya, but objections existed to that route. I have said that it was three times as far, and that it took perhaps six times as long to cover, if winds were contrary. Europeans in Siam used to say that it was a more tedious voyage than from India home via the Cape. And it was not safe. There were often more pirates in the Straits than in the Bay, and the Dutch, who attempted to impose a monopoly of trade that way, were inclined to interfere with rival commerce.

For many reasons of this kind the trans-peninsula route via Mergui was favoured, particularly for goods of high value or small bulk, such as silk and porcelain from the Far East and cottons from India.

In White's time the dealers in this trade were Mahomedans from India and Persia, who had settled in Siam. Neither the Siamese nor the Burmese have ever possessed gifts comparable to the Indians for international commerce and navigation. Though the province of Tenasserim was part of Siam, its native inhabitants had left to foreigners the management of this highly lucrative traffic.

The fact was that the trans-peninsula trade had always been handled by outsiders. When the Siamese entered the area in the fourteenth century, the trade was already in existence, and was managed by Hindus, who had originally come from India centuries before at the time of their early migrations eastward. The Siamese turned the Hindu ruling family into the holder of an hereditary vice-royalty, and so recognized their own limitations as international traders. Though an influx of Indo-Chinese races took place, the big merchants remained Hindus.

By 1677, the year of Samuel White's arrival in Mergui, the situation had changed only to this extent, that the Hindu merchants were no longer in the lead, but had been ousted by Mahomedans.

George White, who, as an interloper, was particularly interested in the coast trade, wrote in 1678, a 'Report on the Trade of Siam'. This report confirms what has been argued above, and shows very precisely the importance at that date of Mergui and Tenasserim as an entrepôt. The Mahomedans had worked up the trade with great ability. They controlled flourishing businesses and with their wealth had become so important that they held also the key administrative appointments. Says White: 'This considerable Trade is at present totally engrossed by the Persians and Moors (Indian Mahomedans) who are in Effect Masters of that part of the Country as well as the Commerce.'

He goes on to explain that the Governor of Mergui, the Viceroy of the Province of Tenasserim, and the Governors of all the principal towns on the overland route between Tenasserim and Ayudhya were either Indians or Persians. So high had they risen that the king's first Minister was a Mahomedan. Over a long course of years this man had advanced his co-religionists until they had become an element of great importance in the state.

Samuel White arrived in Siam at a moment when a reaction was setting in at court against the domination of these Mahomedans. Carried on the wave of that reaction, a few years later he will displace them and dominate the trade in their stead.

IX. THE FOREST BELT

We must now accompany White as he makes his way by the overland route to Ayudhya. As no record exists of this, his first journey, I shall describe the way as I have seen it with my own eyes, adding here and there a contemporary account.

The map facing the next page shows the area between Mergui and the Gulf of Siam. The traveller used to engage at Mergui a country boat, which was propelled partly by sail and partly by oar. Starting early on the flood tide he entered the mouth of the Tenasserim river immediately to the south of the town. The first hour or so was depressing as mangrove swamps covered both banks, excluding all view. But in ten miles the mangrove disappeared, the view opened out, villages, rice fields and palm gardens becoming visible.

The map gives the names of numerous villages, all of which existed in White's day? for during my time at Mergui Chinese porcelain and Siamese bronzes of the sixth to the eighteenth century were dug up at each of them. Some of the places were small walled towns, the moats and ramparts of which can still be traced, of these Tonbyaw, which lies about half-way to Tenasserim, was the largest. It was a Mahomedan settlement and its present inhabitants, still Mahomedans, have the appearance of Indians subjected for centuries to an Indo-Chinese environment.

It was at Ton by aw that I came across an object which brought me close to White, One night I was anchored off the village when a man showed me a bottle, which he had found in the mud of the river bank. On examination this proved to be of English manufacture and of seventeenth-century date. It was made of green glass and was of the particular bulbous squat shape associated with Stuart sack bottles of the reign of Charles II. For all I know this bottle may have been White's property. Its period corresponds exactly with his own. As we shall see, he was no teetotaller. He may well have emptied and thrown it there on one of his journeys.[1]

After Tonbyaw the river enters a wooded gorge, which leads after twenty miles to Tenasserim city. This considerable place was built on the triangular piece of ground formed by the confluence of the Little Tenasserim with the main stream. The land side of the triangle was protected by high walls running along the top and slopes of the hills, the other two sides by ramparts standing over the two rivers. The circumference was four miles. As far as this narrative is concerned the city's significance was as follows.

Big boats, even ships if they were warped up, could reach it from Mergui on the flood tide. Eastwards she route towards Ayudhya lay on the Little Tenasserim, a small river hardly affected by the tide and, farther up, interrupted by rapids. Only small boats could navigate it. Tenasserim city, therefore, was the place where passengers and cargoes were transferred from large boats to small. It was a town of middlemen, Carriers, warehouses and agents, in dose contact with the merchants of Mergui. When, says an ocean-going vessel belonging to an English free trader arrived at Mergui, it was a common procedure for the supercargo to go by boat to Tenasserim, collect and pack there what goods he wanted, bringing the cases down in barges, where they were loaded on to his ship.

From Mergui to Tenasserim the journey was agreeable, for the scenery was good, the large boats tolerably comfortable and, rowing with the tide, the rate of progress was reasonable. But eastwards front that city a dangerous section began. It lay past the two little hamlets, shown on the map, to the

[1] Another relic of White or of his companions, which was found buried by the Tenasserim river and was presented to me at the time I lived at Mergui, was a Stuart candlestick of brass, much pitted by its long immersion in mud, I like to think chat by its light Davenport wrestled with White's accounts, See page 103.

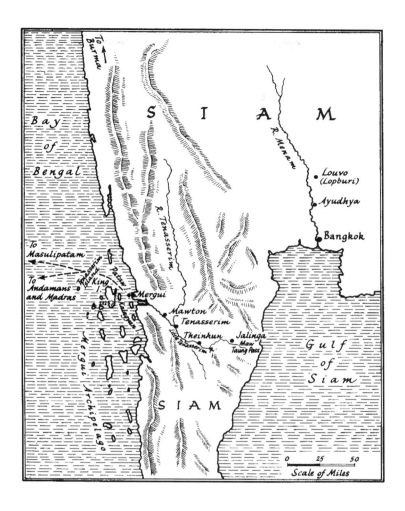

village of Jalinga. The distance was only about forty miles in a straight line, but the journey might take days; in the rains weeks might be consumed paddling against the stream and the rapids. It led through one of the most impenetrable, the loneliest, the most tiger-haunted forests in the world.

The local people, of course, did not mind about mosquitoes, leeches or carnivorous animals. A lonely forest was nothing particular to them. For centuries sturdy boatmen had brought through it cargo after cargo of porcelain, scented woods, silks, calicoes, dyes and copper vessels. But Europeans found the journey detestable.

A number of Preach ecclesiastics had passed that way shortly before White. They were brave, ardent men, intent upon proving to the Siamese the fallacies of Buddhism, but, accustomed to the routine of cloister and Mass in a French country town, they found the strange scene rather intimidating. One of them, Monseigneur de la Mothe Lambert, Bishop of Béryte, has been the subject of a memoir by one of his staff. A few extracts from this will show how the journey appeared to a European of the period, when undertaken during the monsoon.

'Our transport consisted of three boats. Each boat had a crew of three men; a section of it was roofed with thatch. . . . We did our cooking and slept in the boats, for it was too dangerous to go ashore on account of the carnivorous beasts, such as tigers and rhinosceros, and of elephants and wild buffaloes, which teem in the forest stretching away unbroken on both banks of the river.'

The Bishop's biographer then goes on to speak of the swiftness of the current, the foaming rapids, of the coolies wading in the water and dragging the boats round difficult corners or poling for hours and making only a mile. He describes how Monseigneur was nearly drowned: 'The boatmen, unable to make headway against the current, lost control of the boat, which was carried down and dashed to pieces against an up-

rooted tree in midstream. . . . By the mercy of Providence the
Bishop caught a branch and hauled himself up . . . remaining
there for some time surrounded by rushing waters.'

He was rescued, but lose his passport, being obliged to
return to Tenasserim to get a new one and start the terrible
journey all over again. But this was travelling by inexperienced
men, and at the wrong time of the year. Goods were not
transported during the monsoon, which was the close season.
From November to May, when the river was normal, the
passage could be managed with much less trouble.

At Jalinga the river ceased to be navigable. For a traveller
who had made his arrangements a sedan chair was in readiness. Cargo was loaded on carts or porters. A rough track led
away eastwards. After some ten miles you were on the pass,
quite a low elevation, and fifteen miles more carried you to a
road running north along the coast The Bishop, who had no
sedan chair and had to travel in a cart, found the track to the
pass very bad going.

'Our carts afforded us more torture than convenience; in
fact, we were generally obliged to go on foot. They were our
lodging for the night. . . . It was then that the leeches, wrig-
gling in legions from the damp undergrowth, attacked us so
persistently that we could not prevent them sucking our
blood. . . . To keep off the wild beasts, we built a stockade
every night with the cattle and baggage in the centre. . . . We
never passed a night without hearing rhinosceros and, particularly, tiger prowling round us.'

Salt and tobacco juice make leeches let go their hold at
once. The Bishop had no one to tell him this, nor to reassure
him that the rhinoceros does not eat beef or human flesh, a
belief generally held by French travellers at that time.

The journey to-day from Tenasserim across the pass is
exactly the same as it was in White's time. It is not, indeed, so
comfortable, for there are no sedan chairs. I recommend it to
any man who would like the sensation of traversing one of the

last unexplored regions in Asia. No one knows what may be in the jungles extending for hundreds of miles north and south of the track. Besides wild animals and leeches, they reek of malaria. If you lose your way and escape the tigers, the ants will pick your bones. All that is certain enough. But they are also said to contain gold, oil and tin deposits, rare animals such as tapirs, caches of Ming porcelain and pieces of eight,

Taking it all round, Mergui was not too easy a place for the European visitor to enter. On the sea side pirate gypsies gave him pause; eastwards a jungle full of uncatalogued terrors confronted him. Eight times was White to cross the forest, the seventh passage, this time in the monsoon, nearly costing him his life.

At the junction of the track from the pass with the main coast road the country assumed again, a mild and cultivated appearance. The road led first to a small square town, behind a wooden palisade, called Koui; from thence to Preanne, a port on a river mouth, and lastly to Pipili, a large town with brick walls. At either of the two last the traveller engaged a large country boat and, catting off the north-west corner of the Gulf of Siam, came in a couple of days to the mouth of the Menam river, called 'the bar of Siam'. Ayudhya Was fifty miles upstream, but two flood tides carried him easily to the capital.

X. OLD AYUDHYA

The modern traveller is always a little disappointed. Easy communications and European propaganda have levelled the differences between countries. Marvels arc no longer by the roadside. But for White, trudging in his English clothes, or in a palanquin or in a galley, 'This', as

Conrad Says, 'was the East of the ancient navigators, so old, so mysterious, resplendent and sombre, living and unchanged, full of danger and promise.'

The city, which he now saw for the first time, was an integration untouched by European thought and ways, a mart of the fabulous Orient, with an extravagant atmosphere of its own. Fort St. George, Madras, was a piece of England in the shadow, only, of the princes of India; but with Ayudhya the scene closed in; you had arrived at a place entirely unfamiliar, the seat of a strange king, a fantastic court.

For us these eastern corners are mapped and harmless. In our intense sophistication, with our tabulated knowledge of oriental religions and arts, everything we see is a labelled specimen and what princes remain are posed as in a museum. André Gide's observation—'moins le blanc est intelligent, plus le noir lui paraît bête'—is a flattering intellectualism. The intelligent, and we are all that, more than that, find the coloured races stimulating on paper. How titillating often is their approach to some problem of the arts or of metaphysics. With comfortable admiration we look at them as through the glass of our cabinets.

But this was not White's approach. He had arrived at a living place full of danger and promise. Interesting or not, the King of Siam was a real person of great power. To obtain his ear, win the tolerance of his entourage, was to grasp fortune.

There is a Dutch painting of Ayudhya, now in the Rijksmuseum, which shows the city as White Saw it. After the savage loneliness of the journey, it was a surprising place upon which to come suddenly. The directors of the East India Company in 1617 had stated it to have been 'as great a city as London'. Monsieur Véret, the manager of the French Company, meeting the rather disreputable but witty Abbé de Choisy at the bar of Siam in 1685, told that nobleman that it was larger than Paris, with poor houses, magnificent pagodas, an admirable river, a huge population and with countless

boats. Schouten, the Dutchman, writing forty-eight years earlier, gave its circumference as six miles, and said that the walk
were of stone, the main streets broad and straight on a regular
plan, with canals running down one side; that the king's palace was like a town apart, great and magnificent, many of its
buildings and towers being entirely gilded. The Abbé de
Choisy later wrote his own impression:

'We went for a walk outside the town. I stood frequently
in admiration of the strong great city, seated upon an island
round which flowed a river three times the size of the Seine.
There rode ships from France, England, Holland, China and
Japan, while innumerable boats and gilded barges rowed by
sixty men plied to and fro. No less extraordinary were the
camps or villages outside the walls inhabited by the different
nations who came trading there, with all the wooden houses
standing on posts over the water, the bulls, cows and pigs on
dry land. The streets, stretching out of sight, are alleys of clear
running water. Under the great green trees and. in the little
houses crowd the people, Beyond these camps of the nations
are the wide rice fields. The horizon is tall trees, above which
are visible the sparkling towers and pyramids of the pagodas.
I do not know whether I have conveyed to you the impression of a beautiful view, but certainly I myself have never
seen a lovelier.'

Exploring still further one day, the Abbé had a glimpse of
the Siamese at home: 'We rowed down the long canals under
the green of the trees while the birds sang, and passed between
rows of wooden houses perched on posts, very shabby-look-
ing outside, but, as we were to find, clean within. We entered
one of them prepared to see the peasants in rags, but all was
spick and span, the floor covered with mats, Japanese coffers
and screens everywhere. Hardly inside the door, they offered
us tea in porcelain cups.'

So the Abbé, one of Louis XIV's courtiers. What he was
looking at was the distributed dividend of the coast trade. The

Chinese and Japanese brought to Ayudhya silk, tea, porcelain, quicksilver and copper-bronze vessels, taking in exchange such articles as scented woods, pepper, hides and birds' nests. The far-eastern products were largely sold to dealers for transport via Mergui to Golconda and the Persian Gulf. The enterprise of Mahomcdan merchants had made Ayudhya a great centre for the exchange of goods between China and India. They had also found a market for the Siamese home products. As a result, even the common people were comfortably off, far better provided than the ragged starving peasantry of Europe.

At the back of this picture of commercial prosperity sat the lord of it all, King Phra Narai, in his palace, a Forbidden City, surrounded by a triple wall, giving audience to his council of Mandarins, or listening to his Brahmin astrologers. His state was modest compared with that of his contemporary, K'ang Hsi of the Ta Ch'ing, fabulous in his jade pavilions, or of Aurangzebe and his paladins, but he was sumptuous enough with his seraglio, some of the women bought in Georgia, with his Amazons and his Tartar guard. He was exhibited to the public gaze by court etiquette as the lord of slaves. In the panelled audience chamber of the palace, bright with gilding and lacquer, he made his appearance, not in the manner of   Western princes, or even of the Mogul, seated upon a throne and addressing his inferiors like a gentleman, but elevated mysteriously to suggest godhead. The scene was often described by contemporary travellers. Before the audience ministers and petitioners enter, crouching. The apartment is empty. At the end wall stand three umbrellas, tapering to the roof in seven, in nine tiers. Beneath the central umbrella is a curtained window. The ministers take a prostrate attitude on knees and elbows, face downwards upon the floor, their hands stretched forward in the form of a lotus bud. Music sounds and the curtain before the window is drawn aside, disclosing the king, framed over his worshipping slaves like a Boddhisattva floating above the earth. His face is composed and gracious; as far as possible he has put off the materialistic form of a man and has become in his costume, the lines of which writhe up like flames, the centre of an architectural composition, a stylization of the human shape conveying distance and divinity. Introducing the business of the occasion, the chief mandarin begins: 'Since the Divine Word has seen fit to descend upon the King's slave, who is but filth and dust, that person has the temerity to petition . . .' In this ritual the exchange of statements proceeds, till the council listening, if possible more abjectly, the Divine Word pronounces. At that, music sounds again, the curtain is drawn, the king disappears.

Or again, the king would go out. The Abbé de Choisy was the witness of one of his promenades and has described it in these words:

'At four o'clock in the afternoon the King left the palace on Ms elephant. All the principal streets were lined with Foot and Horse Guards. Those on foot were accoutred in helmet and cuirass and held a gilded shield; the Horse Guards, Indian Mahomedans, were well mounted and were magnificent-looking men. Mandarins went before and behind the King, each wearing his hat of ceremony, shaped like a pyramid, and encircled with rings of gold according to his grade. I assure you that the cortège had a royal air and was very strange. I feel that Pharaoh on the banks of the Nile used to parade in the same splendour.'

When the king went thus in procession through the capital, the fiction of divinity and unapproachableness was still maintained, for the people were not allowed in the streets, were not allowed even to watch from their windows. Bamboo screens were erected in front of the houses and through the interstices of these peeped the crowd, as at an ineffable mystery.

That was how the government of Slam appeared from without, but within there was every convolution which intrigue could devise. As in all autocracies, the mandarins who had the king's car were the real masters, They maintained the ritual to hedge him from their rivals.

XI. WHITE MEETS PHAULKON

Making his way down one of the canals, White landed at his brother's house. The reader will recall that George White was associated with a Greek called Constant Phaulkon, who had come out to the East with him seven years before. To this remarkable person Samuel was now introduced.

By one who had met him, Phaulkon has been described as a man of medium height, full of fire, with something dark and unhappy about the expression of his face, but nevertheless agreeable to talk to, and, when he had a mind, of the most engaging manners. He possessed a remarkable breadth of outlook and, without being well-read, seemed to know everything, for his conversation was sparkling and he was a great linguist.

His origins were obscure. Emerging from the underworld of the Levant, he went to England in his teens, pressed by a vague ambition to make his fortune. He was one of those rare and fascinating youths who mature early and by their brilliance, industry and charm captivate all who meet them. Though of formidable genius, such persons do not at first alarm, for they combine usefulness with servility, but when their talents and guile have lifted them into power they arouse a terrified loathing in the hearts of their opponents.

By one of those strange chances, which make history, George White had met Phaulkon in England and engaged him as his assistant. He was now twenty-nine years of age, which for men of his type is fully mature. He had had five years' experience of the coast trade towards Persia and, latterly, two years at the Siamese capital. Helping his patron, George White, to make a fortune, he himself had laid by a substantial sum of money. But his ambitions were immense. He had taken stock of the position of affairs in Siam and felt that his time was coming. It was the country, it was the moment, for an adventurer.

When White and Phaulkon met, they warmed to each other. White was twenty-seven, two years Phaulkon's junior. There was a certain resemblance between them. Both of them were brave and crafty; they both regarded the East as their prey. Entirely unscrupulous, they differed more in degree than in kind. White had a sense of actuality, of what could be done in certain circumstances. He wanted money, not glory. Phaulkon had the unbridled imagination of genius. He saw himself something far more extraordinary than a rich man. But he had as yet taken no part in public affairs. His activities had been confined to trade. It was as a man of business that he was then considered to have great ability. Business ability it was which would bring him into prominence, for important problems confronting Siam at the moment were business problems.

In his brother's house, with such a man as Phaulkon to speak to, White had every opportunity of appraising the situation. It was exceedingly complicated, In a book of this kind I can do no more than indicate the main elements, so that the preposition which George White and Phaulkon were about to make may be intelligible.

The reader will recall the general layout of affairs in 1677. The East India Company, as a company, was concerned chiefly with the purchase of cotton goods in India and their sale in England. As individuals, its members in the Bay of Bengal were interested in the coast trade to Siam, That trade was managed by Mahomedans and shared by interloping Englishmen, who assisted in some cases the Company's employees to make money in it privately.

Yet this was not the whole picture. For many years the Company had considered that the Siamese trade was not altogether a coast trade. The Japanese came to Ayudhya and they brought articles which were saleable in England at a profit. But they dealt with the Dutch and the Mahomedans. Though the Company had maintained agents in Ayudhya off and on from the beginning of the century, they had never been able to get into the Japanese trade. This was due to the opposition of the Dutch, who, with their headquarters in Java and a fine factory with twenty-five European assistants in Ayudhya, kept out all intruders. They were so strong that thirteen years before Samuel White's visit they had lain in their ships at the bar of Siam, and by a blockade had forced the king to give them a monopoly of those items in the Japan trade which interested them. In addition, they found it worth their while to join in the coast trade to the extent of importing goods into Sum via the Straits of Malacca.

This threat to Siam's independence worried the king and his advisers. The Dutch were steadily swallowing the island kings of Java and Sumatra, They might swallow Siam.

For a number of years the direction of Siamese commercial affairs had been in the hands of a minister, called, in the English letters of the period, Ophra Synnoratt. He was a Mahomedan and it was he who had assisted his co-religionists on the Mergui overland route, giving them more concessions and administrative posts than they had ever enjoyed before. He justified this to the king and to the Siamese mandarinate on the ground that their prosperity would balance the Dutch menace. In point of fact, the policy was partly successful, for the Dutch found they could not compete with the Mahomedan traders. Though the Indians had to unload at Mergui and handle their goods across the peninsula, they were able to undersell the Dutch in Ayudhya, though the latter had shipped straight from India. But there was a growing objection to the Mahomedan ascendancy in spite of their check to the Dutch. The latter were still strong enough in ships to dominate the gulf. The Mahomedans could do nothing on the sea to protect Ayudhya. Moreover, they were alleged to be disloyal to the crown and to have themselves designs of seizing the country. Finally, it was said that they were dishonest on a grand scale and that the king did not get his rightful dues.

This Ophra Synnoratt died about the time of White's visit. His death synchronized with a reaction against Indian dominance. His place was taken by a Siamese mandarin. The king, looking round for assistance in his weakness, saw in a new light the agents of the East India Company, who had long been resident, as I have said, in Siam, but who had made little headway. He began to smile upon them, offering better land for their factory, free timber for building, tin concessions, promising to buy English broadcloth (obviously a useless article in a permanent temperature of 75° to 90°F.), making it clear that if they worked up their position they would be given a share in the Japan trade. He desired chat there should be less of the petty trader about them and more of the national venture. He suggested that they might send him from England gunners and engineers.

The little men representing the Company at Ayudhya were dazzled. They wrote home: 'This King from our arrival to the present hath treated us with a civility beyond expectation, and his respects for your honours are such that should we seek a Comparison to express it this side of England, we should be to seek.'

In the calmer atmosphere of London the directors were not so optimistic. They did not see exactly where the profit was coming from, nor had they the smallest intention of spending money on engineers and gangers. It was to be plain business and modest business at that. But they replied: 'Because you apprehend that it may be a means to introduce a trade to Japan and that the King is so desirous of a trade with us . . . we have resolved to make an essay.'

They sent out £5,000 worth of woollen manufactures.

Now, this policy to encourage the East India Company against the Dutch and the Mahomcdans suited George White and his free-trading friends as much as it delighted the factors at Madras. It meant, if successful, that the interlopers, and the factors in their private capacity, would make fortunes from the coast trade. If the Company, as such, was strengthened enough from home to take and work the concessions which the king was ready to give it, then all the English in Ayudhya. even the hangers-on and the beachcombers, were in for a good time.

This was the inside information which George White was able to give his brother. There is little doubt that he and Phaulkon at this stage of Samuel's enlightenment must have put to him proposals which may be summarized in the following way:

'You must know that the coast trade is of two kinds, the merchants' trade and the royal monopoly trade, for the king has a sole right to the primary acquisition and sale of elephants, saltpetre, tin, lead, betel nuts, and scented woods. A merchant who desires to sell in Siam or export to India any of these goods must buy them from the king on pain of death.

'Moreover, the king himself directly exports these articles on his own ships from Mergui. As you know, the royal ships have been officered and manned heretofore by Indians. But with the present policy of encouraging the Company and Englishmen generally, the king wants English captains for his merchantmen. He thinks Englishmen will be more honest, or less cunning, or at least less able, as having fewer confederates, to deceive him. They are also better seamen, and his ships will be held in greater respect.

'Phaulkon and I could get you such an appointment. I need

not enlarge upon the prospects. As captain of one of his majesty's ships with cargoes for Golconda, you would be in a very favoured position. Besides a much larger salary than you draw at present, you would have room on board your ship for cargoes of your own and you would be able to dispense patronage to your countrymen in the Company, assisting them in their private trade for a consideration. Such an appointment means joining the service of the King of Siam, or rather being lent to that service by your masters. But they, you may be sure, will agree, for it will be greatly to their advantage to have you in place of an Indian captain, I am told that the king proposes to make several such appointments.'

This was a splendid opening for a young man of twenty-seven, and Samuel accepted the proposal with the warmest feelings of gratitude.

There is no record of how George White and Phaulkon moved the authorities at court. But it must have been done through the new chief minister. From what we know of the manners and customs of the country, we can assume that the two Whites and Phaulkon, after preliminary inquiries and the sending of presents, waited on the minister at his house. After a delay, no doubt of some duration, they were ushered into the presence. There was no question of a chair, even of a seat on the floor. The chief minister lived in great state. The three of them, with their shoes off, had to crawl. But that was customary for merchants at the time. The minister was no doubt very affable, as he wanted a man like White. His recommendation duly reached the king, A royal audience followed, accompanied by more presents, more elaborate crawling. Phra Narai was probably cordial. He had charming manners, when he chose, 'an engaging air, a sweet and obliging carriage to strangers', says Père Tachard, the Jesuit. On that day the king smiled on Samuel, crouching below there in his knee-breeches and long coat, and sent him down a trifling gift according to custom.

When the time came for White to rejoin his ship, it was arranged that he should return to India in his present employ and that, on arrival there, application would be made formally by the King of Siam's agent on that coast to the Council of Madras for the loan of his services. He left probably in October 1677.

XII. ELEPHANTS

Sailing from Mergui, White reached Masulipatam, The king's agent there made under instructions a formal move. Quoting White's own account written in London eleven years later:

'It happened in time of my being there (Masulipatam) that the King of Syam's Agent applied himself to the Chief of the Companies Factory for a person well qualified to navigate a Ship of the King's betwixt that place and the port of Mergen. To which employ he was pleas'd to recommend me.'

It was an easy matter when all the authorities concerned were agreed.

On appoint ment White transferred his residence from Madras to Mergui, taking his wife along with him. It seems that a daughter, called Susan, had been born to him by this time. In what house he lived we cannot guess, but it was certainly not the stockaded mansion of future years. Nor do we know who were his companions and friends, though there were many Europeans in Mergui and, according to the practice of the time, they probably resided together in one street or quarter: 'Europeans live as near one another as they can, and tho' their Houses do not join, yet a few Bamboos only part their Yards; whence they have a long Street near the River wholly to themselves.' This was written by Lockyear of Achin in Sumatra, but it may stand for Mergui.

As the captain of a ship, White's house was probably on the water-front. Built of wood, with a thatched roof, it stood on posts, and, facing west, received the breeze from the harbour, The shipyards were in the vicinity. The house he Was to occupy later was in a more commanding position, but in the same neighbourhood.

His duties brought him into close official relationship with the mandarins in charge of the port and of the royal trade, who were, as we have seen, Mahomedans. He had to receive under their orders the cargoes of monopoly goods which were for delivery in India. No doubt he made frequent journeys to Tenasserim, the main emporium. There was much to be learnt His rise a few years later to a predominant position would not have been possible had he neglected to study the trade. He was, of course, far more able than the ordinary sea-captain. In that school of Mahomedan traders, a rascally school, he learnt all the tricks of the East.

It was a free life, preferable to living in Fort St. George, where the President and council were ubiquitous with their petty regulations, standing on their dignity and interfering in the private affairs of junior employees. Moreover, the distractions in Mergui were superior. Not only was the climate better, but the delightful archipelago gave facilities for fishing, bathing and parties. Food, too, was much more plentiful; the fruit was unequalled as was the fish; oysters, eggs, chicken, pork were to be had in abundance.

Though we have very little information about White's activities at this time, the Masulipatam factory records are precise that in 1680 he was engaged in the elephant trade: '19 March 1680 Ship Derrea Dowlat belonging to the King of Syam, Samuel White Master, arrived from Tenassary with elephants.'

This trade in elephants between Siam and India was very

old. There were always wars in India, and in old wars elephants had a tactical importance similar to that of tanks today, Siam was the great reservoir of elephants for Hindustan. The forests were full of them and over a long course of years the Siamese had acquired a remarkable technique in their capture. When tamed, they were brought to Tenasscrim, placed in great flat-bottomed boats and floated down to Mer gui on the tide. There they were embarked on the ships, It was no easy job to manage such 'Overgrown beasts', as Bowrey calls them. The ship lay by the wharf and a strong gangway was put across, over which the elephants were driven on to the deck, from which they slid down into the hold on sloping planks. There they were secured. 'They bringe in Some ships from 14 to 26 of these vast creatures', says Bowrey, who was fascinated by the subject. The ships had to be built 'exceedinge Stronge' for such stock, and we may assume that White's command, the *Derrea Dowlat*, was a fine stout vessel. Her name recurs again and again in this narrative, bandied about eastern seas until the House of Commons at last is petitioned to pronounce upon her.

With the elephants safely in the hold, each provided with at least seventy banana trees as provender for the sixteen or twenty days' crossing, the anchors were weighed and the ship set forth. It was an anxious time for the captain. The elephants had to be kept quiet. in this connection the ever-unfortunate John Struys is our authority, for in May 1650 he spilt his soup over an elephant in the hold of the *Posihorse*, on which he was a mariner. Here is his story, from *The Perrillous and most Unhappy Voyages*:

'About noon when the dinner was ready, I went to the Cook for a bowl of hot broth, which having got I came to bring it to 2 of my Comrades and passing by the Hold, one of the elephants wound me about the legs with his Trunk (or snout) that I came tumbling down, Plates and all, which being scalding hot. fell upon the Elephant's back, and made him roar out and stamp, that the ship tumbled and shaked again, This so amazed the Commander chat he came running out of his Cabin to know what was the matter. Here I was in a great strait fearing to cry out, being sensible that he was a choleric man and yet durst not stay below for the Elephant, who if he could have come at me would have trodden me as flat as a Flounder: but considering with my self that the Captain would assuredly come to hear of it, one time or another, and if I stayed long I was sure this beast of vengeance would assuredly send me to my Grindsir I cryed out and the Commander in all haste sent one to pull me up. As soon as they got me upon the Deck, he gave orders to tie me to the mast, and commanded a fellow to lick me lustily with a rope's end.'

The captain may seem to us harsh, but he knew that once elephants got restive, it was as dangerous as a cyclone. Bowrey has a story of an elephant, excited whether by soup or by something else is not stated, that 'with all the force he cold possibly, did run his tooth through the Ship Side' and sank her, the crew hardly escaping in their boat.

But White seems to have mastered the technicalities of elephant transport, carrying out his duties so efficiently that when his first two years in the Siamese service were finished, the chief minister asked the head of the factory at Ayudhya to get sanction for the Continued loan of his services, 'as he had given very good satisfaction in the discharge of his office'.

This extension was sanctioned and White continued in his appointment, which was proving as lucrative as Phaulkon had led him to expect, for he wrote himself afterwards that 'his Majesty was graciously pleased to let me in a large measure partake of his Royal Bounty and favour'.

He was indeed in favour with everyone, particularly with the Madras factors, whom he obliged by carrying their private cargoes. There is a letter from Samuel Wales, chief at Masulipatam, in which White is spoken of as arriving there with 'concerns of Mr. Hatton's, Mr. Tivill's and Mr. Wynne's in copper and also 70 chests of copper of Mr. Matthew Main-wareing's'. The arrangement was working very well. The English, both within and without the Company, were beginning to get a comfortable share of the coast trade, thanks to the facilities which White was able to give them.

I said that White was in favo or with everyone, but the Mahomedans must be excepted, for he represented the new policy of ousting them from, power. In Mergui no one dared to interfere with the captain of a king's merchantman, on the other side, however, the King of Golconda's Governor of Masulipatam, in sympathy with his co-religionists at Tenasserim, and in trade relations with them, made difficulties. He was a man called Ali Beague, It began in the matter of a business deal between him and White, in which White considered that Ali Beague had tricked him out of £600, a large sum in seventeenth-century values. In September 1681, the southwest monsoon blowing up fresh, the same Ali Beague caused him to leave Masulipatam without certain ship's stores, including cables, with which he had promised to provide him, In consequence, when White found himself on a lee shore off Mattaban and anchored, his old cables parted and he was cast away.

News of this catastrophe reached Masulipatam in January 1682, when rumour had it that White was drowned. This was later shown to be false, for information revealed that he had refloated his ship and was safe In Mergui, a fact 'which occasioned great rejoicing in the town' of Masulipatam, for no doubt the factors had ventures of their own on the vessel. In any event they disliked Ali Beague as much as did White, He had made himself thoroughly disagreeable in 1681 by refusing clearance from the customs, until duty was paid, of the copper which White had brought for Mr. Hatton and the others. By an arrangement Company cargoes, including goods owned privately by its members, had not to pay duty before entering the factory, but on the ground that the goods in this case were

Carried in a Siamese ship, the other cargo of which was not entitled to free entry, he made his claim. His object thus in standing on the letter of the regulations was to discourage factors using a Siamese ship captained by an Englishman, as opposed to a Mahomedan. Samuel Wales was very angry and even asked the head office at Madras to take the matter up officially.

White's clash with Ali Beague was destined afterwards to have consequences of much importance. in the event itself there is no indication of future complications. The officials in the Golconda and Mogul administrations were generally found rapacious and slippery. But Ali Beague's conduct working in with other elements in the situation was to result in a combustion which eventually involved White in the drama it is the object of this book to describe.

During this period he lost his wife, Mary. A second daughter, called after her, had been born. The circumstances of her death arc unknown,[*] but the birth of two children in seven years, without a change home from a climate which, though not actively unhealthy is relaxing, and much ignorance about tropical diseases—any of these is sufficient to account for it. one of my predecessors in office at Mergui, Mr. J.S.Furnivall, made in 1917 the interesting discovery of her gravestone. out walking one day in the town he noticed an Indian Washerman pounding clothes on a slab in the manner of his country. His eye caught an inscription upon the stone. on Investigation this read;

. . . RE LYETH T . . .

BODY OF MA . . .

. . . SAM WHI . . .

THIS LIF . . .

O DONI 1682

. . . *Ergo Resurgam*

[*]But see appendix 4.

It was beyond question Mary White's headstone. Where her bones now lie, no one knows. Mr. Furnivall rescued the stone from the washerman, who in his pounding of it symbolized the hatred in which White, as will transpire, was held by the Indians. He set it up, strongly reinforced, at the entrance to the port under an ancient tree, where it now stands. With Mary's death, White was left alone upon that shore to face his strange fortune. His two little girls, Susan and Mary, he sent home to England.

XIII. PHAULKON EMERGES

During the period I have just described (1677–82) White made at least one trip to Ayudhya, when he saw Phaulkon again. That was in 1679. Events had moved and were to move faster.

The king had continued for quite a time to smile upon the East India Company. The London authorities, realizing that they had a chance of business, if they sent a competent man to represent them, selected a Mr. Richard Burn a by. He arrived in 1678. Everything was in disorder, no proper books, business done on loose papers, the broadcloth from England quite unsaleable, the English staff quarrelling among themselves and borrowing money for private trade from the king on the security of the Company.

Burnaby tried to reform matters. But a furious dispute broke out between him and a man called Lambton about debts, which hurt the Company's reputation. Dividends failed to materialize. The London office became more disillusioned than ever.

George White, who had been most anxious to get the

Company on its legs and induce it to embrace its great opportunity, now offered to assist Burruby and actually worked as joint chief with him from March to October 1679. But it was no good. The Company was a broken reed.

When the king saw that the directors had no intention of coming into Siam in a big way, with engineers, gunners, ships and capital, he began to think he would have to look elsewhere for the outside assistance he required. It was impossible to build up a policy in collaboration with such a poor lot of men.

At this point Phaulkon emerged. He obtained the ear of the new Siamese chief minister, the man always referred to as His Excellency the Barcalong by contemporary writers. It seems to be agreed that he accomplished this feat by a masterly exposure of Mahomedan ambitions. The Abbé de Choisy, an accurate observer writing immediately afterwards, may be quoted: 'Monsieur Constance is a very clever man with a great head for business. He disclosed the rascality of the Mahomedans who were in power before he began to interest himself in politics. That is how he raised himself to high office.'

Phaulkon made the Barcalong's flesh creep by a detailed account of what they were plotting to do. 'The Mahornedans saw how great was their power . . . and so believed that without any risk they could undertake all, supplant the Siamese mandarins, rifle their houses, and even in a short time make themselves masters of the King's storehouses and of the King himself, if he should refuse to embrace the Law of Mahomet,' as wrote the Jesuit, Nicolas Gervaise.

Phaulkon drove his arguments home by pointing to the clannishness of Mahomedan kingdoms. They had all—Persia, Golconda and Achin—sent embassies to Siam. the main object of which had been to convert the king to Islam. The country was full of Malay followers of the Prophet, formidable men of war. A combination between these elements and the Dutch would be enough to overthrow the kingdom.

These revelations only confirmed what the Barcalong and the mandarinate had long suspected. The arrest and torture of certain Mahomedans were suggested. Phaulkon advocated, however, a constructive policy which would have its indirect effect The Siamese were too weak to resist these men if they were suddenly provoked to violence.

The Barcalong, now much impressed by Phaulkon, demanded to know the details of his solution. He replied to this effect. 'As His Majesty has perceived for some time, assistance from outside the Kingdom most be sought At first there was reason to think that the English Company might come to the rescue. They have been offered large concessions to encourage them to strengthen their position and in alliance with this state to disperse the dangers by which it is encompassed. But they have made it plain that as a commercial concern they have no ambitions of the kind. It is useless to look to them any longer. But there is another strong nation in Europe which has shown its interest in Siam. namely the French. Their missionaries, many of them gentlemen and men of education, have been coming and going between this country and France for years. I am well acquainted with their views. Our task is now to persuade them that there is a great field for French commercial expansion in Siam. Let the King smile upon them as he has upon the worthless English Company. Rouse their interest, and their character will lead them to engage with us, both politically and commercially. Their King, Louis XIV, has graod ideas. He may be induced to send us engineers, gunners, even soldiers and warships.'

There can be little doubt that this was the substance of the advice tendered by Phaulkon about the beginning of the year 1680. It was accepted by the king and his council as sound. No other way existed of lifting Siam from the morass into which she was sinking. The Siamese by themselves were too backward to stand against those with whom the development of navigation had brought them into contact. There was no

Siamese navy, and the army, though large in numbers, was only good enough to fight the Burmese or the Cambodians.

Adopting Phaulkon's policy meant adopting him. There was no one else in the kingdom at all competent to deal with the French. His promotion was sudden. He was raised to the mandarinate in the third class with the title of Luang Wizaijen, and, subject to the Barcalong, was made head of the department of foreign trade, This gave him administrative control of the royal monopolies. He became at once the man through whom all business connected with commerce had to be transacted, The English Company would learn to their cost what that meant.

His first step was to stage a conversion from Protestantism to Catholicism. His next to induce the king to send an embassy to France.

He knew that an interval must elapse before he could get to close quarters with the French, and during that period he proposed to work with a body of Englishmen under his direct control, He would recruit the best he could. He would tempt from the Company suitable persons by promises of large pay and good prospects. He would organize the free merchants, obtain the services of sea captains. Already he had one good man in Samuel White—George had gone home in 1681. He now induced Richard Burnaby to leave the Company, together with his assistant called Ivatt, a person of diminutive stature. With the help of these people a start must be made.

The two key positions in the country were Mergui and Bangkok. the latter a fortress mounting eighty guns, some miles inside the bar of Siam. In Mergui he must post his best Englishmen, displacing the Mahomedan officials. A fleet must be organized there for trade and defence; the place must be fortified. At Bangkok he would put a Frenchman and strengthen its walls.

This enormous programme received the king's enthusiastic

endorsement. The Barcalong was all admiration. The court mandarins, though they found the pace hot and were not altogether carried away, decided to lend their support and suspend judgment.

White was again summoned from Mergui and arrived at Ayudhya in the autumn of 1683.

XIV. LORD WHITE

His Excellency the Lord Phaulkon, though not titular first minister, the Barcalong holding that rank, was now very powerful. Since White had seen him last in 1679, four years had elapsed. In the interval his manner had become more imposing, chough to the brother of his patron and friend he was affectionate and good.

It was November when he unfolded to White, Burnaby and lvatt his plans for their advancement. He said the king had sanctioned their elevation to the mandarinate and their appointment to administrative posts on the Bay of Bengal. White was younger than Burn aby, being not more than thirty-three years of age. He was to be made a mandarin of the third rank and the post he was to occupy was that of Shāhbandar of the port of Mergui.

The word Shāhbandar means in Persian 'King of the Haven', and was the title all over the Indian seas for the officer in charge of a port. But in White's case it was to imply far more than the term 'port officer' might be supposed to connote. He was to have under his charge the collecting and managing of all the king's revenues in the whole province of Tenasserim and to be chief commissioner of his maritime affairs on the Bay of Bengal.

The king's revenues referred to were the monopoly revenues. White was to be superintendent of the royal trade in Tenasserim; that is to say, in respect of the commodities already enumerated, it would be his duty to capture, collect, dig for or grow them as the case might be, and to sell them at the king's price to merchants or to ship them on the king's ships and dispose of them on the east coast of India or beyond. As chief commissioner of maritime affairs, he would have to develop and strengthen the port of Mergui, building merchantmen and frigates in its dockyards and fortifying it with batteries and stockades. For that purpose he would be given at first grants from the central treasury and later, when the revenues from the royal trade began to come in, he would be able to transfer sums from that head to the other. He would not be paid a salary, but would take a stated percentage from the public moneys.

Burnaby was to be made mandarin of the second grade with the appointment of governor of Mergui. As such he would be head of the general administration, of the town. But he would be expected to consult White on all matters of importance and give him what help he might require in carrying out the new policy, such as by supplying labour or suppressing disorders. It is clear that Burnaby, though a grade higher than White, was to be rather Ms adjutant than his superior.

Ivatt was to be posted to Masulipatam as the agent for the monopoly trade. When White's ships arrived there or at the other Coromandel ports, Ivatt was to superintend their unloading and the sale of their cargoes and to procure cargoes in exchange for their return journey.

The effect of these three appointments was to take from the hands of the Mahomedans the key positions in Tenasserim. The Viceroy of Tenasserim was, as we know, a Persian. The office had become hereditary in his family. He was left where he was; he still had the duty of collecting the ordinary revenue from land and was generally responsible for law and order outside Mergui town; but, compared with White, he was a nonentity. In addition to him there were four other mandarins in the province, some of whom appear to have been Siamese. It seems that the viceroy himself lived in Mergui and likewise at least one of the others, his post being that of judge. The remaining mandarins were in the city of Tenasserim.

Such was the brilliant promotion which Phaulkon held out to White and his two companions. He had summoned them to Louvo, the king's summer palace, a day's journey north of Ayudhya.acharming place where Phra Narai spent a good deal of his time from November to April hunting elephants. He seems to have enjoyed that sport more than any other. He did not shoot the elephants, he captured them and he was always hoping to catch a white elephant, a new one, for there was already one specimen in his stables, magnificently caparisoned in scarlet broadcloth from England.

Louvo was a small town, only a mile and a half round. The palace looked over the river; the inner apartments were approached on the town side through three courtyards. In the first was a garden, 'not very large', writes de La Loubère, 'for the paths would not hold two people abreast nor the alleys more, but all being planted with flowers and with a variety of palms and other trees, the garden, the summer-house and the fountains have an indescribable air of freshness and simplicity, which is delightful.'

Through a grove one reached a doorway leading to the second courtyard, which was surrounded by a white wall, delicately sculptured, with niches in which were placed pieces of Chinese porcelain. Overlooking this courtyard was a building with tiered roofs and with a large upper window.

In this second courtyard Phaulkon, White, Burnaby, Ivatt, with the Barcalong, the ministers and court mandarins now assembled. It was the early morning, the time of the first audience, in the last week of November 1683. The courtyard was half in shadow, fresh but warm. The whole company lay prostrate on carpets. Presently music sounded; the large window under the tiered roof was unshuttered and the king was disclosed to view. Titles were conferred upon the three Englishmen and they were invested in the robes and with the insignia of their new offices.

The official costume of the court of Siam consisted of a brocaded robe and a conical hat with gold rings on it, the number of rings corresponding to the wearer's rank in the mandarinate. It does not seem that White and his companions were expected to wear Siamese costume even on official occasions. There exists a contemporary drawing by a Frenchman showing Phaulkon at a royal audience. Though prostrate on knees and elbows in the Siamese manner, he is wearing a laced coat and breeches in the European style.

XV. APOSTATES AND RENEGADES

The turn affairs were taking in Siam was not altogether lost on London in spite of the distance. There was evidently something very wrong; the factory was making no progress; profits were not coming in. But the reasons for this failure were far from clear. News of the rise of Phaulkon and the formulation of his French policy had not yet been received or was not understood.

It was decided to send out a reliable man to make inquiries and, if necessary, to close the factory. A Mr. Strangh was selected, one of the staff in the London office. He was considered a solid painstaking assistant. With him was to go Thomas Yale, a younger brother of Elihu Yale, the rising man in the Madras establishment. Their salaries were fixed at £50 and £30 a year respectively. The mission, in short, was a very modest affair. Its personnel was decidedly middle class and it carried no letter from Charles II, chough the occasion was of importance, for the whole future of English trade east of India was involved. That the directors were taking so little trouble to make an impression shows that their hopes in Indo-China were nearly gone and that they had decided to concentrate upon India. They did not realize at this date that the evacuation of Siam exposed them to danger in the Bay of Bengal, if Mergui were developed by the Siamese.

Strangh and Yale sailed from London in December 1682 on board the *Mexico Merchant* with a cargo, the sale of which was to pay the cost of the mission. They arrived at the bar of Siam on Ist September 1683, just before the investiture of White and Burnaby, Totally ignorant of Phaulkon's new importance, they had no conception that on a broad view of national politics he had weighed the Company and found it useless for his purposes. They did not even know that all business would have to be transacted through him. In short, they had no idea what was going on.

The news which met them as they came up the river was rather staggering. Ten months before their factory had been burnt down with all it contained, including the books.

After Burnaby had joined Phaulkon, a person called Potts had succeeded to the direction of the factory. He was a drunken and dishonest rascal, heavily in debt. The magnificent jobs which Phaulkon was handing out to Englishmen roused his cupidity, but when he was refused one he became embittered and abusive, writing to his principals that Phaulkon 'domineered and insulted with great and insufferable insolence', that they 'must unavoidably root out this bramble who is now arrived at the helm of this Government', and saying about the town that he was a powder monkey, a Greek and a cabin-boy, all of which remarks were reported to

Phaulkon. Potts then burnt the factory down, either by mistake when he was drunk, or on purpose as the best way of destroying the record of his debts and of his mismanagement.

It was Strangh's first duty to go into this matter and hold an inquiry upon Potts. But he found it very difficult to make headway. There was no one to help him. Potts protested his innocence, said he could bring the whole town to prove it. When Strangh asked him to call his witnesses, he produced a Dutch beachcomber, who on being taken aside by Strangh proved to be drunk.

Strangh did not know what to do, where to turn, how to find out anything. He had never been to Siam before, knew nothing of the language or the people. His ignorance was so extceme that on arrival he was even unaware of the name of the capital He had been introduced to Phaulkon; Ivatt had done chat much for him. He had even had dinner there and the Greek had made a few polite remarks. But he was totally in the dark as to what it all meant. The Barcalong gave him an audience, but Phaulkon remained present throughout. It did not lead to anything. They seemed to have no time for him. A ho use was allotted for his use, but he complained in his diary that it was 'a mere dogge-hole, more like a prisson than a dwelling house'. Most of the Europeans seemed to look askance at him.

At last he found a man called Gibbon, 'an ould Standert in this place', he calls him, 'though troubled with the impediment of hard hearing'. With this decayed old creature tottering after him, he tried to collect debts owing to the Company, but no one would pay and, when he asked the Barcalong for assistance, that minister refused to have anything to do with the matter.

Trouble pursued him. About eight o'clock one night, when he was sitting in the lower room of his kennel, word was brought that two men wanted to speak to him. Before he could rise, a couple of Dutchmen appeared, 'one iff not both, very drunk'. Yale, who was upstairs, had to hurry down and help Strangh to hustle them out. Potts had sent them—perhaps to beat him.

A few nights later Potts was arrested for loitering outside Phaulkon's house with intent to waylay and murder him. He was put in the pillory, though he protested that he was only selling beer. Rascal or not, he was English, and Strangh was shocked. The news brought home to him the set against the Company. He became more and more discouraged. He made propositions to the Barcalong, Phaulkon always being present, but his requests were ridiculed. They said he was a long way behind the times. He was still talking about interlopers and their suppression, when His Excellency was forming a service of his own from interlopers. One day Phaulkon told him plainly that the Company deserved no consideration and would get none, unless it was prepared to take up affairs seriously like the French. Even that hint did not enlighten him.

He began to hate Phaulkon. Yale, on the other hand, was getting on very well with him. They did a little private business together. What worried Scrangh most of all was the cargo on the *Mexico Merchant*. He could not sell it. That meant a dead loss for the voyage, as well as closure of the factory. He went again to Phaulkon, but obtained no satisfaction.

As a last resort he decided to petition the king direct. I have said that His Majesty was at Louvo, hunting. Strangh set out for that place with a Mr. Crouch from a ship in the harbour, as Yale refused to go with him. On arrival at the summer palace they heard that the king was hunting elephants some way out of the town. Accordingly they started after him on foot and when far beyond the walls saw him in the distance with all his train, the king himself 'ridding upon his Oliphant'. They ran to present their petition, but could not catch him up. The cortège passed on and Strangh was foiled again.

They were putting up in Luovo with a Mahomedan and

when the man, in compliance with the regulations about strangers, reported their arrival, the Barcalong sent a message to say that he desired to see them the following day. Strangh was glad, Perhaps at Louvo he might get a private interview. when he could complain about the way Phaulkon was treating him.

Next morning, the 28th of November, at eight o'clock, he presented himself at the minister's house. While waiting outside, he was astounded to see Phaulkon arrive and with him Samuel White, Richard Burnaby and little Ivatt. He then learned they were to be made mandarins next day and given appointments at Mergui. This was a shock to him. There was a Captain Paxton, too, a well-known interloper, in nothing but a shirt and drawers, evidently on close terms with the others.

When word came down that His Excellency would see him, he climbed the stairs, made his obeisance and observed with annoyance Phaulkon whispering to the Barcalong, and White in the background. It was too much. He thought of asking them to withdraw, but dismissed the idea. It would cause a scene. So 'notwithstanding all that crew I delivered myself', he records.

One cannot help admiring Strangh. Misinformed, powerless, involved in a situation beyond his comprehension, he was not afraid to speak out boldly what he thought. He accused Phaulkon before them all of double dealing and usurped authority, and asked permission to close the factory and leave the country at once.

The Barcalong heard with stupefaction. So English, so downright an approach was very embarrassing. Though his rank was higher than Phaulkon's, he had not the smallest intention of listening to a complaint against the king's favourite. When Strangh was done, he replied shortly that he was very busy, but that the Lord Phaulkon would attend to him. At that he appeared to fall into a doze. Phaulkon whispered with White a moment and then, turning an angry face to Strangh, asked him if he realized to whom he was speaking, a prince of Siam. Had he been other than an ignorant stranger, such an insult could not have been overlooked; a Siamese would have been tortured for less. As for winding up the Company's business in Siam, so much the better; it had been miserably managed. He should have his pass to depart.

Strangh, who had attempted to interrupt, now broke in to say that he was not afraid of threats and that the truth ought to be spoken before kings, let alone princes.

Phaulkon desired to know if that was all; he could not have the Barcalong disturbed any longer. When Strangh said that it was all and that he wanted only a pass to be gone, the Barcalong, 'as if raised from Sleepe', muttered that he was anxious to obtain in exchange for country goods some iron railings and gates in Mr. Strangh's cargo, as the Lord Phaulkon was building a grand new house. So that was the upshot. Strangh was to provide Phaulkon with an ironwork door for his courtyard.

But he had still more irritations to bear. He was kept waiting the whole of December for the pass. His patience or his nerve failing him, he left Louvo secretly without it and was 'disgracefully brought back to the Factory with innumerable indignities and abuses more'. At last, on January 2nd he found himself safe on board his ship. Lying at the bar of Siam out of reach of danger, he gave vent to his indignation in a letter to Phaulkon, which for force of style and colour of phraseology is a contribution to the prose of the seventeenth century. All the English hatred of upstarts and adventurers, foreigners and despots is behind its passion. With a roll almost as thunderous as Sir Thomas Browne's he begins:

To MR. CONSTANT PHAULKON
From WM. STRANGH, *dated from the Barr of Syam*
2 *Jany* 1684
'I have two of your scurrilous and false imputations of the

16 and 24 Deer to answer, with a little larger explanation of
the brief though ample import of my just and parenetic
charge to you of the 23rd Deer, such as may suit your im-
polite weak capacity, which has been jumbled through your
sudden and surprising elevation to a soaring Lordship and a
heathenish Grace.'

Phaulkon's head had been turned, he went on, he had lost
his head; as prince of a heathen realm, he thought he could
speak to Englishmen as if they were crawling blacks, he, a
Greek, if you please, a fellow who had risen from the gutter.
Colloguing with his native slaves he had sunk to the lowest
subterfuges.

'The firing of this Factory was not done without some
cursed treachery (which Heaven detect!) and though I cannot
charge you with it as a matter of fact, yet I cannot excuse your
indirect clandestine practices, in setting so many cunning and
crafty engines, and corrupting and treacherously seducing
little Ivatt—a Lord forsooth!—to your practices and faction.'

Phaulkon was 'the bellows of that flame' which had consumed the Honourable the East India Company's property
and hopes, though in Burnaby and George White's time he
had been glad to take a loan from it, a loan free of interest.
And not satisfied with extirpating the Company from Siam.
he must needs treat him, Strangh, abominably, baffling and
spying upon him since his landing.

'At my arrival, to prevent my obtaining true knowledge
and information, not only how the Company's affairs were
carried on and ruined by you, but of trade of this place, on
the principle of your own self interest, fearing my approach
would be prejudicial to your monopolized trade of this kingdom, you sent your fluked engine and creature Ivatt to congratulate me.'

And when Phaulkon found himself ignored, when Samuel
White, another creature of his, by a gross breach of confidence, told him that Potts had called Mm a powder-monkey

and a Greek in his; Strangh's, presence, and when he found that they refused to bribe him, he turned against them, though he had no authority to do so from his master, the king, and had prevented them even from selling their cargo.

'You, by the abused authority of your great Master, favourer of our Nation and not acquainted with your Pranks and Tricks, have not only privately but publicly, some on pain of forfeiture of life and goods, others with threatening and imprisonment, forbidden and hindered all Merchants and Brokers so much as to peep or come near the Factory, either to buy or sell with us.'

He, Strangh himself, had had a narrow escape; fallen among persons disaffected to their God and country, renegades and apostates, men who would take service with pagans and spit like the unspeakable Dutch in the face of their Saviour to obtain a competence, he must congratulate himself on having emerged alive, though, like the dog in the story, without his tail, for he had lost every farthing he had invested in the venture.

The letter ends with a solemn indictment and a threat, 'I have done with Siam, yet I hope the Honourable Company has not. . . . Therefore in the Name and on behalf of the Honourable Company I do by these presents solemnly and in Optima forma PROTEST against you, Constant Phaulkon, to be liable to answer and make satisfaction in cither body or estate for all the above-mentioned damages and great losses.'

Signing this truly remarkable document, Strangh sent it ashore and weighed from the bar. The East India Company never set foot in Siam again.

PART TWO
THE DAVENPORT PAPERS

XVI. WHITE TURNS FILIBUSTER

The elevation of White to the mandarinate at Mergui and the flamboyant exit of Scrangh from Ayudhya bring the introductory sections of this book to an end. These, perforce, covered a large field and a number of years; in the space available they could amount to no more than a sketch, in which emphasis was laid on certain typical events to the exclusion of a great quantity of detail In the present part the attention is concentrated almost entirely upon Mergui. The period is short, from December 1683, when White arrived as Shāhbandar, to December 1687, when he left for England. The main authority is the Davenport Papers. What precisely these are will be found discussed in the Appendix. Their chief characteristic is the detail in which they describe the extraordinary dilemma into which White fell in 1686–7. Their author, Francis Davenport, did not arrive in Mergui till March 1686. For the year 1684 and 1685 information is comparatively meagre, though enough is known to prepare for what follows. But from the moment Davenport appears, the curtain is lifted and we are able to observe White and his companions in their speech and daily life, almost as completely as if they were characters in an historical novel, for in Davenport's style they live for us with the intensity of an artist's creation. When in a few pages from now I am able to chronicle his capture, the spirit of this narrative will undergo an immediate transformation. From a methodical effort to present the data for a judgment on White it will become a close description of a number of sensational events.

There arc certain implications in White's new appointment which may conveniently be brought out in this place. Inasmuch as Strangh had left Siam to report to his principals that Phaulkon was the Company's great enemy and that White was his creature, the English official attitude to White was likely to become disagreeable, White, moreover, was a cog in Phaulkon's larger policy of remodelling the country with

French support. These elements of his position were calculated in the long run to range him against England. But unofficially White's good post in Mergui gave the staff at Madras great hopes of making money. If as a mere captain on one of the king's ships he had put business in their way, as Shāhbandar he should be able to give them greater facilities. Phaulkon's intention of displacing Mahomedan merchants, if it meant that the Company's private trade would have wider scope, was commendable. It all depended upon how White behaved.

We must keep in mind that White was a young man. I have said that he was not more than thirty-three years of age at this time. It is possible that he was only thirty. But, thirty or thirty-three, he had in his hands wide powers. For all practical purposes he was in control of a province. The amount of supervision which the king and Phaulkon could exercise over him was very limited. I have shrunk from overloading this book with an account of the Siamese administrative system. The mandarinate was elaborate enough in theory and its officials were under strict control from the boards at the capital. But White's appointment being a special one, and part of a change in policy, the routine regulations had less force in his case. His situation was exceptionally independent.

On taking over charge of his duties at Mergui—if such an expression can be used in regard to White—he delayed not, as he afterwards wrote, 'to give notice to my friends in the Companies service at Fort St. George, Masulipatam and Bengal, humbly tendering my best services to their Commands in whatever I might be useful to the Publick and their private Concerns'. By this Setter he intimated to them that the facilities he had been able in the past to afford them as individuals would be continued. As the Company itself had no trade via Mergui of any importance, the matter of rendering it assistance hardly arose. Yet, when there was occasion to oblige it, he did not refuse. Shortly after receiving 'their kind congratulations' on his promotion, the *Golden Fleece*, one of their ships with a very valuable cargo, sprang a desperate leak as she was making for home down the Bay of Bengal. Mergui was the nearest port and she put in there for assistance. White laid himself out to help. His slaves unloaded her; she was dry-docked and her goods warehoused free of charge. When she was refitted, he allowed her captain, James Cook, to provision her at the special rates fixed for the king's ships. The vessel then sailed for England, when the remarkable return of £190,000 was realized on the venture. This episode is significant. It proves that Phaulkon's treatment of Strangh and of the Company in Ayudhya was dictated partly by personal disagreement and partly by the conviction that the Company was of no use to him as a political asset in Siam. But he had issued no specific instructions that it was to be unsympathetically pursued in the bay, As not only a rivalry but a threat was inherent in his French policy, it must be supposed that in 1684 he did not see fit to show his hand. When he became more powerful, having obtained French support, so his lieutenant White took less and less trouble to consult the interests of the Company.

If he reader will turn to the map of Mergui harbour in chapter xxxv, he will see marked White's house at the spot where it seems most likely to have stood. I went into this question rather carefully on the ground and, after weighing the references in the authorities, I have come to the conclusion that the house was situated within the main town on that part of the ridge which slopes to the creek at the south end. It stood probably some fifty feet above the water of the harbour. Steps led down from it to a private wharf. it consisted of a main building and outhouses and was surrounded by a stockade. Like other houses in the town, it was made of wood and stood on posts, the part underneath the main floor being used as a warehouse. A few guns were mounted in front. A gateway led through the stockade. Within its considerable compound, in various buildings, resided his assistants, his English and Indian servants and his slaves, From its windows the full panorama of the harbour was visible, the eye carrying over the bar past the point Pata of Pataw and on to King Island, with Iron Island blue on the north-western horizon.

Adjacent to it was a shipyard on the creek, which was the southern boundary of the town. In Mergui the tide rises eighteen feet at springs and, as the neighbourhood was stocked with the most excellent timber and the native inhabitants were noted carpenters and shipwrights, it was an ideal place for building merchantmen, on White's arrival there were a few ships, but no men-of-war except an old sloop called the *Prosperous.* It seems that in 1684 a certain Captain Coates joined him, This man he put in command of her.

When White settled down to the development of the trade with Golconda, he found that Ali Beague, the governor of its chief port, Masulipatam, was no more agreeable than he had been in the past. By exactions and corrupt practices he caused losses to White's ships. Ivatt was continually writing across to complain, White had his instructions to give the king's trade a name in the bay and to suppress Mahomedans, If his merchantmen were subject to delays if the captains were insulted or called upon to pay illegal dues, there was only one remedy —a show of force against Golconda, That kingdom, though it possessed a large army and was powerful on land, had no navy. White, moreover, had never forgiven Ali Beague for cheating him and, by withholding cables, for having caused his shipwreck three years before. It was the time to repay these injuries.

Accordingly, in 1684 he represented the state of affairs to Phaulkon, saying that the moment had come to bring the Indians to heel. He asked for sanction to seize merchant ships belonging to Golconda until Ali Beague paid compensation for the losses he had inflicted. He added that the Pegu officials of Burma, some of them Mahomedans, were equally high-handed and that prizes might also be taken on that coast. Phaulkon obtained the king and council's sanction to White's proposals, who was directed first to make representations at Golconda for compensation, and if these failed, to fit out the *Prosperous* under Captain Coates and send her to make prizes, But care must be taken not to interfere with the East India Company, which had a factory at Masulipatam, and at Mada-pollam, close by, Phaulkon knew that though the Company had no warships at the moment stationed in the bay—for, as we have seen, it was set against political entanglements and overhead charges of such a kind—warships would come out from England eventually if it became a vital matter of defending the trade. Until French support had arrived there was no hope of Siamese warships, even if captained and largely manned by Europeans, meeting successfully an English fleet. It was essential not to alarm the Company at this stage.

On receipt of these orders from court White, who was excited by the prospect of prizes, wrote to Ivatt at Masulipatam, that in making his claims for compensation he was to insure their rejection by asking too much. The *Prosperous* Was got ready. Early in 1685 she sailed. Captain Coates's instructions were to make as many prizes as he could on the Indian and Pegu coasts, but not to offend the Company. On the contrary, he was first to go to Madras, tell them there what he was about to do, buy ammunition and stores, and recruit for his crew more Europeans. The captain, who was a regular old sea-dog, went off in high spirits to attack single-handed the kingdoms of Golconda and Pegu.

Hardly had he sailed before White received further letters from Ayudhya cancelling the sanction to proceed to warlike measures. The explanation of this sudden change appears to have been that the Indian merchants of Mergui, traders of old standing with Masulipatam, afraid that the projected war would cause them loss, sent a deputation to court which, bribing its way with the pro-Mahomedan section of the mandarins, succeeded in getting the sanction cancelled. Phaulkon was over-ruled; he was not so completely the autocrat in 1684 as he became in 1685, when the arrival of Louis' magnificent embassy gave him a great personal triumph. He was obliged to order White to recall Coates by sending a fast sailer after him.

White was much annoyed by the 'fickleness and irresolution of the Syam Courtiers', and he decided to disobey the new orders. So bold a course shows that he believed Phaulkon would be able to shield him. But he does not seem to have reflected that, if he seized vessels belonging to another state without his government's authority, he became a filibuster and maintainer of pirates. It appears, at least, that he was prepared to be such for the time being, provided he was covered later, as he believed would be the case. How rash a course this was and how fraught with unforeseen consequences the narrative will disclose.

What White actually did was this. A new ship had recently been launched from his yard called the *Dorothy*. It was intended later to fit her as a frigate; her guns had not yet been installed. He had a commander for her, a Captain Cropley. This man WAS given orders to sail after Coates to Madras and deliver two letters to him. One letter contained the orders of recall issued by Ayudhya, the other was a personal letter from White to Coates, telling him to pay no attention to the government's change of front and to carry on as before. He would be protected from all ill consequences and handsomely rewarded. To make his intentions less obvious, he was directed to pursue the following tactics. He should sail to Madapollam, which was within the jurisdiction of Ali Beague, before the monsoon broke in May or June and there order three sloops, for there was a good shipyard in the place. When these were nearly complete at the end of the monsoon, he was to pick a quarrel with the governor of Madapollam, a lieutenant of Ali Beague's, alleging that the sloops were being unlawfully held back. He could then proceed according to the original plan and take prizes, as they offered. After Cropley had delivered these letters, he was to return to Mergui in the *Dorothy*, when the work of fitting her as a frigate would go on.

XVII. A PIRATE IN A RIVER

When Captain Coates received the letters, he was quite satisfied. As a simple ruffian, it never occurred to him that he was stepping to the wrong side of the law; or, if he had some misgivings, he got over them quickly, believing that Phaulkon and White would regularize his position later, if questions were asked. He had had a good reception at Madras, They had met him before; he had been the round of those ports many a time. His old friends were delighted to see him so well set up, in command of a heavily armed sloop and with plenty of money, for White had granted him from the Mergui treasury ample funds for the expedition. He told them, unofficially of course, what he was going to do and they all heartily concurred that the time had come to teach Ali Beague a lesson. He recruited with their help some English seamen, filling up with a few Dutch, Danish, French and Portuguese beachcombers and roughs. Little Ivatt had come down from Masulipatam and made himself very useful, but he suddenly died in March. That did not, however, permanently damp their spirits. They gave Coates a final send-off dinner. Some time in early May he set sail for Madapollam, his lockers and magazines well stocked with gunpowder and cannon-balls. He reached Madapollam Road without incident and came to anchor. In pursuance of his instructions contracts were placed with the Indian shipwrights for three sloops, The small English community under their chief of council, Samuel Wales, welcomed him. There were more dinners and entertainments. Coates, who was 'flusht with money', gave return parties and lived extravagantly. The monsoon, generally a dull time, passed in the pleasantest manner. He became very friendly with a Portuguese don, called Joseph dc Heredia, who had an armed ship of his own and now joined forces with him. A Captain Alexander Leslie, also, who at the rime was living at Madapollam with his wife, Mary Leslie, and their young children, accepted his offer of an appointment in the Siamese navy. The Mahomedan authorities suspected nothing. Probably the claim for damages had not been made in case it put them on their guard.

By November Coatcs's money was spent and he thought the time had arrived to get to the real business. He was on the best of terms with the local English, Wales and Mrs. Wales, and a good number more. He felt that he could count on their approbation, no matter what he might do. It so happened that there came in to Madapollam a ship belonging to the Armenian millionaire, John Demarcora. This man had originally lived in Madras under the protection of the East India Company. He had bout up his fortune by trading with Pegu in Burma, where he held an official position. His ship, which was called the *New Jerusalem*, was laden with a very rich cargo. It seems, indeed, that it was a treasure ship, the dream of all pirates. There were rubies, pieces of eight and other valuables on board. I should like to be able to state the valuation with certainty. The figure £500,000 was given later, when a claim was made. Whatever the exact value, it was a colossal one, and Coates as soon as he received the information decided that he must have the ship and all it contained. There was a small legal difficulty—John Demarcora was not a subject of Golconda. Coates was prepared to operate against Golconda on White's sole authority, but there was not even that backing for the seizure of the *New Jerusalem*. It was then pointed out that Demarcora, inasmuch as he was a mandarin of Pegu, was a subject of that state. White's orders included the seizure of Pegu's ships. Coates decided that this would cover his contemplated action. It was true that no claim for damages had been presented to the Pegu authorities, not even of the perfunctory kind made, if it was made, by Ivatt at Masulipatam. Coates was not checked by the lack of that; satisfied with his excuse, he set to work.

His first step was to send a peremptory demand ashore to the Indian shipwrights that his sloops be delivered forthwith. They replied with civility that they were not quite ready. Coates found the reply ample provocation. He immediately declared that Ali Beague was dishonestly withholding delivery to the loss and insult of his great master, the King of Siam. He would have to take measures, he said.

He lay in his ship, the *Prosperous*, at the bar of Madapollam. The *New Jerusalem* was ten miles up the river near the town of Narsapore. On 21st November 1685 he got out his boats after dark, In them he placed a picked body of men, heavily armed, and before midnight sent them up the river under the command of his chief mate, William Mallett. They passed the custom house unchallenged, passed sleeping Narsapore and stealthily approaching the *New Jerusalem* seized her before her crew could make any resistance. Lying near was a ship called the *Redelove*, the property of the King of Golconda, They seized her also. Word was then sent to Coates that all was in order and he came up with Don Heredia at dawn.

At three o'clock in the afternoon they brought the *New Jerusalem* down as far as the custom house, firing several shot from the guns she carried into the town of Narsapore, which stretched along the bank, and frightening the inhabitants out of their houses. She anchored by the custom house.

This bold seizure of a very rich ship in the middle of the

night caused a great sensation. The Mahomedan governors of Narsapore and Madapollam repaired at once to the English factory. Samuel Wales, the chief, was away at Masulipatam and they asked his assistant Charles Fownes to get in touch with Coates and find out what it was all about.

Fownes went on board the *New Jerusalem* and met Coates. To the question of what he meant by his nocturnal seizure, the captain replied that he was merely taking security for the completion of his ships on the stocks. At that point he said nothing about his commission to make prizes. Fownes, much relieved, reported to the Golconda officials that Coates would return the Armenian's ship when satisfied by the delivery of his sloops. Nothing more happened that afternoon. Next morning the *Redclove* was brought down to lie with the *New Jerusalem*.

As Golconda possessed no armed vessels with which to resist Coates, the governors of Narsapore and Madapollam continued their line of the day before and sought to get the factory to control him. They sent for the factory's chief clerk, a Hindu, and pointed out that as Coates was English, had been entertained and fitted out at Madras, fêted and encouraged at Madapollam, they proposed to demand satisfaction for his outrageous behaviour from the East India Company, The chief clerk replied that Coates was a servant of the King of Siam, that he was in no way countenanced by the Company and that none of the staff had any information as to his orders or designs. He had been entertained only because the Company, having interests in Siam. wanted to create a good impression there.

So the matter rested for a day or so. Fownes wrote urgently to Wales asking him to come back; the Mahomedan officials wrote to All Beague asking for troops. The don threatened Fownes and induced him to deliver eight cannon in the factory's godowns. Coates remained on the *New Jerusalem*, going through her papers and inspecting the fabulous loot. He selected £4,000 worth of the rubies and put them aside for himself in Case of accidents.

As Wales did not arrive, Coates became more arrogant. He said that if the factory did not give surety that whatever demands he might make on the King of Golconda would be granted, he would take other measures. This letter upset Fownes so much that he asked Mrs. Wales to remonstrate with Coates, She was a young woman of strong character, whom he had met frequently during the entertainments of the monsoon. Chaperoned by the factory doctor, she went on board his ship and on his own. quarter-deck told him what she thought of his last preposterous demand. But she failed to bring him to reason, He refused to see that he was jeopardizing the existence of the factory. When it was pointed out to him that the local authorities would revenge themselves upon the Company, which had no troops, ships or fortifications, he replied that that was their affair and that he was only carrying out the orders of the King of Siam. They, of course, were not aware that he was without legal authority for his acts. They now bitterly regretted that they had countenanced him at first and Madras was asked to recall the seamen recruited there.

At last on November 27th.aletter came from Wales refusing to stand surety and warning Coates formally that any damage he did to the subjects of the King of Golconda would result in retaliation on the Company at Madapollam, and adding that in the whole matter it would have become him far better 'first to have made demands for his Master, the King of Siam, upon the King of Golconda, and, upon refusal of the same, in a further manner to have proclaimed War, and to have proceeded like a Man of War, and not a Pirate in a River, and so near an English Factory.'

Coates's only reply was to pour a broadside into Narsapore, weigh anchor from the custom house and take the *New Jerusalem* and the *Redclove* down to the bar. Captain Leslie was so much attracted by these proceedings that he joined Coates that day, embarking on the *New Jerusalem* with Mary and the children. Meanwhile the Mahomedan officials had got together a force of 150 men armed with guns, fifty of whom were Rajputs, formidable mercenaries. Had Coates not fallen down to the bar, they would have boarded him by the custom house.

He now made his great mistake. As a pirate, for he was nothing more in spite of his claim to be taken as a man-of-war captain, he should have sailed away. He had a prize which would have set him up and White, too, for life. But he had not the nerve. Like so many predatory governments since, he wished to cloak his robberies in a decent phraseology, he wanted to make it appear that it was a real war, not freebooting. Accordingly, he blockaded the harbour mouth and seized all passing rice-boats, burning them after transfer of their contents to his ship.

As he took no trouble to identify the owners some of the boats he burned belonged to Robert Freeman, President of the Masulipatam council.

This was a very stupid act, for it turned the Company violently against him. It was contrary to White's instructions and to his practice of obliging the factors in their private trade. From a troublesome man, Coates became an enemy. Madras later fitted out the sloop *Thomas* and, with soldiers on her, sent her against him. But that took time; Madras was two hundred miles down the coast. Coates had still leisure to continue his depredations. on December 2nd Wales had arrived, bringing Robert Freeman with him from Masulipatam. They sailed down to the bar and saw Coates. He repeated his story about the injuries sustained by the Siamese government at the hands of Ali Beague and defended his seizure of the *New Jerusalem* on the ground that John Dcmarcora was a subject of Pegu. Freeman and Wales expostulated with him; they told him he was not behaving like an Englishman; that he was ruining his friends; and, worse, that Ali Beague had issued

Orders to his subordinates to stop the Company's trade throughout his jurisdiction.

Somewhat struck by this, Coates consented to go up the river in his boats and continue the discussion in the factory near the custom house. He took his guard with him. While they were talking there, John Demarcora himself pleading for restitution and arguing that he belonged not to Pegu but to Madras, news arrived that the Mahomedan soldiers were marching on the place to take Coates. Without a moment's hesitation he hurried to the waterfront and rowed down to the bar as fast as he could. Freeman and Wales sent after him a bill for £545,000.

A supreme effort was now made to bring him to reason. They argued him round to his first declaration that his seizures. were made to force delivery of his sloops. Very well, they said, we guarantee you your ships; now hand back Demarcora his valuables; if you have any other quarrel with Ali Beaguc, negotiate about that separately afterwards. Coates had not the nerve, as I have said, to be an out-and-out pirate. Like a fool —for that was White's opinion of him later—he disgorged the valuables, which apparently were worth hundreds of thousands of pounds, keeping only the paltry £4,000 worth of rubies which at the time Demarcora did not notice were missing, and cargo worth £2,700.

Freeman and Wales were overjoyed at this diplomatic success, on December 22nd they reported to Madras that the affair was as good as finished. Everything else seemed small after the return of such loot. 'On the 13th we concluded the business with Mr. Coates, who delivered all John DaMark's things and only keeps his ship (the *New Jerusalem*) and the King's (the *Redclove*) till his own or the King of Siam's is finished and put into the water . . . and the only dispute is a parcel of burnt boats and paddy, which Mr. Coates will make no satisfaction for till Alley Beague does the like for the wrongs and damages done by him to the King of Siam. What the final conclusion may be we cannot yet guess at.' The Indian authorities were mollified. It was felt that the Company was not really in league with Coates. The embargo on trade was taken off.

But they had not altogether done with the captain. When he thought of the enormous restitution he had made, he began to feel that he had been worsted in a battle of wits. Who was this John Demarcora? He was only a merchant stranger. The Mahomcdan officials and the Company supported him, because he was rich and influential, because they had shares in his venture. That must be the explanation.

Coates became melancholy and then he became angry. Raging, he piped up his men and embarking with them in his boats rowed to Madapollam landing stage. It was December 30th, a bright cool morning, the wind N. E., just rippling the river mouth. On the quay he paraded them, and announced that he proposed to seize the governor and hold him to ransom. They set off towards the palace, about fifty in number, armed to the teeth, as rascally looking a band of cut-throats as ever stepped through a pirate story. The troops were not in Madapollam, but at Narsapore, a few miles up, and the police were powerless, but a man ran to warn the governor. He closed his doors and sent a messenger to Wales.

That unfortunate gentleman, who so lately had been congratulating himself on his cleverness, turned out the factory guard in a hurry. Putting himself at their head and supported by his factors, his trumpeter and his peons with their Company badges, he took a short cut through side streets and intercepted Coates before he had readied the palace. He began at once to expostulate with him, pointing out that his intention, if carried out, would cost them their lives. Coates would be safe in his ship, but they had to stay and trade on shore, They would be murdered in their beds one night. In any event it was ruin. But Coates waved him aside and ordered his men to quick-march. Wales followed brokenly behind, pleading for sense. in this manner they arrived at the governor's palace.

But, as we have already seen, Coates was nor a real pirate. He had neither the courage nor the conviction for that desperate career. There Was a great deal of bluff in his make-up. When he saw the gates closed and the preparations made to resist him, he became much more amenable. He said he had only come ashore to see about the delivery of the sloops. He consented, with a little pressing, to have a conversation with the governor, who promised that the vessels should be ready in a day or so. With that assurance he turned his men about and marched back. This was practically the last of the captain. He saw that he could do little more at Madapollam and that it was time for him to go elsewhere. He may have heard that the sloop *Thomas* was coming up from Madras to fight him.

First he took delivery of two sloops (afterwards called the *Robin* and *Mary*), transferring to them the armament of the *Prosperous*, which was put on the scocks for repairs. At this point he handed back the *Redclove*, the King of Golconda's ship, but not the *New Jerusalem* and her cargo.

Before leaving, however, he decided on a few exploits, as on reflection he had not yet made war on Ali Beague. He would at least tweak his nose before his departure. In February 1686 he sailed up again as far as Narsapore, where the authorities had erected a battery behind a teak stockade. At 10 a.m. he opened fire on this. The artillery duel lasted all day, The Indians, however, had no trained gunners and not a ball hit him. But his bombardment put their guns out of action and the stockades catching fire they evacuated the position, His men landed at their leisure and carried the guns on board the sloops, where they came in useful to complete the armament. Coates felt that this was a real battle and he was very pleased, in theory, of course, for a sloop to take a land battery was a great feat, but in this case the circumstances were hardly normal, as the guns were harmless.

His kit act was to take a trip round and set fire to the villages on the banks. He burned Rameswaram and Antravdi and threatened Narsapore itself. He also burned the *Prosperous* on the stocks, as she was useless to him now. This was enough to satisfy honour. With the don and Leslie he lay off at last, He had still the *New Jerusalem* and ordered Leslie away in her to the coast of Pegu to take there what prices he could. He sent the sloop *Mary* back to Mergui to report progress, Mrs, Leslie and the children travelling by her. He himself went north in the *Robin* with the don's ship, the *Sancta Rosa*, of 400 tons, a new vessel which it seems had also been built at Madapollam. The don's crew was French and Portuguese, and he had forty-five prisoners taken from the rice-boats, whom he had made slaves. The arrangement was that the *Robin*, the *Sancta Rosa* and the *New Jerusalem* should return to Mergui in April or earlier if they took further prizes.

We are able to sum up Coates's exploits at Madapollam in terms of cash, for the amended bill was sent in later. In its first form it had been, as recorded, for £565,000. After the return of the Valuables, it was cut down as follows:

Charge for sending the sloop *Thomas* from Madras to catch Coates. It did not arrive in time	£315
Loss of interest suffered by East India Company through delay in shipping cargo for home, due to Coates's interruption of trade at Madapollam	£1,918
Value of *New Jerusalem* with fittings	£4,050
Value of cargo left in her after the restitution of the valuables	£2,700
Rubies stolen and not restored	£4,050
Other items missing and general expenses	£4,500
Total	£17,513

Of this total £10,800 reprcheated valuables which had passed into Coates's possession, a sum equal to £50,000 in modem currency. But multiply £565,000 by five and it will be easy to understand White's rage when he heard the news.

XVIII. THE CAPTURE OF DAVENPORT

On the return of Captain Cropley on the *Dorothy* from Madras, where he had delivered to Coates the orders which had seat him filibustering to Madapollam, White now had a ship with which to filibuster himself. Cropley on landing reported that he had noticed near Iron Passage a merchantman called the *Meet Faqueer Deun* of Masulipatam, White told him to put about at once and capture her. He accordingly did so and brought her into the harbour. Among those on board was a Mr. William How, whom White made his steward and accountant. This ship had a valuable cargo, estimated as worth £25.000.

If White expected that Coates's actions at Madapollam, a thousand miles away, would escape notice until such time as he could settle the matter of disobedience to orders with Phaulkon, he had no such hope in the present case. When the prize came in, it was visible to the whole Mahomedan population, who would, he Was sure, petition Ayudhya at once. He saw that he must forestall them and wrote to Phaulkon, telling him what he had done and suggesting that the king and council's acquiescence might be obtained by representing the capture as a lucky omen. We are not fully informed on this point, but the reference to it later by Davenport is sufficiently explicit for anyone who remembers the importance attached to astrology by eastern kings. Evidently the place and date of the seizure were such as to make an exceptionally good impression in such quarters. Phaulkon, as we know, had been overruled in the matter of Coates and he saw in the present seizure a chance of getting his way. With this hint from White about a happy astrological conjunction he piloted the affair successfully through the council and the king's sanction was obtained. This regularized White's position at law in the particular case; but, though the sanction could be taken as applying to the whole matter of Coates and Golconda, the letter conveying it contained no reference to the war itself.

White, however, felt that Phaulkon was behind him and that all would be well. He decided to take what prizes he could. The *Meer Faqueer Deun* was reconditioned, armed as a frigate and renamed the *Revenge*. A certain Captain English, who had recently been engaged by the Siamese government, was placed in command. In the open season of 1685–6, while Coates was at Madapollam, English, accompanied by Cropley in the *Dorothy*, was sent to prowl off the coast of Pegu. There early in 1686 they seized the *Traja Raja*, a ship belonging to an Indian merchant who lived under the protection of the Company at Madras. On board there were several respectable Hindu traders from that town. The ship had just left Syriam, a port near the present city of Rangoon, and was on the way to Madras with a valuable cargo. These explanations were given to Cropley and English, when they seized her, but were not accepted. The men were Indians; that was good enough. They were taken to Mergui and thrown into prison by White. There they remained for eight days without food or drink, until they were in the frame of mind to which it had always been his intention to bring them. Taken from gaol in an exhausted condition, they were brought before him.

He knew who they were and that he had no shadow of

authority to seize them, but he was not going to release them until they made it worth his while. The conditions were simple, £1,350 down and a paper signed by all to say that he had done nothing to them and had taken nothing from them. They signed and paid. White then released them and cleared the *Traja Raja*, though his last act was to demand and get from their Indian master a matter of £150 in gold and cash, his earrings and a parcel of rubies and musk.

White, as we shall see, was always careful to have his papers in order. His piracies, robberies and embezzlements were done under the cloak of an unimpeachable file. The merchants, of course, complained when they reached Madras and White eventually was sent the bill. But that was long afterwards and we shall come to it in due course.

The *Traja Raja* was the most sensational of White's seizures because the merchants were so cruelly treated. Their cries for help as they lay in their godown prison near the docks were heard all over the quarter. But it was by no means the only Case during the period October 1685 to March 1686. Cropley and English were very successful. They brought in a total of seven ships to Mergui and a number of others had to pay a heavy squeeze on the high seas to avoid seizure. But they made one bad mistake; they captured and took into harbour a ship belonging to Robert Freeman, the President at Masulipatam.

All this time White had been very careful to continue the promotion of the Madras factors' private trade. His intention was to give them such an interest, almost the interest of an accomplice, in his filibustering, that in their official capacity they would look the other way. The *Revenge*, for instance, dropped in at Madras in 1686 and delivered business letters addressed by White to Freeman and others. But this seizure of Freeman's ship by White's careless lieutenants gave much offence, for, though White let her go at once, she was delayed and interest was lost. Coates had already taken some of

97

Freeman's rice-boats at Madapollam. It was this sort of thing which eventually irritated the Company so much that they turned on White.

But in 1686 he was master of the bay. He seized what ships he liked. He preyed on all Mahomedan and Hindu commerce. There was nobody to oppose him. As no real war existed between him or rather between his master, the King of Siam, and the governments of the unfortunate persons whose property he stole, he was to all intents and purposes a pirate operating on a large scale.

As soon as Phaulkon entrusted him with the authority carried by the office of Shāhbandar, he must have decided to go in for freebooting as a quick way to riches. For years he had been a pilot, captain and merchant on the bay; lie had seen the peculiar defencelessness of its traders, who ventured in ships armed only sufficiently to repulse the attacks of native pirates, rovers like the Saleeters, who could only take a big ship if she was in distress or anchored carelessly under the islands by a pirate nest. When he was given the power, when his yards turned out ships and the treasury armed them, he became master and under cover of his position plundered the merchantmen who were not strong enough to oppose his frigates. Though Phaulkon supported him, it must not be thought that the value of the prizes went to the treasury. As we shall see, White had his methods. The treasury got something, Phaulkon had his share, money was distributed at court, but White took each time a substantial sum for himself. The terror and loathing with which the Mahomedan traders of Mer gui now began to regard him can be imagined. This was the man whom Francis Davenport was shortly to meet and describe in his diary.

It happened in this way. As already recorded, Captain Leslie left for the Pegu coast on board the *New Jerusalem* in February 1686. In March he captured off Cape Negrais a vessel belonging to a merchant of Bengal, which was on her way from Syriam to chat country. Her name was the *Quedabux*. He brought her into M ergui on the 13th. On that ship was Francis Davenport. This Davenport was what we should now call an American. He originally came from Boston, where his father was a captain. I have mentioned the strange chance by which he had travelled out to India in 1670 on the same boat as George White and Phaulkon, It was alleged afterwards by his enemies that he left America for England and, in turn, England for India on account of complicity in certain criminal offences, but whether his life was as disreputable as his detractors declared is open to doubt. He was certainly a man of education and some birth, socially White's equal. A sailor by profession, he was a qualified navigator with a scientific bent. on arrival in India he did not attach himself to George White, but entered the employ of the East India Company, sailing to Tonkin as boatswain and to Bantam as gunner. In 1680 he was on the list of Hugli pilots. In 1686, the year of these present events, he navigated on behalf of the Hugli factory a ship called the *Hopewell* to Burma. He suffered shipwreck on the Coast of Pegu and, getting ashore alive, was sold into slavery by the Burmese authorities, for if, wrote Hamilton, a 'stranger has the misfortune to be shipwrecked on their coast, by the laws of the country. the Men are the King's slaves'. From this misery Joseph Demarcora, the brother of John Demarcora, whose ship. the *New Jerusalem*, Coates had taken, redeemed him 'at his vast charge' out of humanity. He then shipped at Syriam on board the *Quedabux* for Hugli to report to his principals. As we have seen, his ship was Captured by, of all ships, the *New Jerusalem*, the property of his deliverer's brother, and he was brought into a port where the brother of his old acquaintance, George White, was now Shāhbandar.

On the morning of March 14th he was allowed to land under a strong guard at the wharf below White's house. He went up the hill at once to see him and at the door met Mr. William How, who like him had been captured and was, as I have said, White's accountant. How introduced him Into the presence of the Shāhbandar.

Davenport then put his case. Captain Leslie had seized the *Quedabux*. He was not going into the rights of that, though he must say that she was not a Golconda ship. But he himself was English, he came from the East India Company settlement in Bengal and was merely a passenger on the *Quedabux*. As the King of Siam was not at War with the Company, there was no reason, he supposed, why he should not continue his interrupted journey to Bengal by any available ship.

White was very cordial. There was no objection, he said; a ship of his own was leaving the very next day for Hugli with a cargo of elephants, was already anchored, indeed, below the bar; Davenport could take a passage on her. He would even let him have a supply of fresh provisions at once, as he understood that his private stores had been eaten by the sailors of the *New Jerusalem*.

In the course of the day, Davenport had an opportunity of observing White more closely. When the native captain of the *Quedabux* was brought *in* by Captain Leslie, his captor, White pointed out that as from all accounts the *Quedabux* belonged to a subject of the Mogul, and had nothing to do with Golconda, Leslie had exceeded his instructions in making a prize of her. This was rather startling news, for Leslie thought he could seize any Indian ship leaving Burma. It had never occurred to him to distinguish subjects of the Mogul from those of Golconda or Pegu. He believed he had White's authority to capture anything afloat which did not obviously belong to the Company. But White chose in this case to take a scrupulous line. He told the native captain that he would send the *Quedabux* on her way at once after recruiting her with water and bananas. His reason is obvious—he was afraid to consummate a piracy before a witness like Davenport.

The Bengali, astonished at this apology, passed at once from dejection to impertinence. He intimated that the mere release of his ship was not enough, that she wanted repairs, that the elephants he had on board were indisposed and must have treatment on shore, that all this would take time and might prevent him leaving before the monsoon. He ended by saying that he reserved the right to demand on behalf of his employers damages for the delays caused by his wrongful seizure on the high seas.

When White heard the Bengali (probably a native of Chittagong) talking in this strain, his caution forsook him, he fell into a violent rage and, shooting that the ship was to be unloaded at once, ordered some rubies and other valuable merchandise on board to be banded over to him. 'As for you', he said to the Chittagonian, 'you shall have the elephants delivered to you to be maintained at your own charge. If you would not take the first offer of liberty, you shall stay long enough before you shall have a second made you.' This reduced the native captain to his former servility and he made no difficulty about signing a paper, written in Persian, to the effect that he was staying in Mergui till after the monsoon of his own free will.

Next morning Davenport sent his chest ahead to the ship below the bar which was to carry him to Bengal White had procured the fresh provisions and these had been put into a boat, which was alongside the wharf. Before stepping into it, Davenport decided to go up and say good-bye to the Shāh-bandar. White was amiability itself. He told Davenport that it would be most obliging of him if, when he reached Bengal, he could manage to explain to all concerned that the *Quede bux* was remaining at Mergui at the desire of her commander, strictly at the commander's request. He then wished him good-bye, 'with a great deal of Courtesie'.

Davenport left the house and descended to the wharf. As the boat was pushing off, a man came running with an order to stop her. She put back and Davenport was told that White wanted to see him again. He returned to the house and White said: 'For some reasons I have, I think it not convenient that you should go on chat ship to Bengala.' On second thoughts he evidently felt it unsafe to let him go; he had seen what was too like a piracy. At this sudden change, Davenport was much surprised and disturbed, He had observed White the day before alter quickly from a good to a bad humour. He seemed a man of sudden impulses.

White presently continued: 'I intend nothing to your prejudice, but have a mind to do you a greater kindness than you are aware of.' He then offered him an appointment in the Siamese service.

DAVENPORT: 'I have never in my life served any heathen Prince, Perhaps such an engagement might debar me the privilege of returning home, when I should have a mind to it.'

WHITE: 'If you will serve me, I will order matters so to your advantage that you will have no occasion to repent your stay on shore this monsoon.'

DAVENPORT: 'There is the unhandsomeness of taking that, or any other employ, until I have first appeared before my late masters and given them an account of the loss of their ship.'

WHITE: 'I shall give you fifteen taels a month to assist me in my particular affairs and in the month of August next I will put you in master and supra cargo of a ship of my own, which I am resolved to send to the bay, which would be abundantly more to your benefit than to go now as passenger, when you must expect to lye a whole monsoon at home out of employ.'

Davenport accepted this attractive offer and, if we consider his circumstances, it is only surprising chat he made any demur. Just rescued from slavery, he was probably destitute, particularly if he had adventured anything upon the *Hopewell*, a total wreck. Fifteen taels a month was a remarkable starting pay. At that date a tael was worth ten shillings. The salary offered was therefore £90 a year. A factor at Madras only received £20 a year, Elihu Yale, second in council of Madras at that date, was paid at the rate of £100 a year. Davenport was therefore being offered practically the salary of a member of council in the East India Company, with in addition immediate prospects of a lucrative private trade. At the moment White had urgent need of a clever and educated man to assist him. That Davenport was very competent these pages will testify.

After accepting White's offer, Davenport's first act was to get his chest back from the Bengal ship at the bar. He had just time to scribble a note, explaining where he was, to his principals at Hugli before the ship sailed. He then moved into White's house, where a room was found for him.

Next day, March 16th, White handed over to him all his papers and account books. These were in the greatest confusion, for Mr. How was not an experienced accountant. The most urgent matter was the treasury books. These had not been passed by the revenue board at Ayudhya since December 1684. Urgent orders had been received to balance them up to the first of the current month and to submit them before July. Davenport therefore had to wrestle with the entries for the whole of 1685 and for the first two months of 1686. White promised him a clerk to write out the fair copy. He began work at once.

That afternoon two Englishmen arrived from Ayudhya overland. They were Thomas Yale, brother of Elihu Yale, and a Mr. James Wheeler, who was an interloper. He had originally been employed in India by the East India Company, but had gone to Ayudhya, attracted by the favour there extended to adventurers and by the large salaries which Phaulkon paid. We met Yale last in Ayudhya with Strangh in 1683, when he and Phaulkon had got on well together. After returning with Strangh to report to Surat, the Company's headquarters on the Bombay side, he had been sent back to Ayudhya in 1685 to explore ways and means of repairing the breach.

But the situation was hopeless, for a great French embassy had arrived. He was now returning to Madras on a peculiar mission.

Some little rime before, his brother Elihu had promised to procure for the King of Siam, as a private deal, some remarkable rubies. Ivatt negotiated the affair and Elihu was paid a large sum of money. The stones, set in jewellery, were sent to Ayudhya. On their examination by the king's experts, they were found to be of small value. The charge Was considered grossly excessive. The affair caused a scandal at court and there were people who said that Phaulkon was mixed up in it. His friendship with Thomas Yale was cited. While there may have been no truth in this accusation, Phaulkon felt obliged to take a decided line. He was now sending the jewels back to Elihu by the hand of his brother Thomas, together with a request for a refund of the money paid. White had instructions to place at once a ship at Thomas's disposal for his transport to Madras.

This episode throws a great deal of light on the realities of the situation, Here was the brother of the first merchant in Madras after the President, himself a senior member of the East India Company, travelling from Ayudhya with an interloper and putting up at Mergui with White, the man who for the last eight months had been preying on Indians in the bay with four frigates, the captains of which were hardly distinguishable from pirates. Yale's business is the return of jewels after an abortive private deal between Madras and Ayudhya. When we call to mind that afterwards Elihu Yale, becoming President of Madras, made such an enormous fortune in so unconventional a manner that he was not allowed to leave India for some time pending inquiry, and when we remember that he was succeeded in his office by Thomas Pitt, one of the most theatrical interlopers of the succeeding period, we are obliged to conclude that at this time there was less difference than might appear on paper between the Company

merchants and interlopers. The premier interest of both was
a private fortune as quick as possible.

We should avoid picturing the East India Company as it
afterwards became when it added India to the Empire. Ia
the 17th century it was still only a monopoly concern in
which the King of England was interested and whose members were half chartered merchants and half private adventurers. That was why it was natural for Thomas Yale to sit
down to brandy with White at Mergui. Moreover, coming
from Ayudhya. he had probably only a vague notion of
what had been happening in the bay. But the time was soon
coming when Phaulkon's French policy would force the
Company to identify itself more closely with the general
overseas interests of the English people. That Phaulkon, by
returning the rubies, was now making a private enemy of
Elihu Yale, shortly to be the Madras president, would give
added heat and motive to the latter's official animosity.

XIX. CAPTAIN COATES AND
HIS OPIUM

Next day Captain Coates arrived on the *Robin*. His
crew landing in high spirits paraded the streets, as if
they had been real men-of-war's men back from
fighting the enemy, and boasted to all they met of their exploits on the opposite coast, particularly the taking of the
battery at Narsapore.

Later in the day Coates himself went up to report his arrival
to White. Yale was sitting with the Shāhbandar. It was rather
an awkward moment when the captain, with the ingenuous
air of the faithful bloodhound, stepped into the room

expecting congratulations. White, who had received information by the sloop *Mary* of what had happened at   Madapollam,
had a great deal to Say to Coates, much of it disagreeable, but
this was not the moment to say it with Yale listening and
ready to repeat all he heard when he got to Madras.

Davenport, who was watching the comedy with his shrewd
eyes, writes:' 'twas easy enough to observe that Coats's
Reception by the Shabandar did not correspond with his expectation, though, because strangers were present, the best
side was put outermost on both hands.' The fact was that news
had reached Ayudhya of Coates's doings at Madapollam and
White had received orders to send him to the capital as soon
as he returned. White had told neither Phaulkon nor anyone
else of his having given. Coates authority. It was assumed at
court that he had turned filibuster on his own. As he had not
been very successful and had offended the Mahomedan interest, he was in a dangerous position if White did not stand by
him. However, serious talk was postponed till Yale was gone.

A ship was got ready, the *Dorothy* (Captain Cropley). On
March 20th Yale departed, being accompanied on board by
White, Davenport and Coates. These three remained with
him drinking last toasts as the *Dorothy* dropped down the harbour, the *Robin* following behind to take them back to Mergui. At the bar farewells were exchanged and White and his
companions were rowed to the *Robin*.

On the way back up the harbour, White finding himself
alone with Coatcs, began to hector him about his exploits. He
had been ordered to make prizes of Golconda ships; what had
he done? He had taken the *Rcdclove* and the *New Jerusalem*,
but had given up the former and the valuables on the latter.
In addition he had seriously annoyed the Company. The
upshot of the season's cruise, which had cost a lot of money,
was no plunder and a bad reputation. Had he returned with
plenty of loot, all could have been arranged at court. The
valuables he had surrendered would have been, ample to have

made any view prevail there. But how were they going to shut the mouths of their enemies with no money? The outcry against him was most violent.

Coates pleaded his best endeavours.

WHITE: 'You must prepare to go to Syam and there give an account to the king of what you have done.'

COATES: 'I did you good service in revenging you on Ally Beague, the Hobledar of Mechlipatam, by putting the country into a combustion. This was done in observance of your private orders to me. Instead of being blamed, I expected you should according your promise Skreen me from his Majesties displeasure. I exposed myself meerly to it for your sake.'

When they disembarked at the wharf 'they came to so high words that Coates in a great passion openly slighted the Shabander and the Lord Phaulkcon'. They mounted the hill abusing each other. On reaching the house Coates in a loud and desperate voice ordered his surgeon to bring him an ounce of opium. From this he pinched a lump, which he rolled into a pill, and protesting that he was a much wronged man, made a great show of swallowing it. But actually, he stepped into the next room an instant and took it out of his mouth. Returning and going up to White he began protesting again, pointing to the ounce of opium, showing the big bit out of it and saying reproachfully: 'your unhandsomeness has made me take the pill.' He then flung the opium out of the window and, assuming the attitude of a man who had not long to live, he bemoaned the misfortune which had given him so hardhearted a master.

This acting deceived White. He thought Coates had really taken poison and 'seem'd mightily touched at it'. The garrison surgeons, both French, were sent for urgently. They examined Coates and said they could detect no sign of opium.

The scene, however, had been sufficient to change White's mood. Nor was he sure that the surgeons' diagnosis was correct.

WHITE: 'I shall engage Life for Life that if you but go up to Syam I will bring it about so that all your proceedings shall meet with his Majesties approbation and you will not want all the Favours and Honours you can desire.'

At this speech Coates calmed down, but still maintaining the farce took antidotes. Next morning he allowed himself to appear quite well. Nothing more was then said about his exploits on the coast Don Heredia arrived shortly afterwards and was given similar instructions to proceed to Ayudhya.

During the following days Coates prepared for his journey and made his papers over to Davenport, Amongst them was the huge bill of damages handed to him by Wales. Even though the total had now been largely reduced by his return of the valuables, the items detailing his damage to Company property still remained, It was an awkward document to explain away. A copy of it might be sent to Ayudhya. The day before he left (April 21st) Davenport found him sitting in a very melancholy attitude.

DAVENPORT: 'What makes you so?'

COATES (producing a paper); 'Read this.'

It was White's letter to him to disregard the king's orders and to do what mischief he could to Golconda, It assured him that White not only would bear him out, but would make it redound to his great advantage and honour at court.

COATES: 'Has Mr. White's demeanour to me since my arrival at Mergen corresponded with those splendid Promises he made me in this Paper? Is it reasonable that I should be turned over to Syam to give an account of my proceedings at the Coast, when Mr. White was the only person who put me upon that Action, and for whose sake alone I thus embroil'd myself?'

DAVENPORT: 'My opinion is that the exhausting of so much of the Kings stock by your twelve months stay at the Coast, without any advantage, was the main reason which made Mr. White loth to pass your Accounts. But Mr. White, being sensible that those orders may at any time be produced against him, there is no question but he will use his utmost endeavours to obviate all blame that the Lord Phaulkon could transfer upon you.'

COATES: 'Nothing troubles me but that, my first commencement of the breach at the Coast being point blank contrary to the King of Syams pleasure, I see no way to save myself but by letting the King understand the truth of the matter, which could not but be of hazardous consequence to Mr. White.'

DAVENPORT: 'I have little to say, but I advise you to be of good Courage and yet very cautious how you prejudice your old and experienced friend.'

A conclusion to be drawn from these conversations seems to be that Phaulkon's power was now so great that White was safe so long as he befriended him. But there was a growing clamour. To protect him, Phaulkon might find it necessary to sacrifice Coates. Yet summing it all up, Davenport felt that probably Phaulkon and White would carry off the day and that it would be unnecessary and therefore most unwise for Coates to try to save himself by prejudicing his master.

XX. WHITE INCREASES THE PACE

White does not seem to have been alarmed by the complaints, which he must have known were being sent to the court against him. He continued on his course, if anything increasing the pace, making money by every means at his disposal and taking no precaution to placate anyone. The shadow of Phaulkon, falling round him like a magic garment, had made him invulnerable—or so he appeared to assume, for his actions at this stage can only be explained on the assumption that he thought he would never be Called to account. The news filtering down from the capital gave him every reason for confidence. No doubt he had had a long talk on the stability of Phaulkon's position with Thomas Yale and Mr. Wheeler. They may very well have advised him —and this would account for Yale's affability—that Phaulkon was never stronger. Now in the first class of the mandarinate, the acknowledged chief minister, counsellor and favourite of the king, supported by the majority of the court officers, his policy had been triumphantly vindicated by the arrival the previous September of Louis XIV's splendid embassy, of which I shall have more to say later on. There is no question of it—Phaulkon was all-powerful at this date, and in a country like Siam that implied far more than in England. White felt that he had the soundest reasons for believing that he was safe. Phaulkon was his friend; Phaulkon himself favoured the filibustering in the bay. The sole question was whether he could resist the Mahomedan pressure, which had support in the council, White believed he was strong enough to do this successfully now that the French had arrived. There was nothing to be afraid of. Let Coates go up.

And as I said, White now put on the pace. His captains seized the *Sancta Cruz*, a ship of 350 tons burden belonging to the brother of John Demarcora, the Joseph who had ran-somed Davenport from slavery. Joseph was also a mandarin of Pegu and the seizure of his ship with her cargo was made on that ground, but White's subsequent disposal of her solely on his own account rates this Capture as plain piracy. When the *Sancta Cruz* was brought into port, instead of unloading and warehousing her rich cargo, entering the same in the king's ledgers and reporting to Ayudhya for orders, he put some of his own men on her and sent her to Achin at the north end of Sumatra, some 500 miles down the coast, there to sell her cargo as a private venture of his own. As he could not spare many men, he retained most of the Armenian's crew but held Joseph Demarcora and his son prisoners against a possible mutiny. There can be no doubt that Phaulkon heard of this affair, but in what light it was represented to him by White, we do not know. Presumably White reported that the cargo was suitable for Achin and that he would credit its value later, but, as will be shown, White was faking his accounts. once he got money into his hands, the king saw very little of it.

This affair of the *Sancta Cruz* moved Davenport to a risky action. He was under a permanent obligation to Joseph Demarcora for ransoming him and he felt he must try something on his behalf. Unknown to White he wrote personally to Phaulkon, who had come out, as we have seen, on the same ship with him in 1670, and presuming on this dared to intercede for his friend Joseph, making bold to say that his ship and cargo 'had been taken from him under pretence of his Majesties Authority'. Since no inquiry was instituted as a result of this letter, we must conclude that Phaulkon was prepared to wink at White's actions. There may have been an arrangement between them to share privately in such ventures, for it is noted later by Davenport that White and Phaulkon were business partners in the Japan trade at this time. But it also appears that Phaulkon did not know how much money White was making and that White did not want him to know.

In addition to the seizure of the property of merchants trading in the bay, such as Demarcora, White was making money by normal trade. In April the *Delight* arrived in Mergui- It is interesting to observe that in spite of White's increasingly bad reputation, the factors in Madras were still in business partnership with him. The *Delight* was owned jointly by White and a Mr. Lucas, who was actually on the council at Madras. The cargo valued at about £3,000 was also their joint property. It was sent to Ayudhya overland and sold there by Francis Heath, a private merchant from London and White's agent at the capital. Later in the month the '*Agent*' arrived with a cargo of which White owned one-third and two interlopers from Bengal the remainder, On these, Davenport says, he played a nasty trick. In his official capacity as Shāhbandar he refused to allow them to land their part of the cargo till they had paid lain a substantial sum.

These activities having occupied White to within a week or so of the break of the monsoon, which always arrives in Mergui early in May, he resolved to take a short holiday, The weather is at its most oppressive just before the S. W. wind sets in and a trip to the islands was likely to be refreshing. He combined with this excursion the charting of some of the channels on the south of the harbour, Davenport added to his other accomplishments that of marine surveyor, and together they made an exploration with the line of the various exits round the south of Pataw and out to King Island. They had a party of friends on the two new sloops, *Robin* and *Mary*, and when the monsoon began to blow up and it became rough in the outer archipelago, they turned back and fished under cover of King Island. In this beautiful scenery, a fresh wind blowing from the great bay beyond, they enjoyed themselves for some days, bathing, exploring, sailing and dining. White was carefree. His money affairs were going very well. He had already remitted considerable sums home by means of bills of exchange arranged by his agents in the Persian Gulf and the Red Sea.

Suddenly he received orders to proceed at once to Ayudhya and give an account of his administration. This was a tremendous shock. The orders contained no reasons; he was to proceed forthwith, that was all. So the storm had broken. The anonymous letters and secret complaints from the numerous persons who had suffered at his hands had at last, it seemed, obliged Phaulkon to send for him. What had Coates been saying? Did this mean that Phaulkon, powerful though he was, could no longer defend him, or was Phaulkon himself angry with him? It was impossible to say. He could not hope to escape ruin in either event, for he knew only too well how irregularly he had acted. He had been in high spirits all the holiday. He now became melancholy and reserved. The rest of the party saw there was something serious the matter. In silence and constraint they all hurried back to Mergui.

XXI. WHITE IS RECALLED TO AYUDHYA

W hite's first inclination was to refuse to go to the capital. He was not at all sure that it was safe. Once out of his own jurisdiction he would be at the mercy of people who now could not get at him or who were afraid to speak openly in case he heard of it and punished them. Moreover, there was a chance of his being thrown into prison. Being an Englishman might protect him from the bastinado—the usual punishment for officials out of favour—but imprisoned he might be. Phaulkon had thrown Peter Crouch and John Thomas, Company merchants, into a dungeon because they had refused to sell him some nails; he had caused Samuel Potts to be flogged and exhibited in public with a board round his neck. Captain Lake of the *Pruduent Mary* had died in prison. These things or worse might happen to him. Not to go to Ayudhya would of course be ruin, but to go might put his life in jeopardy. As a sailor, White had a dread of being cut off from his ship. A ship in the harbour represented freedom. As long as he had that, he could get home. And he had saved some money. With these thoughts uppermost in his mind, he drafted a letter to Phaulkon, stating that his health was indifferent, certainly not sufficiently robust to sustain a journey in the rains through the forest. He added the touch that in any event he could not suddenly leave his work without great prejudice to the administration.

But before he sent this letter, another messenger arrived from the capital, followed quickly by a third, each of them the bearer of an order for his immediate departure. From neither of them could he obtain any precise information as to the cause of his recall.

Thinking the matter over, he decided that he would have to go. Flight at this moment would be most inopportune. After all, there was nothing to show that Phaulkon had turned against him. All these months he had written him no word of reproach. It must simply be that his enemies had secured the ear of a section at court and that Phaulkon was obliged to send for him. Once in Ayudhya, his friend would devise means of proving to his accusers that his conduct had not only been irreproachable, but had redounded enormously to the glory of Siam. Had he not made Siam for the first time feared in the bay? His captains, Leslie, Coates, Cropley, English, flying the king's flag, had taught the Mahomedans they could no longer insult His Majesty's servants. He tore up his first letter and addressed Phaulkon afresh, saying that he was glad of his lordship's invitation to visit the capital, as it would enable him to engage with his superiors during the close season of the monsoon in necessary discussions on the policy and measures to be adopted in the next open season; that had it not been for a tour he had undertaken during the preceding weeks to survey the frontiers, he would already have written to beseech his lordship for permission to come and kiss his hand.

He felt better after despatching this letter, more confident that Phaulkon would see him through any unpleasantness which might arise, so sure that all would be well that he decided to increase his personal estate by some adjustments of the king's accounts.

The treasury books, already referred to, had by this time been brought into some semblance of order by Davenport. Among other entries they comprised the military and naval pay rolls, with the names of the soldiers in the garrison and the seamen on the ships. There was a pleasant balance in the king's favour, In order conveniently to appropriate this sum to the private head of his own credit, White inserted sufficient names of imaginary payees to engulf it. As Davenport puts it in his coloured style: 'he invented a Muster Roll of so many mens names (who for ought any man knows never were in rerum Natura) as swept out of the Kings stock 135 Cattees (£1,350), as clearly as if they had been lain on a Drum-head in the face of a Regiment.'

Stores were troublesome to keep account of when away, so by entering those on the king's books, valued at £2,760, as disbursed and distributed among the ships 'the King's Godowns were clean swept and the Sha b anders fill'd". After all, had he not said that his departure would greatly prejudice the public service?

White's next anxiety was to see that his private affairs were in such a posture that no matter what happened in Ayudhya, he or his heirs might realise his estate. Mr. How, the steward, was given charge of his house. An inventory was made of the furniture, utensils and ornaments. He wrote a number of private letters with instructions that they were to be handed to those of his captains who had not yet come into port. These contained his orders for the disposal of their cargoes.

He then turned his attention to Burnaby. We have heard nothing of him since December 1683, two and a half years before, when he and White travelled together down to Mergui, The fact is that Burnaby was a nonentity and that he was treated as such by White. Phaulkon's idea had been that they should consult frequently and, though working within their respective spheres, should take joint responsibility for important decisions. With this end in view he addressed despatches to them both together. But this did not suit White. There was so much to conceal about his actions that he could not take another into his confidence. Besides, he wanted no one's advice, particularly advice which might have been contrary. Burnaby, moreover, was notoriously indiscreet. But he was also easy-going and, when White broke the seals of letters addressed to them both and failed to show him the contents, he raised no effective protest.

One matter, however, had seriously estranged him of late, He had been given no share, not even a fractional share, of the prize money from the many seizures, which had enriched White. They had not spoken to each other for some time. But looking round, White came to the conclusion that Burnaby was the only man in Mergui to whom he could entrust that part of his personal estate as yet unrealized in cash and remitted home. He went round to see him, and, having a great power of charming people when he so desired, soon had him devoted to his interests. In his hands, therefore, he put his plate, a small box of rubies (presumably those he had taken from the *Traja Raja*, the *Quedubux* and perhaps from Coates) and a number of other jewels. He authorized him to open his letters and explained how to dispose of their cargoes if his merchantmen came in.

It is clear from these careful arrangements—always characteristic of White where his private interests were concerned—that he could not be quite sure whether he would return to Mergui as Shāhbandar. Nor did he know how long he would be away.

All this settled, he had his clothes packed for the journey. Davenport, whom he considered invaluable, particularly in a crisis of this kind, he was bringing with him. His party, consisting, besides Davenport, of Captain Leslie, John Turner the clerk, with a Mr. Ware in charge of his black servants and the baggage, left Mergui on May 20th.

XXII. THE SORROWFUL
JOURNEY

As we have seen, the monsoon had already broken. Before May 20th violent downpours must have swept in from the S.W. The weather was bound to have been very crying for a journey. Drenching showers frequently were falling, the humidity was high, with the temperature about 90°F. during the day and 75°F. at night, though after a heavy squall there would be a drop suddenly of 15 degrees. On such occasions there is much danger of a chill, followed by fever, and the rain revives the mosquitoes and the leeches. In the soaking undergrowth of the forest tracks these pests swarm to the attack, insalubrious at any time, the jungle now was dangerous to cross.

They made their first stage to Tenasserim as usual in country boats and comparative comfort. There the fourth of Phaulkon's messengers was waiting. In haste they were paddled up the interminable river to Jalinga, passing the rapids of the now rising stream. Two sedan chairs were in readiness. Into these White and Leslie climbed and were carried off through the jungle as fast as their bearers could take them. Davenport mounted an elephant, leaving Turner and Ware to follow with the baggage carts. They took the track to Peranne, a town on the shore of the Gulf of Siam. At that place two more pursuivants were found. The impatience of the court for his arrival began to get on White's nerves. Davenport has the phrase: 'This hurrying of those Messengers at the heels one of another, gave Mr. White no small jealousie, that all was not well.' At Peranne they left the land route and embarking on sailing boats made the bar of Siam in a few days. During this part of the journey by sea, which permitted of some concentration of thought, White 'wishing himself no Shabander', went over his position with Davenport. The secretary was told to make a note of those items in White's admiiustration, which might require the most explanation at headquarters, so that he could think over in advance what answers to give. Davenport has left in detail these items for our inspection. They are of considerable interest.

The matter of the contrary orders to Coates seemed 'the deepest and most unanswerable charge they could lay against him'. He had started a war contrary to orders. But Phaulkon by his subsequent acceptance of prizes taken into Mergui had condoned the breach at Madapollam. That was all right, provided that Phaulkon would or could stand by him. But if his enemies were strong enough, to persuade the king that Phaulkon should not have advised sanction of later seizures, then he was left to face the plain charge of disobedience in a matter of great importance. It all turned on Phaulkon. He believed Phaulkon had the power. But supposing news of his other misdemeanours had reached his ears, news that he had been cheating the government, or worse, cheating his friend and patron of his share. The *Sancta Cruz* which he had appropriated altogether for himself—that would be difficult to explain. The only line to take there was to swear his intention from the start had been to pay the value of the cargo later, But why had no report been made? He forgot to report in the press of public business. Would that do? But there were other matters. He had seized a number of ships, but had let them go when the Indian merchants on board had given him private consideration amounting to 5,000 pagodas, £2,400. He had taken the precaution to report that matter. He had written to Phaulkon: 'The Merchants on their departure freely made me a small present, which for its inconsiderableness, I hope may pass for a perquisite of my office,' If Phaulkon had heard the presents amounted to £2,400, would he hold chat sufficiently inconsiderable? He might or he might not.

Then there had been his practice of forcing importers of cargoes to sell him any goods he wanted at his own price, when he would then resell the goods to the town merchants at a higher price—a much higher price. That had been an abuse, certainly, and one which had done him much harm, for it had sent so many Mahomedans complaining behind his back to the king. How was he going to explain that, so as to make it appear he had acted to the king's advantage? It would be very difficult, because, unfortunately, there were occasions when some of these goods had been sold by him to the king himself as stores for ships and the like, but not at the original price he had paid for them. And what about his box of rubies? That was crown property.

Another matter which troubled him was his complete neglect to fortify Mergui. He had been specially selected for that task, which was regarded as urgent in view of the repereussions a forward policy in the bay was certain to provoke; large sums of money had been placed at his disposal for the purpose. But he had done nothing, nothing at all; and, now that he recollected the facts, he had credited to his private account the total allotment. There had been some talk in the town about that. It was a thing you could not hide, Burnaby, too, had felt strongly that, as the work was connected with the town, he should have got his share. Perhaps the most stupid thing of all was his neglect to consult and give percentages to the local mandarins in charge of the other civil departments. These people knew what was going on and now would all be witnesses against him.

The case looked bad, as bad as could be. He could not explain these charges away. There was just the one hope, Phaulkon. But would he be ready to cover up so much?

'Thus was', records Davenport, 'the remaining part of our passage spent by him for forming fit answers for what he had recollected as most like to be alleadged against him, and being from hence forward more than ordinarily dejected in his spirits, the day before we got up to the City, he was taken with a strong fever.'

XXIII. WHITE'S DESPERATE
SICKNESS

They reached Ayudhya on June Ist at 6 p.m., a fast journey of twelve days from Mergui. The court was not in residence. The king had moved to his summer palace at Louvo, a place more than another day's journey up the river. In spite of his increasing fever, White, with Leslie, left for Louvo next morning, Davenport staying in Ayudhya to execute some commissions.

On June 6th Davenport received a letter from Leslie to say that White was 'desperately sick, almost past hopes of recovery'. Davenport at once took boat for Louvo, arriving there on June 8th. He found White in lodgings opposite Phaulkon's palace. Coates and the don were at his bedside. He was delirious. They all sat up with him. That night Was the crisis. Next day his temperature Came down. Davenport went to him when he could speak. He said he felt very bad and desired him to put his private papers in order in case of his death. They were in his escritoire. An inventory should be made of his personal estate and the accounts should be balanced. For a fortnight Davenport worked on this, nursing White till he grew convalescent. He had been very ill, having no doubt contracted malignant malaria during his journey through the forest belt.

When he was able to walk about in his room, Davenport showed him the statement of his affairs. It was encouraging. He had saved a substantial sum. Safely to his credit in England were 1,574 cattees of silver, equivalent to £15,740. At Mergui with Burnaby, his plate, jewels and the rubies were valued at £3,220. In partnership with Phaulkon in the Japan trade he had £4,000. This represented a total of £22,966, equal at a conservative estimate to a hundred thousand pounds sterliog to-day. He also had a good sum of cash in hand for immediate expenditure at court, as required. The review of his financial position cheered him.

Davenport was then directed to make out two statements, one containing details of his whole estate, which should be sent to his executor, Heath, at once. Heath was in Ayudhya. The second statement should contain only that part of his estate represented by his partnership with Phaulkon—the £4,000. That was to be left loose among his papers.

After a further week of convalescence White felt that he was strong enough to wait on Phaulkon. It was now July 1st. During these weeks, though he lived opposite, Phaulkon had made no direct inquiries about his old friend's condition. All seemed very cold and most unlike him, though the Lady Phaulkon, who was Japanese, used sometimes to send across the road 'what she thought might be grateful to him and proper for him'. It was therefore without his usual freedom and familiarity that he approached his patron's new and magnificent residence, with its iron gateway, Strangh's unwilling contribution, its courtyard full of liveried attendants and guards, its private chapel, its extensive and handsomely appointed rooms. He sent in his name. Three days successively flunkeys told him that his lordship was engaged and could not see him, He waited about in the courtyard, bareheaded in the rain and chilly wind, standing longer than he was well able, and 'much dejected at the alteration he observed in his Lordships Carriage towards him, he fell into a relapse'.

His fever was not so violent as before, but it was accompanied by a grievous pain in the stomach. He went back to bed. Coates and Davenport, faithfully watching up with him, thought his condition hopeless. Feeling that his last hour was come, he dictated between spasms a letter to Phaulkon.

This letter, as we have his private memorandum on the major lapses of his duty, is pleasantly ingenious. He began by a complaint of, an astonishment at, his lordship's coldness towards him. He had enemies—that he knew—enemies who had secretly poisoned his lordship's mind, but was not the calumny of disappointed persons the experience of all men in 'publick and weighty Employment'? 'Having now one foot in the grave,' he continued, 'I can safely aver (and nothing troubles my conscience now so much as that) how I have always been more Zealous for the Honour and Interest of my Master the King than in my Devotion towards my Creator, under whose afflicting Hand now I lie,' The sentiment here has been lifted rather too bodily out of Shakespeare to ring true, but perhaps White hoped that Phaulkon had not read *Henry VIII*.

He concluded the letter saying he desired to know how he had offended, so that he might throw himself at his lordship's feet 'in confidence that his Lordship would not take delight in plucking down the Building which his own hand had raised'. Phaulkon replied so impressively that I must give his letter in full.

July 10, 1686

'RIGHT WORSHIPFUL,

'We know no reason you have to charge us with Strangeness in our deportment to you, when you consider or observe our general Carriage towards all other persons, which we hope is not offensive to any man in particular. The jealousie you express of having private Enemies, who endeavour to estrange us from you, as'tis on our part altogether Causeless; so it not only argues you culpable of something you would not have discovered, but highly reflects upon us, as if we took pleasure in harkening to the malicious tattling and detraction of over busie men, to the prejudice of those we have thought worthy of so considerable a Trost, as we, upon mature deliberation, thought good to confer upon you: Nay, Sir, we must be plain, and tell you. The Shabander has no other Enemy, that we know of, than the Shabander, which your own hand will evidently make appear.

'That you arc now reduced so near the grave is a matter of

trouble to us, and that you may not hasten yourself thither, Ice us, as your Friend, persuade you to Temperance. As for the Protestation you make of your Zeal for His Majesties Honour and Interest, give us leave to tell you, that it is no miracle to see a man drive on his own Covetous designs, under a pretext of promoting his Kings interest, though we do not desire to charge you with being a Court Parasite.

'The satisfaction you desire shall be granted to you, so soon as you are in a condition to be Examined by our Secretary, who should long since have been sent to you, had we not understood your Indisposition, and be cautioned to be plain, fair and moderate in your Answers, to whatever Queries he proposes to you; avoiding all Passionate Expressions or Gestures, which may do you much harm, but cannot avail anything to your advantage.

'It will be no small pleasure to us to find you as innocent as you pretend, nor shall we ever take delight to ruine what our hands have built up; but if we perceive a Structure of our own raising begin to totter, and threaten our own ruine with its fall, none can tax us with imprudence, if we cake it down in time. There is your own Metaphor retorted, and the needful in Answer to your letter of yesterday's date, concluded with our hearty wishes for your recovery, as being

Your friend

PHAULKON'

White read this letter with confusion. He found some of the sentences Very tare'. There was now no doubt about it; he had been sent for to give an account of his behaviour before a commission of inquiry. Phaulkon might deny the tattle of malicious tongues but clearly information had reached him that White's administration, as chief commissioner of His Majesty's maritime affairs at Mergui, left much to be desired. on a further study of the text, however, White's spirits rose, He got the impression that Phaulkon was going to stand by him.

The letter is so revealing, that it repays further comment In the first place, the use of the plural by Phaulkon and his weighty style suggest the great minister, the mandarin of the first grade, the king's privy adviser, the man who had brought the French to Siam and who was now awaiting the arrival of a French army. The reader will observe that I have refrained —and I shall continue to refrain—from making an attempt to present an estimate of Phaulkon. He cannot take second place in a book on White. But I must supply sufficient information about him to make White's career intelligible. Below I shall state some of the influences from outside Siam which bore upon his policy at this date, I invite the reader to await that statement and meanwhile to bear in mind that the Phaulkon whom White meets in 1686 is a bigger man than Strangh saw whispering with the Barcalong in 1683. He was now, for the moment at any rate, master of Siam and a figure in world politics. White knew, of course, that he had achieved a diplomatic coup by his success with the French, he saw the great state in which he lived, but he was sufficiently versed in the actualities of an oriental court to realize that, powerful though he was, he had to walk with caution, giving his every action an air of legality. He could not clear him by a stroke of the pen, All the formalities had to be observed.

The meaning of the letter may now be clearer. In the first paragraph Phaulkon suggests that he has reached such a position in the state that he is obliged to keep all men at a certain distance. He cannot, as of old, collogue with White, I interpret the second paragraph as conveying that as Phaulkon had chosen White for the Mergui appointment for reasons of state and because he held him on ma tore consideration to be a suitable man, mere gossip could not modify his conviction that, if White himself chose to work for him, he was fully competent for the post. In the next paragraph the reference to temperance is interesting. There is no doubt that White was a heavy drinker at times. The later extracts from Davenport will prove this. But it may be to moderation in speech and conduct that he is recommended. White was a very violent man. Lack of self-restraint at this moment would so embroil him in difficulties that he wo did be beyond the rescue even of Phaulkon. That this may be the interpretation is borne out by the particular warning of the next paragraph, where White is told he must submit quietly to the inquiry. If Phaulkon were to save him, he must let Phanlkon save him in his own way.

The sentence where he answers White's protestation of zeal is also full of subtle innuendo. It suggests that he had read Wolsey's speech in *Henry VIII*. White was not a court parasite, but a blunt adventurer. It was hard to think of him at any court.

We see the character of White emerging from behind the starched magnificence of Phaulkon's periods—a passionate fellow of strong individuality, with no conception of the tact and care necessary for his protection among the multitudinous and cunning complexities of the palace of Phra Narai. We have, too, a glimpse of Phaulkon, smiling behind the veil on veil of his circumlocutions.

The last paragraph is also significant, I may not be able to save you without exposing myself to undue risk, says Phaulkon, well aware that the association of rulers with disreputable instruments is one of the most potent causes of their downfall.

An interval followed the receipt of this letter, for White was still very weak. He and Davenport spent the rime in talking over their prospects. He no longer feared imprisonment and dismissal. What he was afraid of now was a transfer to another appointment. He knew that Phaulkon was giving Frenchmen important posts and that more Frenchmen were expected, Coates came in one morning with a rumour that Monsieur le Comte de Foorbin, a young gentleman in command of the Siamese fort at Bangkok, might be sent to Mergui. White's anxiety to retain his position of Shāhbandar was twofold; his interest and his safety both commended it. He knew the ropes there. The place suited his methods. Nowhere else could he trade so well. His ships, too, were out on ventures, Moreover, it was well away from the capital, and the government would always find it difficult to know what he was doing. Most important still—his thought before he left the place—he could get away quickly by ship if things went wrong.

The rumours carried in by Coates disturbed White to such a point that he wrote to Burnaby telling him that affairs in the capital were upside down, that he could no longer count on Phaulkon and that the French were supreme. He asked him to collect all his effects, and if he were not back in Mergui by October, to send them to India. An effort should be made to get in all sums due to him and to sell any stores in his warehouses. He went on to advise Burnaby that his own best course was to withdraw, while he still could do so.

This distracted letter showed how apprehensive White remained. The delay in settling his fate was destroying his nerve. His health was not fully recovered. He had been in a tropical climate for eleven years without a change home.

However, July 15th was fixed at last as the day for the examination of his papers. The board consisted of Phaulkon himself and the next most senior Siamese mandarin. The papers were in English, and they were all in Phaulkon's possession, who had no difficulty in withholding those he thought White could not explain. The board duly and at length considered what was before it and declared White innocent of any misdemeanour. After it had adjourned, Phaulkon sent for White privately and said: 'Well, Sir, you are cleared, but you must know that you owe your escape to me as I owe my self and all I have to your good brother George.' Phaulkon then handed White the famous instructions which Coates had received to ignore the king's orders, saying: 'If I have frowned on you, read this paper and 'twill satisfie you that I have reason. And I make no doubts that your Accounts, if thoroughly scann'd, would appear notoriously unhandsome.'

To this White made no reply, judging best, as he phrased it afterwards to Davenport, 'to hand[1] a Sail in time than carry a Mast by the Board'.

Phaulkon continued to admonish him with these words: 'I hope this will be a Caution to you for the future, nor are you to think that though I love you well, yet would I ruin myself to skreen you.'

Phaulkoa knew that those court mandarins, who had pressed the case against White on representations from the Mergui petitioners, would not be deceived by a mock inquiry. They would wait until they saw a chance of catching White in so flagrant a misdeed that he would be forced to abandon him. His power had averted the danger for a time, but if White continued in such courses, he was certain to be broken.

The minor matter of Coates and the don now offered no difficulty. On the general ground of the fine manner in which he had shown the flag of Siam, and without any reference to orders, accounts, mistakes or any other unpleasant topic, Phaulkon made Coates an Admiral. presenting him with a gold-hilted sword and a rich coat. But the title carried no salary and Coates felt cash down would have been preferable. At the moment he was penniless, having surrendered the Armenian's rubies to White or squandered their value.

Indeed, talking it over afterwards with White, who appeared to bear him no malice, he attributed his escape to his destitution. They did not look at his accounts or reports, as there was nothing to be got from him, if irregularities were proved. ''Twas my Happiness', said he, 'that I was not worth the Fleecing.'

But Coates was a plain man and he did not know what was going on behind the scenes. White and he owed their escape to the French, for unless Phaulkou had held that trump card he could never have supported his men against the

[1] To lower.

Mahomedan interest. If is worthy of note that the king does not appear in these transactions. When Phaulkoa Informed him that the allegations made against White were without foundation and that a properly constituted board had found him innocent, he did not interfere.

XXIV. THE FIERCE FIGHT WITH THE MACASSARS

Attention was now distracted from these matters by a sudden and alarming event. When a minister becomes very powerful and a king does not exercise his powers, malcontents plan rebellion and contemplate massacre. A conspiracy to dethrone King Phra Narai and assassinate Phaulkon was being hatched. The leaders kept out of sight, but there can be no doubt that they were the Mahomedan merchants and mandarins, together with the Siamese courtiers whom they had won over into opposition to Phaulkon. Their tools were formidable. They induced the Macassars to rise.

These Macassars were Malays who had fled under the leadership of their prince, Dai, from Macassar, the principal city of the Celebes, when some years before the Dutch captured it. The prince and his followers found asylum in Siam. King Phra Narai received this proud people honourably and gave them a quarter outside the city among the other quarters reserved for resident foreigners.

Now Malays at this date had a reputation. For reckless savagery and contempt of death there was no one like them in Siam. Contemporary writers all emphasize their passionate louring nature. Bowrey, writing in 1679, speaks of them as 'a very sullen illnatured people'.

Crawford says: 'The Siamese are favourably distinguished from their neighbours the Malays by the absence of that implacable spirit of revenge.'

Gervaise, writing just before the rising, noted: 'The Malays also are established here and are in greater numbers than could be desired, for they are Mahomedans and are known to be the worst people that can be found in the Indies, and to them are imputed all the crimes committed here. often they are really guilty of them for they are naturally wild and cruel. . . . They would always be inciting to rebellion in the State if they were not checked in their desires through punishment. . . . But their great numbers are to be dreaded, they are so fierce and so given to sorcery.'

Turpin, writing eighty-five years later from documents supplied to him by the French missions, is equally emphatic. He says, describing the rebels: 'This singular people deserves to be known. It is new to find in a climate predisposing to softness such marked ferocity, They did not employ firearms. Such weapons they regarded as inconsistent with personal valour and as detracting from the value of bodily strength and from skill with the sword: using them made it impossible to taste the full savour of vengeance.'

These were the fanatics whom the disaffected party roused by the cry of' 'Islam in danger'. The rebellion was fixed for   July. The king and Phaulkon, as we have seen, were at Louvo. The rebels' plan was to burn the city of Ayudhya, plunder the palace and then march on the summer palace to overthrow the king. Six hours before the projected insurrection, information leaked out and a large number of arrests were made. Phaulkon went down to Ayudhya and the leaders were put to death.

But this was only the beginning. The execution of their comrades, far from intimidating the rest of the Macassars, stimulated them to a pitch of rage. If they had risen in religious excitement, if the *coup d'état* had been projected as an adventure, a fresh motive was now supplied, the fiery motive of revenge. There was a preliminary brush at Bangkok, when the Comte de Fourbin, with his garrison and artillery, had the greatest difficulty in overcoming fifty of them. In September their main body at Ayudhya broke out.

The king had returned from Louvo to the capital and had offered them clemency provided that they laid down their arms and disclosed their accomplices among the mandarins, But they would have nothing to do with this and stood upon their defence in their own camp outside the city. A most vivid account of what then happened is preserved in a letter written that month by Samuel White to his brother George. It is not clear whether his health permitted him to join in the fighting which ensued, but the letter suggests that he was on the spot or near it. The style is vivid and accurate. As the only long document bearing White's signature, except his subsequent petition to Parliament, it is of special interest. But of course, Davenport may have drafted it.

After the king's unsuccessful attempt at a peaceful settlement the Macassars made a bold move. On September the 10th, says White, their prince 'attended by the whole Crew of desperate Votaries, all arm'd with Creases and Launces, went to the Palace Gate; whence he sent word to his Majesty, That in the sense of his late Error, and reliance on his Royal word, he was come to ask his Majesty's Pardon, and promise a peaceable demeanour for the future; and to that end desired admittance to throw himself at his Majesties Feet, To which he was answered, That the posture he then was in, did not correspond with his pretences, but if he would at first surrender his Arms, and Command his Attendants to do the like, his Majesty would readily grant him liberty to come into his Presence, and confirm the Pardon he had already on that condition offered them; whereupon the Prince peremptorily replied, he would never be guilty of so base a submission as required the parting with their Arms; adding that he was not insensible of an approaching great storm: But, says he, tell the King that I am like a great Tree, well Rooted, and shall be able to endure any ordinary Shock; but if the Storm comes so violently on that I cannot longer stand it, he may be assured my fall will not be without ruin of much under wood; and since I cannot be suffered to speak to the King with my Arms, if he has any further business with me, he knows where to find me at my own House.'

The authorities realized that this was a nasty situation. If they annoyed this prince further, there would be a sanguinary amuck by the palace gate, 'Resentment was seemingly smother'd' and the prince was induced quietly to depart.

It now became evident that drastic action was essential. Accordingly, the Macassars were secretly surrounded in their camp. Phaulkon decided to direct the operations in person. Besides calling up seven thousand Siamese troops, he asked all the Europeans in Ayudhya to help him. Sixty of them came, including a number of English captains and French gentlemen. Among them was present our old friend Captain, or rather Admiral, Coates—his last appearance on this stage.

The Europeans were delighted at the prospect of a fight. White represents them as in a foolhardy boyish mood, 'having more Resolution than Conduct', and 'Emulous of showing themselves every man more valiant than his neighbour'. The attack began:

'The Lord Phaulkon in Person, accompanied with sixty Europeans, having first in the night blockt up the small River, and so surrounded the Macassers Camp with about two Hundred of the King's Galleys and Boats, that they could not possibly fly, on Tuesday the Fourteenth Instant at break of day gave order for the Onsett, intending first to have fired down all the Houses before them, that so they might force their Skulking Enemies to an open fight, who otherwise would have the opportunity of Murdering all that came near them, and yet keep themselves unseen: But alas! the

Rashness of some of the Chief Europeans hurried them on at once, to the breach of Orders and their own Death, and that without any damage to the Enemy; For Captain Coates, and by his Example and Command, several others Landed before the time on a small spot of a dry point, where the Macassers, e're they could well look about them, rushing out of the Houses Dispatcht one Mr. Alvey, newly arrived in the Herbert, and forced the rest to take to the Water again, in which hasty retreat, Captain Coates with the weight of his own Armour and Arms lost his life in the Water, the rest with much danger and difficulty recovering their Boats.'

So ended poor Coates, thinking to overawe the Macassars as he had the Indians at Madapollam. There was something likeable about him, perhaps because he never made any money. The *Herbert* mentioned above had arrived from England a few days previously with a Captain Udall in command, who carried a letter from James II. to Phaulkon. He was among those who had offered their services and, attached to the chief minister, he was watching the fight. This inaction did not suit him at all, but as it was manifestly the act of an idiot to land he restrained himself for three hours, while the Macassars were harassed by artillery and driven two miles higher up the river, leaving their houses in flames. At last he could bear it no longer and out of all patience, 'not withstanding all his Lordships earnest disswasions from it, would needs leap ashore, where he had not been long, with several other English in his Company, c're a parcel of Macassars, in disguise of Siammers, by hawling a small Boat along the Shoal-water, got so near them, undisccrmed to be Enemies, as to reach them with their Launces, at which time it unluckily fell to Captain Udalls lot to lose his Life.'

Captain Udall's brother, expressing himself as graphically under cover of an extraordinary orthography and without stops, describes the same events. He is worth quoting to show how correctly White or Davenport could write in comparison.

'Nothing would searve brother and one or two more but they would goe a shoare. for they were Vropians and thouse dogg If they se them but land would Runn from them although they ware perswaided to yecontrary and told they ware Desperate Villings and would Runn to ye mussels of there gunns and Crease them yet this advice could not disswaid them a shoare they would goe and ware no sooner lauded but Mr. Alvie . . . was immediately Creast Capt Coats one of the King of Siams men of War r Captaines nock was nockt in to ye water and Drowned and Brother with some more being landed in a place half a mile from them was immediately kild.'

When Phaulkon saw the resolute going ashore of Udall and his violent end, he followed after him, though he knew from a longer experience of the Malays that to expose himself to a hand-to-hand fight, when he had firearms, was against all sense. Yet he went ashore, and he had as narrow an escape as any man who came off with his life. For the Malays made a fanatical rush upon him with their lances and had it not been that one of his black body-servants flung him into the river and swam with him to the boats, he would have shared the fate of Coates and Udall. He had to hang on to the offside of his boat's stern, while his men, firing at close range, with difficulty prevented the Macassars from reaching him.

White, in his effort to explain the extraordinary fact that the Europeans with their guns, loaded for close-range fighting with small shot. could hardly keep off the Macassars, observes in a striking sentence that they were: 'A sort or People that only value their Lives by the mischief they can do at their Deaths; and regard no more to run up to the very Muzzle of a Blunderbuss, than an Englishman would to hold his hand against a Boys Pop-Gun.' Their desperate valour was beyond all experience of Europe. Turpin in the book already quoted speaks of one of them, lanced in the stomach by the Comte de Fourbin, who still advanced, forcing the point deeper into his body, till others hewed him down.

After Phaulkon's escape from death, four Frenchmen fell, among them a gentleman of quality, Monsieur de Rohan, bearing one of the oldest names of France. The day was still doubtful when after four hours' fighting Phaulkon was heavily reinforced by Siamese troops, who began picking off very briskly any Malay who showed himself beyond the cover of the bamboos and bushes fringing the muddy banks. 'At length the Prince himself was slain by the Captain of his Lordship's Life-guard, and about three a clock the fight ended.' One last episode may be related in White's words:

'There was no Quarter given to any Macassars in this days fight, save only the Princes Son, a Boy of about Twelve years, who after his Father's fall came on undauntedly with his Lance presented at his Lordship; but drawing witkin reach, and perceiving his Lordship in the like posture ready to entertain him with his Lance, his Heart failed him, so that he cast away his weapons, and threw himself at his Lordships Feet, who received Win with all Courtesy and brought Mm unbound to his Majesty.'

But the affair was not to end on this note of chivalry. The king and Phaulkon had received too severe a shock; it had been too bloody a day. Such rebels as were taken alive, when the whole camp was occupied next morning, could not be spared. That implacable spirit of theirs made them too dangerous. Die they must and die horribly, for those mandarins behind the scenes, who had dared to loose such demons upon the king's majesty, must be appalled. So, tied to posts, they were abandoned to the tigers. These famished brutes were secured in such a way that at first they could only reach the extremities of their victims. After they had devoured their hands and feet, they were given more chain and so methodically ate them alive.

Turpin states that the French missionaries approached the tortured men, holding out the crucifix and calling upon them to renounce their false gods, Allah and his Prophet. But the

Malays refused to hear them, refused all their spiritual consolation, and turning from the priests with a livid sneer 'seemed only touched by the cruel vanity of the knowledge that they were dying'.

They had a secret which escapes us.

This atrocious scene closed a rebellion which might have swept Phaulkon away, had it not been handled at once with resolution. To contemporary observers it was a sinister indication of the state of the realm. Some hint of the apprehension which prevailed, of the anxiety to obtain information on what was intuitively felt to be a threatening future, is given by the strange story of the fare of Captain Udall's body. After a post mortem by the Dutch doctor, which revealed a multitude of mortal wounds, it was buried neat the Dutch factory. Two days later, his officers from the *Herbert*, going ashore to visit the grave, made the startling discovery that the body had been disinterred, stripped naked and tied upright against a tree. In agitation they cut the bonds and reverently buried it again, piling over the place a cairn, of heavy stones. Next day they repeated their visit to ensure that all was well. As they approached the spot, there again was the body against the tree in the same position. Horrified and baffled, they sank it in the river.

Alexander Hamilton comments as follows: 'This strange Resurrection left Room for various Conjectures, but the most probable seemed to be that some Sorcerers took it up and pot it in that Posture, whilst they, by their Sorceries or incantations, interrogate it about future Events, and received answers through human organs. The Matter of Fact, I have heard often affirmed by several who were there at the Time and Saw it, which made me inquire if any people in Siam used to inquire about future Events after that Manner, and I was told that they did.'

The English in their wanderings over the face of the globe have suffered many things, but I cannot recall a stranger than this, to be set up dead as a medium by necromancers in a Siamese burial ground. The ceremony must have taken place at night. It is not impossible to imagine the scene, the stifling heat, the dripping leaves, a rhythm of notes to enchain the spirit hovering near, and at last the voice. Did it speak of more massacre and confusion, for, indeed, those cvils were upon the way?

XXV. PHAULKON OFFERS TO MAKE WHITE PRIME MINISTER

After the strain and excitement of the rebellion had sub sided, there were mutual congratulations. Though the rising showed heat below the surface, its suppression advertised to the country that Phaulkon was still firmly in the saddle. His enemies had failed. Indeed, the leaders had not dared to declare themselves against him. He was in a generous humour and infinitely obliged to the Europeans who had assisted him with such courage and spirit. They were handsomely rewarded.

The final decision in White's case had been postponed during these events; he was still in doubt whether he would be sent back to Mergui or not, Phaulkon was amiable, too amiable, for it appeared that he wanted to keep him in Ayudhya, promoting him at the capital to high office with prospects of the most dazzling, but of the most dangerous, kind.

Speaking one day to Davenport, White said: 'His Lordship made me offer of fifty cattees per month (£6,000 a year), besides the perquisites of my employ should be worth as much more to me, if I would stay here with him,' Phaulkon found himself overwhelmed with work and surrounded by persons whom he could not trust. He considered White an able and faithful man compared to anyone else available. If he would accept responsibility for certain duties connected with the regulation of foreign trade, it would be a relief and a support. Such an offer, White explained to Davenport, was straightforward enough, though not what he wanted. But there was something more, something far more alarming. 'He said I should be Enroll'd in the Court Registers as his successor, in case of his Mortality, but I have with much ado evaded it.' Phaulkon solemnly had proposed that he should become prime minister of Siam, should crawl before the King, manipulate a fantastical court, daily in danger of poison and the knife. White felt he did not possess the gifts, the nerve for such an employment. He had a horror of Ayudhya, cut off from the sea and home.

Phaulkon took the refusal in good part. The letters and despatches brought by the late Captain Udall had contained information which pleased him. It seemed that his reputation, high in France, was making some headway in England, in spite of the animosity of the East India Company. He was quite willing to negotiate an arrangement with James II; it was the Company that was useless and intolerable. He had heard, too, that George White had been working on his behalf in London, George, his old patron, his best friend, still faithful after these years. In a warm mood, he sent again for Samuel.

PHAULKON: 'I find your Brother George so fast and real a Friend to me, that for his sake you may ask what you will.'

WHITE (taking opportunity by the foretop): 'I desire nothing but liberty to return to my former station.'

So it was arranged at last. White went back to his lodgings more cheerful than Davenport had observed him to be since May, when he was recalled from his fishing excursion. They sat down to talk and White, explaining his interview with Phaulkon said: 'I know he wants somebody near him, that might be capable of assisting him with advice, and that he has nobody is his great unhappiness.'

But, White went on to the patient Davenport, he himself could not settle in Ayudhya on any terms, he dare not stay, the situation was too unstable, too incalculable. Phaulkon was rich, laden with honours, outwardly a great and powerful lord; yet, said White: 'I shall look upon my Head to stand a great deal faster on my Shoulders than his, so long as there's e're a Ship or Vessel belonging to Mergen. The whole Kingdom is under a general discontent at this new way of Government.'

White had been four months in Ayudhya. He had heard the bazaar talk, the inner significance of the Macassar conspiracy had not been lost on him. The French were all over the place, the mandarins were slinking about with a queer look, there were extraordinary stories about Phaulkon's designs, It was said that he planned a *coup d'état*, that he aspired to the purple. The mandarinate was profoundly threatened. When the time was ripe it would strike. With a penetrating shrewdness which was to serve him well, White continued to discourse to Davenport:' Whenever this King comes to dye, not only His Honour, but all Europeans for his sake, must expect a Bloody Catastrophe.'

Not as long even as the king might live could Phaulkon count on safety. With a kind of violent horror White confided: 'Though the King should live many years, yet to tell you truly I am not without strong apprehensions that his Lordship stands but in a slippery place; nor would it be a miracle to see a man who hath been raised from so low a degree to such an exorbitant height of favour with a Prince, unable to withstand the shock of an envious Court and oppressed Kingdom; and in case he once slips, how can I or any other dependant on him, expect to keep our footing; so that if once I get to Mergen again, I am resolved never to see Syam more upon such a score as now I came up, but ene

make Hay while the Sun shines, and draw all my Stoc
which now lies scattered abroad, into as narrow a compass as
possibly I can and so be in readiness for any Revolution that
may happen.'

White's point of view is clear. It is that of the man engaged
in a dangerous adventure. There is no preoccupation here
with duty. The reader should get out of his head, if such a
delusion has been in it, that White viewed his important administrative appointment as entailing any public obligation.
If he had ever thought this, if he had ever pictured himself as
the King of Siam's trusted servant, he now abandoned such
fancies. The ship was sinking. The scramble had begun. He
was surrounded by frightful dangers. To think of administrative duties was absurd. Chance had given him an unheard
of opportunity to make money. He had made some; there
was time to make a little more and then he would run for it.

He was able to effect some business in Ayudhya before
starting back, He consigned to George White by the *Herbert*
£2,000 worth- of goods. George and his brother-in-law,
Thomas Povey, were his attorneys and the guardians of
Susan and Mary, his two girls. He now sent them instructions
to lay out the money lie sent home on the purchase of landed
estates on behalf of their wards. In that way, if he did not
survive the troubles he saw looming ahead, his daughters
would be provided for; if he returned safely, he would set up
as a country gentleman. To make certain that these instructions should be safely received, he sent them in duplicate, one
set direct by the *Herbert* and another for Heath, who would
travel with him to Mergui and go home via Madras.

Talking the situation over with Davenport, in whose ad-
vice he placed more and more confidence, he came to the
conclusion that before setting out for Mergui he must induce
Phaulkon to grant him more extended powers than before.
He wanted to be sole master of the province of Tenasserim.
It was impossible in the present circumstances to have to

court the agreement of colleagues, the viceroy, the senior mandarins in charge of the other departments, Burnaby, the civil governor of the town. He must not be in a position where they could interfere with the quick execution of his plans. The delays of council or joint responsibility were now quite out of the question. Control of the port, shipping, customs, authority to raise revenue for port expenses, fortifications, shipbuilding, to press labour—all these powers he had had before and would have again. But in addition he wanted to be absolute master in every department, so that no mandarin could dispute any of his actions. If he could arrange this with Phaulkon, he would concentrate the administrative machine on one object, his own enrichment. With such assistance, twelve months more and he was made.

To provide the right atmosphere for his requests, he decided to give Phaulkon a splendid gift. Making his selection, he presented himself at his patron's residence with six large ruby rings of good quality, two curious sapphires and a couple of Persian horses with silver harness. For the Lady Phaulkon he had 'two Delicate Rubies, one Dia mind Ring with five stones and a striking watch'. The presents were accepted, and the Lady in her turn gave him twenty pieces of the best Chinese silk and some porcelain of the highest value.

After this exchange of presents, White put his case to Phaulkon for wider powers in Mergui He had drawn up sixty articles, the effect of which was to give him the unlimited authority he desired. The mandarins in office in the province of Tenasserim were in this draft reduced to the position of ciphers, though for form's sake a council of seven was to be instituted, consisting of White, Burnaby and the five most senior mandarins. It was laid down that White should bring before that council for its approbation all matters, whether relating to sea or land, in time of peace or war, But the other articles were so drafted that in practice the council had no option but to agree upon all his proposals, Phaulkon signed the articles.

It then occurred to White that, when the council discovered it had no power to differ from him, it might leave everything to his discretion. There were contingencies when this would not suit. To cover these, he added a further article that the members should be forced to countersign, when he desired them so to do, all orders or instructions, whether relating to war or merchandise, which he might see fit to issue to commanders of the king's ships.

Phaulkon sanctioned this also, thereby in sum empowering White to do what he thought fit and, if anything went wrong, to throw the responsibility on the council. The idea in White's mind must have been that this latter facility would be extremely useful, if thereafter he was called to account by the English.

Another little matter arranged between them shows that Phaulkon could not trust his Siamese colleagues. It was settled that White's official despatches to headquarters should be couched in general language fit for the king in council, but that he should submit for Phaulkon's private reading a more particular account of any matter in hand.

Having successfully moved Phaulkon to sanction these adjustments in his status, White now asked for money. He explained that the Mergui treasury was empty at the moment and quoted his accounts. Phaulkon, though well aware of their 'unhansomeness', accepted the assertion and gave him £4,000. With this he was to pay the king's seamen at Mergui what was owing them since June, together with an advance of three months' pay, as it was proposed to send out eight ships during the coming open season. In regard to the future, Phaulkon told White he must keep his budget balanced; no further grants from headquarters could be sent to him. He had authority to raise revenue to the amount of £20,000 per annum by taxation; that sum must suffice for all his expenses.

He added: 'It Is to be hoped that by your prudent management of affairs, there will be in a little time a considerable
Bank of Cash founded in Mergen, so that his Majesty may
reap benefit proportionable to the Vast Expense, which for
these three years past he had been at, in fortifying that Province with Garrisons and Shipping.'

White agreed easily to all this. Having resolved that he was
going to put every penny he could into his own pocket, a
lecture on economy in the use of public money was only
diverting. Once he reached Mergui, with a good ship riding
below his windows, ready at a moment's notice to carry him
home out of harm's way, he would know what arrangements
to make, and it would not be the king who would benefit by
them. Davenport says that White had succeeded in deceiving
Phaulkon as to the size of his private estate, and that although
Phaulkon knew there had been misappropriations, he had no
idea of their large amount. He thought White's entire fortune
was invested with his own in the China trade. In regard to
that sum, White now began secretly on one excuse and another to realize his shares, as part of his intention to get all he
possessed into a small compass, such as jewels or cash.

Accommodating as Phaulkon was, there remained one
point where he refused to meet White. This was in the matter
of Coates's expedition to Madapollam, White begged him
for a letter, wherein it would be stated that Coates had acted
under orders from the Siamese government. This Phaulkon
declared he was unable to procure. White pressed him very
hard. It was a matter of first importance to him. If the East
India Company found our that Coates had acted solely on his
orders, it might go very hard with him. It would then be
piracy.

This did not seem of much weight to Phaulkon, because he
thought White was staying indefinitely in Siam; but for
White, with his idea of making England as soon as possible to
enjoy his fortune, it was common prudence to desire to cover

himself against such a charge. His enemies would at least use it to blackmail him. It would always be hanging above his head. if Phaulkon could secure a declaration over the king's seal that his operations had been authorized, it would be the last favour he would ask.

But Phaulkon refused. It may be that he wished to keep a hold over White, or it may be that to cover him he had told the king some lie and was estopped from telling him another story now. Whatever was his reason, White failed to get the paper he desired. As we shall see, the want of it worried him continually, until he thought of a way of supplying it himself.

On 16th October 1686 he and his party, consisting of Captain Leslie, Davenport and Heath, left Ayudhya. The first stage down the river Menam took them to Bangkok. There White received important news from an English ship which had just come in. The East India Company, alarmed at the rumours of Phaulkon's large plans for commercial expansion in the Bay of Bengal with French assistance, had resolved to occupy Negrais in Pegu and from that harbour to protect their trade at the top of the bay from Siamese privateers. 'Mr. White seemed very much troubled and swore most bitterly he would prevent them,' says Davenport.

They hastened down the coast with a fair wind and landed at one of the small ports near the cross-road to Tenasserim. White, Leslie and Heath posted away in sedan chairs doubly manned over the pass to Jalinga. They were in Mer gui by October 27th. Davenport, with the money on a cart, battled after them and Came in three days later.

XXVI. WHITE MAKES HAY

On arrival White got to work at once. As has been explained, before leaving for Ayudhya he had transferred the balance of the king's stores from the government godowns to his own, the accounts being made to show issue to ships. He now sold these stores back to the king's account and issued them to the ships, thereby making for himself 280 cattees (£2,800).

The next item was to pay the garrison and the seamen's arrears. White used the same method which had been so profitable before—the fictitious list of names. In that way he made 300 cattccs do the business of 546 cattees, which left his private account the better by £2,460.

Davenport began to get nervous. He records: 'I thought this a very smart beginning after his so narrow escape of a severe examination, I wished that I might be freed from such a kind of Book-keeping.'

At Ayudhya Davenport had broached the subject about leaving White's employ. He had recalled to him his promise to let him go after the monsoon. It was now October. He approached him again, when White replied that rumour had it that the East India Company was involved in a war in Bengal against the Mogul, and that it would not be safe for him to set out for Hugli. But Davenport pressed to be allowed to go. He did not want to be mixed up in White's fall, which he believed must come. There were four ships in the harbour bound for Bengal, and Davenport begged to be let embark on one of them, the *Anthony*, in fourteen days' time. To this White finally consented with reluctance.

During the fortnight Davenport was busy from morning till night. There were great naval preparations; every Golconda ship in the bay was to be taken. Phaulkon had given a general sanction, and White decided to interpret this in such a way that he could seize any ships which were not European owned. The *Robin*, Coates's sloop, and the *Dorothy*,

Captain Cropley's fast-sailing frigate, were fitted out and sent to the Pegu coast with instructions 'to bring in whatsoever ships they should meet and could overpower, without any respect to their passes'. This meant that Golcondas ships, Mogul ships, ships belonging to Indian merchants resident in Pegu or living within the territorial limits of the English factories—such as the Black Town of Madras—were to be taken.

Such a programme was a mixture of filibustering, piracy and legitimate prize-taking, White's procedure appears actually to have been as follows. When a ship brought into Mergui was proved not to be the property of a Golconda merchant, he let her go as a rule—for a large consideration. He would then record that the seizure had been a bona fide mistake, easily made as it was difficult for his captains to distinguish one sort of Indian from another.

On November 24th the *Anthony* was due to sail. Davenport brought White the keys of his escritoires and asked leave off for the morning to carry his luggage on board. To this White replied: 'I cannot possibly spare you at this time.' Rather than provoke a scene, Davenport postponed his departure, December being now fixed as the month when he might hope to get away.

He set to work again. There was the greatest activity. After the departure of the *Robin* and the *Dorothy* for Burmese waters, the *New Jerusalem* and the Sancta *Cruz*, the two fine armed merchantmen White had taken from the Armenian brothers Demarcora, were sent off on a trading expedition under French colours, for as they were to go in a direction where the Company's ships were numerous, he judged it safer to disguise their Siamese provenance. More and more rumours were arriving that the Company, infuriated by Phaulkon's behaviour towards their factors in Ayudhya and by White's methods in the bay, intended to retaliate by taking prizes where they could. They had been reinforced from England.

On November the 30th the *Delight*, jointly owned by

White and Lucas of the. Company's establishment at Madras, was Sent with a cargo to that port, Heath travelled on her, carrying £3,000 in gold belonging to White. He was to remit the sum to England from Madras on the security of diamonds, travelling himself to England with the bill. On arrival there, he was to cash the bill and make over the amount to White's attorneys, George White and Thomas Povey, at the same rime ascertaining from them whether all the other sums remitted home by White had been safely received and laid out as directed. These now amounted with the present remittance to nearly £30,000. While at Madras he was to make inquiries what WAS going on behind the scenes. Were they all very angry with White over there? If so, what were they likely to attempt? He must sift truth from rumour and find out whether the Company, alleged to be fighting the Mogul, could or would fight Siam also. And what was the attitude of the directors in London and of King James II? Could there be any truth in the story about a royal proclamation recalling English subjects from Siam? Heath was to inform himself as far as he could and write back to Mergui by the *Dorothy* when she returned. It may seem extraordinary that White was able to send into Madras a ship partly his property and with his money on board. It can only have been done by the connivance of Lucas, who was on the council.

The next item on White's list was the launch of a man-of-war called the *Resolution*. She had been building some time in the Mergui yards and now was ready. Armed as a frigate, she was White's best ship or rather—and it is important to note this—the King of Siam's best ship. Captain Leslie was given the command. She was despatched in December to the Coromandel. Leslie's written orders were to make the Indian coast in 80° N. L. and to seize all vessels of whatsoever kind he met, except English vessels, and bring them into Mergui. If he had too many to bring in, or if rime prevented, he was to sink or burn them, after seizing their cargoes. He was also to land at

Chiskercol, a small Golconda town, capture the Indian governor and hold him to ransom. Should the inhabitants fail to produce the cash, White wrote: 'You should fire the Town, burn or sink all the boats in the River and bring off as many Men, Women, and Children as you can seize.'

He was to repeat this sort of thing all down the coast, avoiding places where English or Dutch factories existed. If the King of Golconda spoke of sending an envoy to Ayudhya, the man should be given safe conduct, but the programme of seizing and burning should continue in any event, till he received orders to stop or till May, when he was to return to Mergui. In the main these operations seem to have been authorized unofficially by Phaulkon, but the seizure of vessels not belonging to Golconda and the fact chat White intended to pocket large sums of prize money—all the proceeds if possible gave the *Resolution's* cruise a strong resemblance to that of a pirate. It was also flying directly in the face of Company interests. Had the *Resolution* not been stronger than any man-of-war White believed the Company had at their disposal, it is doubtful whether he would have dared to send her on such an expedition, in a word, White's idea was to use alleged public grievances against Golconda to cover grand-scale robberies of his own.

Leslie was also given two further commissions, which bordered on treason. He was to drop in at Pondicherry, the French factory about sixty miles south of Madras, and deliver a present from the King of Siam to Louis XIV, and a letter addressed to George White, wherein the view was stated that in 'the unsettled posture which the Affairs of India were posting to', it was not advisable to risk any capital on trade ventures in that direction for the moment. The French were to be asked to transmit the present and the letter at once. When there, Leslie should also recruit as many French as possible by offers of large pay.

At the same time White sent a message of first importance

by another ship to Captain Cropley in the north of the bay. He was to anticipate the Ease India Company and land at Negrais. occupying the same and raising a flagstaff flying the Siamese flag, with a notice attached in Portuguese that the occupation was in the king's name. The notice itself was drafted and despatched. It purported to have been signed in Ayudhya the previous October, though actually White had drawn it up himself. Cropley thereafter was to get in touch with some agents of the East India Company and serve on them a proclamation, in this case a genuine one from the government of Siam, protesting against Yale's behaviour in regard to the jewels he had sought to sell the king. The idea of this was to throw the blame in advance on the Company for anything which might happen.

These citations indicate the pace now set by White. He was making hay while the sun shone with vigour. He intuitively felt that it would not shine for long, but he thought it would shine long enough for him to round off his fortune and get out. It was now January 1687. He believed he had till the following October. In this belief lie fitted out two further merchantmen, the *Satisfaction* and the *Derrea Dowlat*. The first under How, his steward, he sent to Mocha on the Red Sea with a very valuable cargo, worth £7,800. On that he expected at least a cent per cent turnover, which would have enabled him. to remit another £15,000 home, bringing his fortune up to £45,000 (or £225,000 in our values). The *Der rea Dowlat* (Captain Russell), the old elephant ship, was despatched to Achin in Sumatra. White had goods on her to the value of £1,838. Shortly after, he ordered out to Coromandel the sloop *Mary*, sister ship to the *Robin*, probably called after his late wife, with copper worth £400, and the *Success* to Achin with £450 worth of cargo. In addition to ali these ships, he had the frigate *Revenge* (Captain English) with a crew of seventy Europeans, privateering north of Madras.

Summing up, at the turn of the year 1686-7 White had

three frigates, the *Resolution* (Captain Leslie), the *Revenge* (Captain English) and the *Dorothy* (Captain Cropley), the last supported by the sloop *Robin*, prowling about the bay with wide commissions to seize all they met. Simultaneously he had out his merchantmen, armed in the fashion of the day, namely, the *Delight on* business to Pondicherry, the *Satisfaction* to Mocha, the *Derrea Dowlat* to Achin, with the *New Jerusalem* and the *Sancta Cruz*, the destination of which I have not found. Add the little vessels, the *Mary* and the *Success*, and there is a grand total of eleven ships. White had become a very big man. At the moment he seemed to be able to do what he liked. As far as the East India Company was concerned, it was bluff; he had no intention of fighting them openly, if he could possibly avoid it. But he wished that he knew more exactly what Was going on in Madras and London.

Phaulkon had written privately in December warning him that information received at Ayudhya suggested that the Company would attempt a stroke against Mergui. White was advised to send out no merchantmen, for Phaulkon believed the Company had decided to seize any such as prizes against the damages they had sustained. And as for men-of-war, wrote Phaulkon: Frigatts went out on a design against the Enemy should be so well equipt, as to be able to encounter any force the Company could make against them.' Phaulkon was so apprehensive that he advised the transfer of the royal merchandise in the warehouses of Mergui inland to Tenasserim. He counted on French reinforcements later to enable him to show a bolder face.

But White did not accept this advice. He believed, and wrote to tell Phaulkon so, that Madras could not break openly with Siam at once. They would have to get sanction from the directors and that would take time. All accounts suggested that they were busy with operations of some kind in India. He believed there was time enough; merchantmen were still safe, there was money still to be made.

So the month of January passed. Davenport became more and more anxious to be gone. He was certain the crash would come sooner than White believed; the pace was too hot. He went to White again and asked to be allowed to depart on a ship then clearing for India.

WHITE: 'Can you be so unkind as to leave me now when I have nobody but yourself who can assist me in my business or keep me company?'

Again Davenport consented to stay, but positively for one month more only.

He began to notice a deterioration in White, that blunting of the better feelings which is the disease of absolute power. There was an unpleasant instance of this on January the 12th. A Mahomedan came up for trial before the Siamese magistrate on a charge of having broken Into the godown under White's house the previous May. There was no evidence and the man was about to be discharged, when White sent down a request chat he should be detained in custody a further ten days, pending additional inquiries. The magistrate, overshadowed by the great Shābandar, complied. The man, however, escaped from prison and fled to Tenasserim. He was pursued by the Shāhbandar's order and brought back. They took him directly before White, who happened to be in a very bad humour at the moment. Turning upon the unfortunate man in a blind rage, he ordered a policeman to decapitate him, The Indian's relations and friends begged for mercy, wept, grovelled. It was no good; the Shāhbandar, beside himself, roared at the police to do what he told them. A Siamese with one blow struck off the man's head.

In February White received a stiff' letter from Phaulkon, which shows that from rime to time the minister attempted some control over his subordinate. This was about Negrais. As we have seen, in the flush of his independence White had ordered Cropley to occupy a piece of Burma to forestall an alleged attempt on the same place by the Company. Phaulkon told him to recall Cropley and evacuate Negrais at once 'and to be more cautious for the future how he proceeded in such weighty Affairs, without first advising up to Court'. A man called Highoe was sent by White next day to tell Cropley to embark the soldiers he had landed, but to leave the inscription standing, Cropley had been busy as pirate in addition, for on February 3rd a prize taken by him. arrived in Mergui, an Indian ship with a Company's pass, that is to say a ship owned by merchants living in the Company's factories. White decided it was unsafe to keep her and allowed her to proceed, but he detained the passengers, who came from Madapollam, and made slaves of them. It was in this connection that an English pilot on board the ship was heard to remark that 'Mergen was a second Tunis'.[1] In point offset White would have seized the ship and its cargo for himself had not Davenport said to him: 'To add this extravagance to all the rest would be like a man willfully precipitating himself into danger and then putting out his Eyes because he would not see it.'

In Davenport's view White was rash beyond all sense. Cropley, too, lost his nerve. He suddenly arrived in Mergui on February 20th with the *Dorothy* and the *Robin*. He had not completed his duties; he was supposed to have given the proclamation to Yale, to have gone on seizing ships, got into touch with Captains Leslie and English, and not to have returned to port before the end of April. White was angry. Cropley said frankly he was afraid to go on. He observed later to Davenport: 'For ought I know that might one time or another hazard my Neck. I am very sure those proceedings of Mr. White can never end well.'

But White himself was less confident than in Januar. He had received more definite news. On the ship Cropley had seized was a Mr. Noden, the man who made the remark about Tunis. White had talked to this person and had been rather shaken by what he heard. Noden said he had the most reliable

[1] Slave port of the Moors in the Mediterranean.

information that the Company was shortly going to make demands on Siam for damages to itself and to merchants under its protection. They were particularly disgusted with White. When he reflected on this news, he felt it was just as well that Cropley had come back. That gave him the *Dorothy* in port. From this on he would keep a man-of-war permanently in the harbour. With all his ships out, he felt himself exposed to attack and cut off from retreat.

XXVII. DOUBTS AND RUMOURS

After his conversation with Noden, White sent for Davenport. These two men had now been associated together for eleven months. Their relationship was peculiar. White clearly had the highest opinion of Davenport's abilities as a secretary. Davenport, though drawing good pay and being the intimate adviser of his master, WAS frankly alarmed about his own future, if he continued to be identified with a man heading apparently for some violent end. on this occasion, when he appeared before White, the conversation at once turned to what Noden had said.

Freeman's name was mentioned. He was the man, it will be remembered, who had been chief at Masulipatam in 1685 when Coates had rufiled it at Madapollam, and whose private trade later had been interfered with by the capture and detention of one of his ships. There was a rumour that the Company proposed to send him on a special mission to Ayudhya to lay a direct complaint against White to the king. Here again, it all depended on Phaulkon.

Phaulkon was privately in league with him, but he himself

must none the less have his papers in impeccable order. Davenport was accordingly told to go through all the files and put up any passages which might suggest that White had enmity towards the Company or which would give his enemies, if Freeman got hold of them, a handle against him. The secretary set to work. On a considered view the whole embroglio centred on the question whether there was sufficient paper authorization for the Golconda and Pegu war from its start at Madapollam to date. On the files before him Davenport pronounced that White had 'never any Commission from the King of Siam for making war upon the Kings of Golconda and Pegu or their subjects, and that he had no other warrant for so doing but bare word of mouth from the Lord Phaulkon, or, which was no more validity in law, perhaps an. approbation for taking that course in a Private Letter'.

The position was that White, having taken the responsibility for the first step of sending Coa tes, had afterwards never received an order sealed by the King to operate in the bay. There was nothing definite on the file. The condonation of silence, the fact that Phaulkon on his own authority had subsequently agreed to allow him to prosecute what he had initiated, would be a slender defence in an English court.

WHITE: 'I feel very apprehensive of the danger I am in. I did not like it when his Lordship in September last refused to grant me a Commission ex post facto, though I did so earnestly desire it. His Lordship being apprehensive of the issue of these Commotions was resolved if possible to keep his own neck out of the Collar.'

White had enough experience of oriental courts to know that, if the Company retaliated on Siam because of his proceedings, the king would begin asking questions and that would be the end; Phaulkon would be forced to repudiate him. There was no doubt about it; this want of the king's written orders behind his operations was the most serious 'oversight and slip'. He continued: 'Our business must be to study some remedy for it. And now, what do you think best to do in this case?'

DAVENPORT: 'A question of such moment will require time for a deliberate and well digested answer.'

WHITE: 'No, but tell me your present thoughts of the matter.'

DAVENPORT: 'Then, Sir, I know not at present what to advise you other than, if the Lord Phaulkon be sincerely your friend and that you have acted nothing in relation to that war but either what he was privy to before you did it or approved it when done or, if once offended at you for it, hath since been thoroughly reconciled to you again, you once more, notwithstanding his former refusal, plainly lay open to him your oversight in not having a Commission to act by when you first undertook the concern, and to obviate all prejudices that may at any time hereafter, for want of one, accrue to you from the pretences of your own Countrymen, you do now request that one may be granted to you.'

WHITE: 'I know the King will not now grant me one, and that the Lord Phaulkon will do no such thing without consulting his Majesty.'

DAVENPORT: 'Send the Don's[1] ship laiden with Rice as a present to the Governors and Council at Madras for the relief of their Garrison, where you hear there is at present a very sharp Famine, which act would in my opinion so seasonably take off the edge of all their ill opinions concerning you, that in all probability they may alter their minds and totally desist from making any complaints against you at this Court or summoning you hence.'

WHITE: 'I could be glad in all my heart to stand fair in the opinions of the Madras Blades at the cost of three or four hundred Tonns of Rice, but to send it at such a juncture as this, when they are plotting and resolving my prejudice, would look too like a piece of precariousness and fear of

[1] The *Sancta Rosa*, the property of Don Joseph de Heredia.

them; and rather than do anything which may expose me to such thoughts among any of them, I will run the hazard of the worst they can do to me.'

The conversation continued. They went over and over every point, every possibility. If the Company began to make reprisals on Siamese ships, worse if they attacked Metgui, and all on account of White's unauthorized proceedings, Phaulkon could not save him, the mandarins would have his head. If the English took him, he was liable to be hanged as a pirate. If Phaulkon were to falter, if a man like Noden were to get his ear, he would be recalled a second time to Ayudhya and lie could not hope to escape then. The Siamese would either deal with him or hand him over to the English.

The two men talked on. Some possible courses were rejected as unjustifiable, given that White had in honour a duty to the king who had appointed him and to the minister, who was his friend. other courses were too prejudicial to the English, his countrymen. Davenport urged a diplomatic careful line in a position bristling with difficulties. White was disinclined to give in to anybody. Ultimately with him it came to this—his money; if he was threatened with the loss of his money and his liberty to spend his money, the fortune he had built up in eleven years' toil and danger, he would take any desperate course. To an observation of Davenport's, which in this respect he considered weak, he said solemnly: 'you are not wholly unacquainted with those Salvoes, which I reserve as yet in my own Breast for whatsoever exigence or emergency.' He was a desperate man, a passionate proud man. He had set himself up against the East India Company and he could not bear to bow to them now. Rather than that, he would go to any length.

Before White rose to depart, he thanked Davenport for speaking so frankly to him, saying: 'That has been some, if not the major part, of my unhappiness, that I never, until I met you, found one who had Courage enough to disapprove to my face any one Enterprise, that ever I proposed to attempt.'

Davenport and he were, perhaps, closer to each other at that moment than they had ever been, than they were ever to be again. White went on, with a gesture towards the town: 'Here's Mr. Burnaby Is fit to converse with nobody, but his serjeant of police and takes delight in being the Town Pimp and disposing of all the whores to any body that wants one, or keeps company with a parcel of Sailors, that over a Bowl of Punch will lye worshipping him up, till he thinks himself a Petty Prince among them.'

Such a person was no companion, not a man you could talk to, confide in, not even in a place like Mergui, at the end of the world, where there was little choice. Besides, he was a fool of a man, went on White: 'He's so soft a fellow, as to let his own servants cheat him to his face and run away with the Perquisites of his office; for I myself have offered Win Fifty Cattees a year (£500), for that he never made Five Cattecs of, since he came to the place, and to tell him a secret is the same thing as to publish it about the town with a Drum or take a Woman into Council.'

This lack of business instinct seemed to White most contemptible of all, that he should not care to enrich himself, Such a man as that, he continued, was useless in the present crisis. Leslie was away, Cropley was a peculiar fellow, he had no one but Davenport, who had served him so faithfully, He bound him to secrecy and begged him always to speak his mind: 'I enjoin you on all occasions to speak plainly with me, for I foresee there will be no small bustle, especially since Mr. Yale, the mighty Man of Power at Madras, has been so highly exasperated. 'Tis impossible that I should escape scotfree unless I take some timely course to prevent falling into their clutches.'

Then he told Davenport to take pen and paper and to note down what appeared to be the four alternatives before him, the four possible ways of avoiding the evils which threatened from Ayudhya and from Madras. Davenport accordingly drafted these four: (1) to go up to Ayudhya before the English should move and put himself under the King's protection; (2) to stay at Mergui and secretly purchase his reconciliation with the Company by betraying Mergui to them; (3) to fortify Mergui, as might easily be done, until it was so strong that the Company could not take it; or (4) to pack all his remaining valuables and get home in such a way as to avoid falling into the Company's clutches.

When Davenport had recorded these alternatives, White asked him to weigh them well and to tell him within the week which of them seemed most conducive to the security of his interest or of his reputation or both. 'In the mean time,' said he, 'I myself will make it my business to consider them.' And so he left the room.

XXVIII. THE FOUR ALTERNATIVES

It was now March. The monsoon would be on them in six weeks. During its continuance from May till October it was impossible for a ship to beat out of the bay against the S. W. wind and reach home, but it was possible for ships in the bay, from Madras for instance, to make and enter Mergui harbour. This limitation by the weather of White's movements has an important bearing on what follows.

A day or so after his conversation with Davenport and the drafting of the four alternatives, the *Dorothy* returned from Pondicherry. It will be recalled that Mr. Heath was to send White a letter about conditions on that side. The letter with others was delivered. From their perusal White perceived that the intentions of the Company were rapidly hardening. It

seemed that they contemplated in fact an armed move against
Mergui, had already begun action against Siamese ships in the
bay, and had captured his third frigate, the *Revenge* (Captain
English). A French sloop arriving from Bengal the same day
brought him a long-overdue letter from Madras, a 'startling
letter', wherein he was taken to task for his treatment of the
Hindu merchants on board the *Traja Raja*, whom he had
maltreated and robbed, so they said.

All this news, confirming what Phaulkon had written, un-
nerved him for a moment. He wanted to do something at
once and to stop the danger he saw approaching. But he did
not know exactly what to do. He called Davenport and
handed him all the letters.

'Here,' says he, 'peruse them. You'll find that English is
snapt in the Bay, but more than all, the Gentlemen at Madras
arc resolved to have a fling at me for what I had out of the
Black Merchants. Yet if they have nothing else to say to me,
I fear them not.'

Indeed, if it was only a matter of £1,500 or so between him
and Madras, it was of small moment. But there were other
matters, many other matters unfortunately. He wished he
knew more. It was strange, for instance, that in May of the
year before, when Cropley took Thomas Yale over to Madras in the *Dorothy*, nothing particular was said, though it was
after the *Traja Raja* merchants had petitioned the council. It
was stranger still that, as far as he knew, the Company had
not sent a formal complaint about him to Ayudhya. Was it
because they thought it useless to complain when Phaulkon
was in power? Frankly, it was impossible to say. But now
they seemed bent on action. The seizure of the *Revenge* left
Leslie on the *Resolution* alone in the bay. But White could not
despatch Cropley to his assistance. The *Dorothy* most lie in
the harbour.

He sent for Davenport again, It had become more urgent
to secure a document covering the Madapollam affair. He

raised the old question as soon as his secretary appeared. He wanted him to draft a formal authorization, purporting to have been given to him by the council of the province of Ten asse rim under the king's sanction as far back as January 1685, and empowering him to sign instructions to all captains of Siamese men-of-war proceeding against Golconda. That would cover the orders standing in his file without any authority behind them. The council, he argued, was bound to sign such an authorization now if he required it, in view of what had been arranged with Phaulkon before he left Ayudhya. Davenport pointed out that the personnel of the council was not the same as it was in 1685 and that in any event it would not dare to sign such a document without reference to court. A reference would publish a matter far better kept hushed up. Besides it was doubtful whether such a document would carry much weight in an English court of law, if he were being tried for piracy. It could be impugned on the ground that in no circumstances would a local council be authorized to sign such a paper.

At this criticism of his proposal, White, contrary to his request to Davenport a few days earlier to speak out freely without fear of the consequences, replied angrily; 'You need not trouble yourself with that. Draw up the Commission and I will take care of the rest.'

He then dictated a letter to Phaulkon minimizing the danger of a war with the Company, for he did not want to be recalled to Ayudhya for a consultation or for any other reason. He wished to be free to act in his own interests as the situation developed. He went so far as to tell his friend and master that he now had it on reliable advices from the French factory at Fondicherry that the East India Company, if they had ever contemplated such a thing, had abandoned any idea of a move against Siam; moreover, they were in no position to do so, on account of the reported ill success of their attack upon the Mogul empire. Signing this letter, he said no more to Davenport about the proposed commission from the council of Tenasserim.

After getting off the mail, Davenport settled down to consider the four alternatives open to White, He decided to write his reply, for he did not think the Shāhbandar in a state of mind when he could profitably engage him in conversation.

He waited, and some days later White asked him for his views, He handed him the draft immediately. It was an elaborate document, containing a complete review of White's position, as far as the information then available at Mergui permitted.

Davenport began by saying that he would speak plainly, as he had been asked to do.

The first query was whether White should go to the capital and seek the king's protection against the English, As to that, Davenport pointed out that if he went to Ayudhya, he might be summoned thence, as easily as from Mergui, by a proclamation of his own king, James II. There was a strong rumour that such a proclamation, addressed to all Englishmen in Siamese employ, had been or was going to be issued. If he disobeyed it, he would be guilty of contempt of his native sovereign's authority and that would be the end of him, unless he proposed to spend the rest of his life in Siam.

Moreover, there was no guarantee of his safety there for long, for if the Company retaliated upon Siam for alleged injuries, as they had already begun to do by the seizure of the *Revenge*, if they blockaded Mergui, captured Siamese merchantmen, interfered with the trade—possible if they were reinforced from England—Phaulkon's popularity would suffer in the eyes of the king, 'and if once he totters, you must not expect to stand firm'. Furthermore, it was a dangerous thing for White to go to the capital, considering the 'slips of his management', as Davenport phrased with tact the misappropriations of which he had been guilty since he returned from Ayudhya in October.

To refresh his memory, Davenport cited sixteen of the principal 'slips', of these, one was 'the notorious overcharge of Seamen and Soldiers Salaries'—the ghosts in the pay rolls. Then there was selling the king his own stores three or four times over in the space of five months, when White, after placing the naval stores in his private godowns, had by a scries of book entries, not followed as a ride by any issue, transferred them back to the king with a credit entry to himself. That would be difficult to explain at Ayudhya, if it came out, and it would he far more likely to come out there, if White went as a suppliant, than if he remained at Mergui as Shāhbandar in all his authority. Of other matters difficult to explain, could be cited the despatch on several occasions of a king's ship, with a cargo belonging to the king, but described in the manifest as the private property of the Shāhbandar. Then he had encroached upon the royal monopolies—a capital offence under the Siamese law—by forcing the local inhabitants to buy his salt instead of the king's. It was not, perhaps, necessary to mention the occupation by Siamese troops of Burmese territory at Negrais on his sole authority; Phaulkon's letter on that subject was already on the file. Such were the chief charges which could, and probably would, be made against him. There was also—he had almost forgotten it—murder, for he had beheaded the escaped Mahomedan without process of law. Each or any of these matters, if brought forward by his enemies, would be ample to ruin him. He had many enemies, who were only waiting for an opportunity. As long as he held his official position, these people were afraid to   come into the open. Let him leave his post and go to Ayudhya and they would set on him. So much for the first alternative.

Coming tc the second, whether to surrender Mergui to the Company on condition that no proceedings were taken against him, Davenport suggested that there were some things which a man of honour, even for his own country, could not do. Allowing that he had the power to give up Mergui without an outburst of native indignation, which might cost him his life, his own countrymen would despise him for such an act, even, if they should profit by it, for it would indicate cowardice on his part, Were they to applaud it, they would fall under the contempt of all other European nations and under the suspicion of all princes of the cast.

The third alternative—to fortify Mergui and resist any Company force sent against it—was equally unthinkable. He could not stand for Siam against England, for so it would be regarded. To fight against his own countrymen, said Davenport, would 'brand him with Eternal infamy'. At any rate, he could not retire afterwards to England as a country gentleman.

That left the fourth alternative—to get straight home with all the money and valuables he could collect. Davenport submitted that this last course, though not so desperate, was still full of difficulty. If the local people detected him making preparation to leave, he might be prevented. It was now March the 29th. It would be impossible to wind up his affairs, get in his money, load his ship (and the question was what ship, for the *Resolution* had not yet returned, might never return, and the *Dorothy* was hardly suitable for such a voyage) and stock her with provisions before August. The monsoon would break in May and after that he could not get clear. He would have to hide among the islands. There were all sorts of difficulties, some of them could not be foreseen. The Company might send ships to Mergui before August, almost any day now. There was only one proper course.

Davenport then advanced his solution. White should make up his accounts, as correctly as circumstances permitted, and submit them to Phaulkon with a request for leave to return to England for reasons of health. on receiving that permission, he should cross to Madras in the *Dorothy* before the end of April, boldly present himself before the council (having taken care by some means or other to obtain for his file state authority for his actions against Golconda) and making it clear to the gentlemen opposite that what he had done was at the King of Siam's command, any damages sustained by the Company being accidental and, indeed, inherent in the conduct of all warlike operations, he should brazen it out, by this timely submission stopping the mouths of the minority, for it was only a minority who wished to harm him, the few persons like Yale and Freeman whose private interests had suffered. That jewel affair, it was unfortunate to a degree! How much better to have cheated the King of Siam than to have made a mortal enemy of a man like Yale. Many of the others were eight enough; they had shared with White in some of his ventures; men like Thomas Lucas were sound as a bell. But Yale!—still, an early submission and the weight of the rest would carry the day in his favour.

So advised Davenport, signing himself 'your faithful servant'. 'All the Reply Mr. White gave to this Paper at this time, putting it after he had read it into his pocket, was, That he was going to Mary Leslyes and it should not be long before he resolved on something or other.'

In this sudden way Davenport brings Mary Leslie into the narrative, intimating that White was a particular friend of hers. We have seen that she was Captain Leslie's wife and that she had arrived the year before at Mergui in the *Mary*. With her husband out on the *Resolution*, she and White had been thrown together and were evidently close friends.

There were other Englishwomen in Mergui. Mrs. Cropley was English, and there was a Mrs. Tuttie, her husband being one of White's subordinate assistants. Several more probably existed, and with them a number of women of mixed blood, particularly Portuguese, who followed, at a certain distance, English dress and manners. But, perhaps, Mrs. Leslie was more White's social equal. We know he was lonely; his wife's death and his exalted position account for that.

He now went round to her house with Davenport's review of a desperate situation in his pocket. That he discussed it with her goes without saying. She and all the English, men and women, were deeply concerned. What was going to happen to them if White fell or fled? That he had spoken to no one else is clear enough, In spite of what he had proclaimed about taking a woman into council, we may be sure that he turned at least in some measure to this woman for advice.

What he told her, what he dared tell her, we cannot guess. But the town was full of rumours. It was no confidential news which had reached him from the other side of the bay. Indeed, there are few secrets in the East. Art oriental crowd has a marvellous flair for anticipating the truth. No doubt Mary Leslie was much alarmed; she may have pressed him to speak.

Next morning he sent for Davenport.

WHITE: 'Mr. Davenport, I have considered your motion for my going to Madras, but, alas, these Arguments yon urge for the stopping of peoples mouths are not of weight enough to induce me to take that course. If God send me well to Europe, I shall have as fair play at the Law for my Money, as my Adversaries.'

Davenport in reply pointed out that going to Madras would have the added advantage of not obliging him to abandon the merchantmen he had sent out with his own cargoes? particularly the *Satisfaction* and the *Derrea Dowlat*. Very probably the *Satisfaction* would unwittingly call in on the Coromandel coast on her return from the Persian Gulf. But even that argument about money failed to overcome White's dislike of the proposal. As a proud man, he was not going to humble himself that way. 'With an extraordinary concernedness', he said, 'you talk like one who knows but the shell and outside of things. If I was sure going to Madras would keep me from going to Hell, I would choose to be damned rather than go thither to be laugh'd at by Yale and Freeman.'

Working up into one of his violent rages, he continued: 'If ever a ship of the King of England comes to this Port before I am gone, the Commander shall find me as civil to him, as he can be to me, but if once he comes to cell me that I must go with him, and pretends the Kings authority here, by the living God, I'll pistol him with my own hands and afterwards wipe my breech with his Commission.'

Davenport knew what White was like in a passion. There was no talking to him and he began to withdraw, He had reached the next room, when White called him. back, saying: 'Come, I talk what I would do if an English man of War should find me here, but you need not fear, but I'll be gone out of their way.'

So that was his decision upon the four possible courses submitted by Davenport. He would make a dash for it, but if caught, he would fight, should the commander of the man-of-war attempt to force him to go to Madras. The idea of fighting against the English was abhorrent to Davenport, but he now realized that White would do that, if his freedom and his money were endangered.

After pronouncing these words, White continued to speak. He made it clear that he was resigned to the loss of the *Satis faction* and the *Derrea Dowlat*. They could not escape; it would be a miracle if they got through. He counted them as gone already, If anyone offered him five shillings for both, he would accept it. But that was comparatively a small matter. It was his frigate, the *Resolution*, with Captain Leslie on board, that he was thinking about, the only ship on which he could get back to England.

WHITE: 'I am most concerned for Lesly, I am afraid he'll be snapt upon the Coast, and he is the only man for my turn on this occasion, for Cropley I know is neither well effected to me nor fit for the business.'

And the *Dorothy* was not altogether suitable. She was too small a ship for the voyage home with the cargo White intended to carry. And there would be passengers.

WHITE: 'I must of necessity carry my Mary (for so he used

165

always to call Madam Lesly) and her young bantlings along with me.'

DAVENPORT: 'Well, but, Sir, what will become of the Raja Mr. Burneby? Will you leave him here exposed to the fury of the natives or at best to the Kings pleasure?'

WHITE: 'God damn him, I dare not trust him with a secret of such importance. Besides what tie am I under to take care of him? Has not he eyes in his head to foresee the danger? Let him shift for himself. Yet I do not know, it may be when I am just ready to go, I may take him with me. That is rime enough to tell him. Half a dozen plates and spoons, and a few clothes, with it may be fourty or fifty cattees of money (£400 to £500) make up his baggage. I need not much fear his overlading my ship.'

'Thus he broke a off at this time', writes Davenport.

XXIX. WHITE PREPARES TO ESCAPE

On March 25th White told Davenport that his mind was now made up to get ready the *Dorothy*, in case the *Resohition* never returned. It should be given out that he was loading her for a voyage to the Persian Gulf. When she was laden and provisioned, he would send her out of the harbour to a hiding-place among the islands, joining her at the last moment. He explained:

'I will always keep the Barge and Sloope Robin in readiness before my door, and a dozen of Country Boats, divided in four Squadrons continually out upon the Scout, and so whensoever an English Man of War comes in sight, I will set fire to the Town and immediately repair to my ship, where I will give them leave to find me out if they can, for they had

as good look for a Needle in a Bottle of Hay as for me, if I get
but two days start before them.'

This wild plan was sound up to a point. Among the hundreds of deserted islands of the archipelago, no one would
ever find him. These islands were mostly uncharted. Among
their shoal waters, behind their reefs, protected by tidal rips,
hidden in covered bays and coves, no English ship could pursue him. He would be safe there till the wind veered N. E. in
October and he could sail out of the great bay. Burning the
town—that suited him, pirate and ruffian that he was at
heart. A burning town would give the Siamese something to
do. When he fled in his barge, the houses flaming up the hill,
no one would have leisure to follow him. It would be a grand
finale to his adventures in Mer gen.

Davenport transmitted the instructions about loading the
Dorothy. The next item he had to superintend was the packing. In spite of his rages and impatience, there was a methodical strain in White, when it Came to conserving his own
property. He had told Davenport to order a set of new
chests. These were rapidly delivered.

WHITE: 'I would have you pack in the new Chests now
made everything of value in my House, and numbering the
Chests, take an exact Invoice of everything, valuing it at the
real worth in this place, so that I may know both what I have
and where to look for it.'

DAVENPORT: 'Would you please to be present at the packing and rating of them, for your better satisfaction.'

White said he would have time for that next day.

But the morrow was Easter Sunday and Improper for any
business of that nature'. He might burn Mergui, but he would
not pack on the Day of Resurrection. Instead, he gave a great
party for the whole station. All the Europeans on that distant
shore were invited. It was a noble entertainment, says Davenport, White was at his best. He was, of course, the master; his
house was the centre of interest, the place about which rumour

was always busy. Every merchant, every farmer, the bazaar-girls, the water-men, looked up at it, standing above them on its height, as they went about their labours. It represented everything that was important, that mattered. White was a great lord in that place. On this Easter night his windows were all lit; there was coming and going; sedan chairs arriving, the welcome, toasts; without, crowds standing and watching in the darkness. He himself knew that the end was near, some kind of an end, and it mellowed and saddened him. Davenport had hardly seen Mm with a manner so gentle and grand.

'He was very liberal to his immediate Servants, both White and Black, from the highest to the lowest; to me in particular he gave two pieces of Silk very rich, telling me at the same time that he design'd a more Considerable Token of his kindness for me in a short while, and that he gave me that only in course, because he was minded to give all his Servants somewhat on that Festival, which he said he had dcsign'd to have done on the fifth of the month, Ms Birth Day, had he not forgotten it.'

On Easter Monday he was back at his preparations. There was no time for rest. The next point was to get in as much money as possible in the short space he felt was left to him. Certain taxes were due. He would gather these urgently in the king's name and use them for Ms current expenses, some of which were of a public nature. The taxes were on the land, the rice crop having just been sold. He proposed to hurry to Tenasserim and from that centre collect the money. He expected to obtain £2,000 at once. His salt he must also sell As mentioned, he had trespassed on the royal monopoly of that commodity and he had a considerable stock to liquidate. He now devised a plan of forcing the subordinate officials to take it. 'They dare as well be damn'd as refuse to take it, said he.'

He wanted the money particularly to pay the seamen and soldiers, all of whom he had decided to disband and disarm, for he was afraid they might mutiny and seize Mm at the instigation of his enemies, if they suspected that he was escaping. The Mahomedans would arrest him in anticipation of sanction.

So the morning passed in business and accounts, Davenport at his elbow.

XXX. DAVENPORT'S DILEMMA

W hen the day's work was finished, White noticed that his secretary had a dejected appearance, WHITE: 'Mr. Davenport, what's the matter with you, are you not well?'

DAVENPORT: 'Yes, God be thanked, I am very well in health.'

WHITE: 'I perceive then you are dissatisfied in your mind at something or other; pray be plain, with me and tell me what it is.'

DAVENPORT: 'Sir 'tis very true, I am much dissatisfied, both in respect of you and my self, in respect of my self, because you have always been kind to me, yet my circumstances are such that I cannot manifest my Obligation to you in such a manner as I plainly foresee your occasions will require, without my extreme prejudice on many scores.'

He went on to explain to White the exceedingly delicate position in which he was placed by serving him at a crisis, from which he could see very little likelihood of emerging intact.

DAVENPORT: 'If I could go with you to Europe and you should have the good fortune to escape Interception, I shall leave my concerns in the Bay at such uncertainties and expose my self so much to the censure of all our Country-men in India, who are, many of them, but too apt to put the worst

Construction upon every persons proceedings that hath been once unfortunate, that I much question whether in my return to these parts again, I should ever be able to retrieve my Reputation.'

Davenport was a clever man. From the first he had had a disinclination to serve White, but had been persuaded to go on and on against his better judgment. Now he was hopelessly involved with his master. He proceeded: 'If I continue with you in the sphere I now move, untill your departure hence, and then stay behind you, what can I expect but to be exposed, if not to the rage and fury of the Natives, yet to the Kings and your Friend, the Lord Phaulkons, indignation as having been privy to your designed escape?'

That was a poor prospect, but there was a worse ahead. Supposing, before White could leave, an English warship arrived and White resisted, as it appeared he might resist, if he was cornered. 'How can I (pleaded Davenport) preserving my Allegiance unblemished, concur with you in so dangerous an attempt?'

Whatever happened, he Was faced with ruin, unless he could dissociate himself now from White. He then brought out what was in his mind, what had been in his mind so long.

DAVENPORT:' Wherefore I desire you would please discharge me from your Service, so that I may live unconcerned, untill some opportunity presents of going hence.'

WHITE: 'Sooner than detain you in my Service against your will, I will not only dismiss you but give you a small Sloop to carry you to Bengala or whithersoever you would go. But you must have patience till I get my ship secured out of the way.'

Again Davenport had to agree to a delay, though he persuaded White to allow him to hand over his cash account to John Turner, one of the subordinates. For the moment the conversation was at art end, for they went to dinner.

Later they began the packing postponed from Saturday. As

they wrapped up his plate (except a little for daily use) counted and packed Ms jewels, sea-books and instruments for navigation, White returned to the subject of Davenport's position.

WHITE: 'I do not forget the promise I have made you of one thousand rupees extraordinary, besides all your wages. If you will but continue with me and go only to Persia, I will give you the Sloope Robin freely.'

This makes White's plan clearer. If the *Resolution* failed to arrive, they would take the *Dorothy* and the *Robin* to the Persian Gulf, where selling both vessels, they would go home overland. Davenport's share would be the *Robin*. It was a possible scheme, for White had an agent in the Persian Gulf. But Davenport did not believe that White would ever get to Persia.

DAVENPORT: 'I do not doubt your making good your promise in the least, but you cannot well blame me if I desire to be at my own liberty. I will never be backward in any friendly assistance, only reserving my self free from interfering with the designs you have entered into relating to your removal hence.'

WHITE: 'You shall be at your own choice and at your liberty to leave me, when you please. All I desire of you is to accompany me to Tenassery and help to settle my particular Accounts with the Merchants.'

Davenport consented to this, though it was another postponement. But his release from an impossible position now seemed close at hand.

XXXI. THE FORGED COMMISSION

The necessity of having some sort of an official paper to cover his piracies in the bay recurred again and again to White, It was madness to set out for England without something of the kind. But he agreed with Davenport that the council of Tenasserim would never sign such a document. Then an idea struck him. There were five mandarins on the council besides Burnaby and himself. Two of these, the Viceroy of Tenasserim and another, were resident in Mergui. He would get the signature and seals of those two by means of a trick.

Half-way down a large sheet of paper he wrote in English a statement to the effect that all orders the Shāhbandar, Mr. Samuel White, might give to the commanders of Siamese men-of-war, were issued on the authority and under the particular instruction of the council of Tenasserim. The date inserted was prior to Coates's expedition in 1685, two years back. He then sent this paper to the two mandarins in the town by the hand of a messenger, who was instructed to say that his Honour was in a hurry and would they kindly affix their seals above the English writing; it was a pure matter of form; the document referred to the dispatch of a vessel to Bengal The two officials made no objection and affixed their seals, as requested.

When White had the paper back, he sent for his clerk and a Siamese writer, took them into his study, shut the door, and translating the English into Hindustani, for the Siamese writer did not know English, he asked him to turn that into Siamese and write it on the top half of the document above the seals of the members of council. When the writer understood what he was required to do, he began to tremble. He looked so wretched that White asked him what was the matter. He replied that if such a trick leaked out he would lose his head. White began violently to abuse him, but perceiving that the man was terrified and that he might be baulked at this last minute from obtaining what was so essential, he calmed himself with an effort, explaining that the document was for use only in Europe, No one in Mergui would ever see it. The man then proceeded with his work.

When finished, the paper had quite a regular appearance, with the Siamese on top, the seals of the two mandarins, with their names written beside the seals, below. Underneath was the English translation. One detail remained, to certify that the translation was a true one. White accordingly asked Davenport and Turner to attest it. Davenport now saw himself involved in the fabrication of a false document. He tried to screen himself by Substituting for the usual categorical attestation a statement that White's clerk declared that what was written above in Siamese contained the true sense and meaning of what was written in English below. This hedging was enough to annoy White. 'Mr. White frowned and said, I might have been plainer in my Attestation, but however he gave it to me to put in one of the new chests above mentioned, which I accordingly did.'

White's file at last was purged of piracy, it was now good enough for home consumption.

XXXII. THE RETURN OF THE *RESOLUTION*

On April 1st they all set out to find a safe hiding-place for the *Dorothy*. The party consisted of the two mandarins, Burnaby, one of White's men called Threder, Don Joseph, whom we have not met since we saw him sitting at White's bedsido at Ayudhya, Captain Cropley and, of course, Davenport. White deemed it best to make the expedition as public as possible, while it was given out that its object was merely to chart the southern approaches of the harbour. No one knew the truth except Davenport, He sat in the Shāh-bandar's pinnace, heaving the lead from time to time, and recording the depths in his pocket book. After four days of this tedious deception, Davenport, who had been on the look-out for likely places, informed White secretly of a spot which seemed in every way suitable. This was twenty-seven miles south of Mergui, an island ten miles from the shore, with a bay protected from the monsoon, and a magnificent strand upon which, if necessary, a ship could be laid and careened, as there was a difference of twenty feet at springs. The place is now called Mergui Island.

On April 5th they returned to headquarters and, after two hours' stay in the house, White and Davenport hastened up the river to Tenasserim to collect the taxes. The lading of the *Dorothy* was pushed on apace. As it was now only a month from the monsoon, the local inhabitants found this very curious. Surprise led to rumour; people started to guess what was in the wind; the whole town buzzed with talk, on White's return from up-river, one of his informants arrived to say that a Mahomedan merchant, called Namtullah, had been spreading the report that the Shāhbandar was preparing secretly to be gone. White, furious and afraid, had the man arrested, flogged, manacled and thrown into prison. As he was a prominent trader, deputations arrived to intercede for his release. But White refused to see them. People would talk, but at least they should not talk in public. If he could not frighten them enough to prevent memorials reaching Ayudhya about his preparations, he was lost.

This disturbing episode was followed by a piece of the utmost good fortune. On April 23 rd the *Resolution* sailed into port, with Captain Leslie safe and all his crew. It was a huge relief. White could now discard his idea of flight on the *Dotothy*, with a long and dangerous journey through Persia.

On the *Resolution* he would return home by the Cape. She was a fine commodious ship; Mary, her children and a few more, perhaps, could travel on her without overcrowding. The *Dorothy* was unladen, her rig taken out and she was sent to lie at Tenasserim. A spur was put on the work of preparing the *Resolution* for her voyage. There was not a moment to be lost, Though she was the king's property, she lay under English colours in the stream, within pistol shot of the house. To suggest to the populace that she was about to sail on a special mission and so explain the preparations at that unusual season, he informed the mandarins that he had received the king's orders 'to fit and keep her in a sailing posture awaiting the Kings pleasure for her dispatch at an hours warning'. He enjoined his men to provision her immediately with rice, cattle, hogs and what else they could quickly procure. Villagers were to be forced to sell at the king's price anything required. Even in distraction and hurry, almost panic, White's business sense never left him. As he had to depart, he would take the King of Siam's ship, provisioned at a nominal cost. More than that, his flight should be a trading voyage, for a rich cargo was laden upon her. We may assume that all his chests were safely stowed on board at this time.

White had had, God knows, every reason for haste before, but the news brought in by Leslie multiplied his impatience. The captain said that the state of affairs was now very different from what it had been, when in 1685 he and Coates did what they liked on the coast. The East India Company had been reinforced from England. A number of men-of-war had arrived and besides the frigate *Revenge*, White's sloop, the *Mary*, had been seized by them. These details and other information of an impending attack upon Mergui were given by Leslie till 'Mr. White was all in a flame to be gone'. If he was intercepted, they might take him to Madras a prisoner. They knew too much there to be deceived by his false papers. It was their personal animosity that lie feared. He might be hanged, certainly he would be mulcted of his fortune. But who said that he would let himself be caught? His frigate with her twenty-two guns, the fortifications on shore—he would fling the English back if they came to take him. Better fight your countrymen than lose all and hang. So he argued.

XXXIII. DAVENPORT DECIDES TO BETRAY WHITE

I t was in this truculent mood that on April 28th he entered into his last conversation with Davenport, as his secretary, Truly, it was a frantic scene. White sat there in his chair over the harbour, where his slaves hastened with the loading. Davenport stood before him, tactful, watching, his spirit unbroken, though he was in the power of a violent and desperate man. White began grumbling about his ship the *Satis faction* on her gulf voyage, his richest venture. A month before he had written her off as a dead loss, so certain was he that she would be taken. Now Ms feelings overcame him. She had twenty thousand pieces of eight on board her and a cargo worth thousands of pounds. True, he had reimbursed himself tolerably by his adjustments of the king's accounts, by his transfers of the king's merchandise and the king's ships to his private credit. It was not altogether that he was losing £16,000; it was the abominable shame of feeling that the Company was getting them, that they were to go to Yale, that scoundrel Yale, and his rascally friends. Perhaps it would be better to stay till September in the hope that the *Satisfaction* might yet put in.

DAVENPORT: 'I do verily believe that we shall see ships here from Madras before August.'

WHITE: 'Ay, ay, Captain Leslie has given me a very un-welcome Account.'

At the thought of his impotence to stay, of the certain loss of his money, of the triumph of Yale, he flew out and swore: 'God damn, I care not much. I'll make fools of one hundred of the King of Englands Captains.'

This sentence reveals the other side of his character. We have already seen examples of his duplicity. Later he will largely put away violence and call to his aid suavity and cunning. But at the moment his anger was rising and he began to repeat in a furious voice to the patient Davenport what he had threatened before.

'If any of them come hither, before I can get away, I'll be civil to them, but if ever a Kings Captain or Lieutenant of them all comes ashore and tells me that I must go to Madras and should pretend a power to force me thither, I'll be the man that will pistol him upon the place with my own hands, and wipe my Arse with his Kings Commission.'

Then he broke out cursing and shouting: 'What a Plague, dost think I'm to be scar'd with the sight of a Kings Flag at a Boats Bow? No, continued he with a horrid Oath, I know better things; I look upon the best Commission any man has, who comes out upon the Companies Concerns, no better than if I stood by and saw them make it under a hedge.'

Still very angry, he pulled himself up to say what he had finally decided to do: 'However, if I can get a way, I will and if I cannot, whose soevers lot it is to find me here, they shall find Merge n the hottest place that ever they came against in there lives, as simply as 'tis fortified. For I am resolved never to go to Madras, If there come Ten Sail of Men of War to fetch me and if it does come to that pass that I am intercepted in my design, I'll defend the place as long as'tis possible with the Natives and when I can hold it no longer, I'll burn it down, and go to Syam by the light on't, and see who will fetch me thence.'

DAVENPORT: 'Sir, I am heartily sorry to hear this and I would fain hope that you speak not as you mean.'

At this mild reproof by Davenport, who held resistance to the English, his countrymen, to be both bad policy and a wicked act, White became irritated beyond all measure, with frightful passion exclaiming; 'God damn thee, I see nothing will work with thee; and since I see thou art still resolved to prefer hugging thy own fears and jealousies, before either thy own advantage or any inclination to my Interest, and art so unwilling to stick by me, when I have most occasion for thee, e'en get thee down stairs out of my House, and never come near me more, for if ever I hear a word out of thy mouth about my business, By the Eternal God, I'll cut thy Tongue out.'

At this, Davenport immediately withdrew. He had his discharge at last. But the language had soured him. It was so unreasonable. He had served White so well. It showed a dreadful selfishness and a total incapacity to realize his predicament. He was never the sa me to White again. He now felt at liberty to put his own interests first and to save himself, if he could, He withdrew, as I say, and sought his own room, afraid to leave the house in case White might think he had gone out to tell some of the vital secrets of which he was the sole repository, He stayed quietly in his chair, reflecting idly that in England information might be laid before a magistrate of such words as White had uttered against the King's Majesty. But Mergui was not England, not by a long way, and the magistrates—why, to lay any information before them of treasonable expressions against King James, and by the Shāhbandar, their master, 'would be an indiscretion little inferior to Mr. White's'. The more he considered his situation, the more dangerous and desperate it appeared.

Time passed; dinner came on; he remained where he was, About three o'clock he made inquiries. Yes, Mr. White was calmer, in 'a calm posture', they said. He called his Christian servant, Lazarus, and sent up a letter.

The letter is a remarkable document to have been composed after such a scene, I shall not quote it all, but I must give certain sentences, for it is so strange a chance that a man of Davenport's gifts of composition should be found beating out a living in the ports of Indo-China. The reader must have been struck by the evocative power of his writing. The dignified language of the protest lie now submitted upstairs is no less revealing.

'Sir, That this morning I happen'd by the unseasonable declaration of my opinion to hazard your displeasure I can't but acknowledge a great indiscretion, but I hope you will not censure it as an unpardonable presumption, at least if you please to call to mind that plainness and sincerity which you have so often, not only expressed your self highly satisfied with, but charg'd me to continue in the whole course of your service. . . . I now humbly request the friendly performance of your promise, which was that I should be at liberty to withdraw from your employment and live retir'd from all public business. My reasons for this request I have so frequently and fully discount you, that to repeat them now would be altogether needless. I make choice of this way of addressing my self to you, partly to avoid any further occasion of offence, and, if possible, to procure a friendly parting. . . . As I prefer my Allegiance to my Prince and the Duty I owe my own Country to all private advantages, so no less a consideration than a hazard thereof could have made me so solicitous to have declined your service. But however you will do me but right to believe that I shall, notwithstanding my dismission, continue as true to your secrets as your self can desire and as becomes one who hath been accustomed to delight himself in being justly esteemed.

Sir, Your Faithful Servant

FRANCIS DAVENPORT.'

To my mind this letter was dictated by one emotion only,

namely chat of fear. Davenport was deeply agitated by two considerations. To stay on with White involved him in the grave risk of fighting against an English company which had the king behind it. He must leave, but leaving after such a scene exposed his life to danger, for he knew all White's secrets. If White thought it was unsafe to spare a person, who through enmity might betray him, his fate was sealed. White was evidently decided to let nothing stand between him and his liberty. As he was ready to fight against King James, he would think little of putting his secretary out of the way, He could easily have him arrested; the magistrates would make no difficulties. Once detained in prison, he would never emerge alive. It was of final importance to induce White to believe that he parted with him on good terms. The letter was designed to that end.

Like all persons subject to violent seizures by the emotion of rage, White tended to be unusually amenable when that emotion had spent itself. The fact is that he understood quite well that Davenport was in a difficult position, but, as an autocrat, he was angered by his secretary's lack of utter devotion, Yet, as he had to go, on calm reflection it was better that they should part friends.

Each was afraid of the other. In his heart Davenport was resolved to betray White, if that was the only way to save himself. White had decided to watch Davenport and on the smallest sign of his defection to arrest him. It was with these mental reservations that they now met.

Lazarus came in with a summons from the Shāhbandar. Davenport went upstairs. With a false cordiality White began.

WHITE: 'What, Mr. Davenport, then you have no mind to stay with me?'

DAVENPORT: 'Sir, if I have not, I hope you are satisfied in my reason for it.'

WHITE: 'Why, you seem by the tenderness and care of your Allegiance to suspect that I shan't be gone before a Man of War meets with me. But if you will needs go, I will not detain you. You know my concerns and your discoursing them may do me a diskindness, but I have no reason to suspect you in that particular. You may come when you will for your Money and you shall have it. Nor will I forget my promise or be worse than my word to you, though 'tis too late for you to go now to Bengala. I hope you'l come now and then and see us.'

DAVENPORT: 'Yes, Sir, and serve you too in any matter that I can, without apparent prejudice to my self.'

WHITE: 'You say very well and you shall not find me backward in any kindness I can do you.'

Brandy was then called for and they pledged each other. Davenport took his leave, but before he reached the bottom of the stairs, White called him back.

WHITE: 'Mr. Davenport, whither do you intend to remove?'

DAVENPORT: 'Sir, I do not yet know, but I think to Captain Cropleys.'

WHITE: 'Pray tell Cropley I would have him come to me in the morning and receive the Money I borrowed of him last month, for I'll send him and his family up to Tenassery, but don't you tell him anything of that till I speak to him myself.'

DAVENPORT: 'Not I, Sir, but if he removes to Tenassery, it will be very good pretence for me to go along with him, under going again to the hot waters[1] for my healths sake.'

WHITE: 'Ay, so it will.'

This arrangement suited both parties. White was not quite sure of Cropley. With Davenport and him up up the river, he would feel more secure. It would, incidentally, be safer for Cropley's wife and children, in case there was any outburst of popular indignation in Mergui when the *Resolution* sailed. And it would protect the breach with Davenport from gossip, Davenport found the plan good because, dissociated front

---

[1] There are medicinal hot watet springs in the Tenasserim area.

White, he could await the crisis, free to select the best course in his own interests. Accordingly in a day or so, he and Cropley, with Tuttie, and with the families of the two last, rowed up the river. From Tenasserim Davenport kept himself informed of what was happening In Mergui and continued to write up his diary.

During May all the soldiers and seamen were paid off, being sent also to Tenasserim. No one was allowed to proceed beyond that town. The road to the capital was blocked. White saw to it that no messenger or letter, other than his own, should go to Phaulkon, There should be no leakage chat way, A close watch was kept on the Indians. Any Siamese merchantmen which returned to harbour were unrigged and warped up to Tenasserim. White's object here was to prevent the possibility of pursuit. It appears that at this time the *New Jerusalem* and *Sancta Cruz* came safely back.

By June the 14th the *Resolution* was deep laden with a valuable cargo, and provisions for eighteen months to feed forty men were on board. Her berth had been opposite White's house. She was now moved on the ebb and anchored near the main battery on the ridge. White's problem was to get her down to the bar without arousing too much comment. She must ride at the bar for, if he were seen boarding her in the harbour, he might be stopped before she was well under weigh, Every other night, therefore, she was dropped down a short distance, by tripping the anchor and letting her drive, though 'always pretending that her anchor came home and would not ride her.' Thus she was taken out of range of the battery, 'and down so near the Barr, that at any time of the Night, with the first of the Ebb she might drive over the Barr.'

The plan for escape was this. On June the 26th the ebb would start about 9p.m. White had his barge and the sloop *Rubin* anchored in front of the house. With the ebb and under cover of darkness, he and those with him would quietly embark, all the luggage having previously been sent to the *Resolution*. Assisted by the S. W. wind, then blowing steadily, and by the tide, the barge and the sloop would quickly slip down the harbour to the bar, a distance of about four miles. In half an hour or so, they would all be safely aboard, and by dawn the *Resolution* would be deep among the islands, a tract of rough sea between her and Mergui, across which the small boats left in the harbour could not pursue. She would bear south beyond King Island and beat down to Mergui Island, the hiding-place selected, remaining there until the monsoon blew over and in October she could leave for England. But, wrote Davenport, 'it pleased God to disappoint Mr. White in the very height of his expectations', on the 23rd news was brought that an English man-of-war lay outside.

XXXIV. BEHIND THE SCENES IN LONDON AND MADRAS

The intimations and hints, rumours and anticipations, which had reached Mergui from the outer world during the first six months of 1687, had been founded on solid fact. The East India Company *was* exasperated with Phaulkon and White; the council *had* written to James II. and obtained from him a royal proclamation recalling all his subjects from the service of his majesty of Siam; and it *was* proposed to send a man-of-war to Mergui. The account against Phaulkon and White had been gradually mounting up. Sir Josiah Childe, the President of the Court of Directors in London, was a man of very forcible character. He became more and more enraged as news reached him of White's depredations in the bay, more and more convinced that the representatives of the Company at Ayudhya were wasting their time there mildly expostulating with Phaulkon. As he became angrier, so he determined on a departure from the Company's policy of trade by agreement with native rulers, a policy which had guided his predecessors from the time of Sir Thomas Roe in the reign of James I and which had only been modified as at Madras, where fortifications had been built. It could be said that such works were no real departure, for they had been raised by permission of the local monarch out of consideration for the disturbed state of the hinterland. But now Childe was to initiate a new policy, contrary to all their experience and, as the event will show, at that date a disastrous policy.

This was to rely on the admitted superiority of English ships of war at sea, to employ them to seize in reprisal merchantmen belonging to eastern kings who had offended, and, further, to attempt to take possession of seaports belonging to such kings, thereby bringing pressure upon them to right wrongs done and to make reasonable trade concessions. He further intended to keep any territory taken, so that the revenue derived from it would pay for the upkeep of the settlement, This policy he was to seek to carry out, not only against Siam, but simultaneously against the Great Mogul. He was evidently profoundly misinformed of the difficulties. That he formulated such projects at all is of great interest in view of the development of those very theories of eastern expansion in the following century. But he was long before his time and the means at his disposal were ridiculously inadequate.

As it is impossible without confusing the picture to paint the whole panorama of events, I propose to confine myself here to a series of extracts from correspondence bearing upon the situation at Mergui and Ayudhya, These will show how the events, with which we are already familiar from the inside, struck Sir Josiah Childe in London and the authorities in India.

I shall begin by the abstract of a letter from Madras to London dated 25th August 1684, nine months after White's appointment to Mergui, which, shows how that event was taken officially.

'Letters from Siam advise . . . that the King is now remodelling and fortifying his Country, turning out Moorish Governors and putting in Europeans, Mr. Burnaby as Governor of Tenasserim [Mergui], Mr. White as Shabander of Mergui. He invites all Europeans and pays great wages, which draws away many.'

The abstract continues with the hope that the king, though making an attempt to build up his trade with the assistance of interlopers, will not be deflected by Phaulkon from continuing his favour to the Company, it is suggested that if Charles II. wrote personally to Phra Narai a satisfactory settlement would result. It is clear enough from the above that at Madras the appointment of White, even officially, was not regarded as wholly bad; unofficially, as we know, they were delighted at first.

The unpopularity of Phaulkon with the Company grew rapidly. I have already described Strangh's melodramatic exit. The imprisonment by Phaulkon shortly afterwards of Peter Crouch and John Thomas, Company merchants on their way to the Far East, his public punishment of Potts, his insolent manner to many and the death of Captain Lake of the *Prudent Mary* which occurred in the prison where Phaulkon had confined him—all these matters, which happened about the time of White's appointment in 1683, had rendered him odious to the East India Company. Sam Barron, one of their men who remained behind on private business after Strangh's departure, writing from Ayudhya on the 15th November 1684, sums up the view then held by Company merchants on the spot:

'. . . the gross and many abuses to Mr. Strangh, the bloody affronts, persecution and infernal practices against the life and Credit of Mr. Sam Potts and other servants of the Honble

Company would be too long a series to particularize . . . the Greek Faulkon has no other aims than to route and exclude the Honble Company from this trade and in lieu to prefer and encourage Interlopers with a few private Merchants. . . . This Hog has himself the ambition to be called Excellency. . . . And since this monster in nature has had the impudence to defame our Sovereign Lord the King, calling his Majesty King of devils, vilifying the nation and injuring the Honble Company, since he has imprisoned, robbed, and abused their Servants and broken open their letters, with other unheard of, enormous and audacious proceedings as hardly an Indian Prince would dare to put in practice . . . forgetting he was raised by White's craft and Burnaby's folly, and with the Company's stock, I hope their Honours will seek public redress and satisfaction.'

Barron then proceeds to hint how this last may be done: 'How easy this Prince [Phra Narai] is to be brought to terms is obvious from the example of the Dutch in 1649: two brave ships will effect the business.'

In a letter addressed the 24th of the same month, this time to the President of Surat, he writes more definitely in the same strain: 'Some talk as if . . . the Honble Company is resolved and have determined to right themselves of wrongs, damages and injuries sustained in India, which laudable course and magnanimous resolution revives me extremely.'

This refers to the directors' reputed plans against the Mogul, Barron says he hopes this determination will extend to Siam, for the Siamese deserve to smart also. The time has come, he urges: 'to give this Indian world the due impression of their Honours' puissance . . . so that none shall dare in the future to domineer over and trample on the English. . . . In the conduct of this affair my humble advice is to send four ships, whereof two should be of fifty or sixty guns a piece.'

Finally, he describes how he attempted to obtain the king's ear against Phaulkon:

'I could not get 3 or 4 Englishmen, of any note out of the
100 or 150 that were this year here, to join with me for the
delivery of a Petition (by which I thought to have renewed
my former complaint to the King) against the Greek, every
one of them siding and creeping to him, both in hope of
profit and employment and out of fear, since he has now
brought to pass, what he declared in time of Mr. Strangh,
that he would make the English 'ere long creep to him like
dogs; and indeed this Country since this Villain has been in
play, has been fit only for those who could flatter and command vice, how enormous soever.'

As an ironic commentary on these violent words it may be
mentioned that in the following year Barren joined Phaulkon.
But the extracts show well enough the way affairs were tend-
ing. It was taken that not the King of Siam but Phaulkon and
his men were the enemies of the Company, If Phaulkon was
overthrown by an armed demonstration, all might yet be
well with the trade. At the moment it had ceased to exist.

Barron's view shows pro-Company feeling in Ayudhya. It
is now necessary to quote the views of the Surat council, the
head office of all the settlements in India, including those in
the bay. Their advice to the Court of Directors will take the
narrative forward another step. After getting into touch with
Strangh and Thomas Yale, who had taken ten months on
their voyage via the Straits from Ayudhya to Surat, the
council wrote on the 29th November 1684 to London.

'According to what advice we have Phaulcon, in all appearance, will not stand long; his behaviour towards the
Merchants of these parts hath been such that none will adventure thither, and many have complained much of him; and
he in appearance is really a very naughty man. However, if he
continues in favour, we shall write to him and gain from him
what we can for your interest till your pleasure be known,
and we are the most intent on this chat if possible by the King
of Siam's means your Honours may get a trade to Japan.'

Some kind of crash in Siam Was therefore anticipated as early as 1684. With their close experience of Indian conditions, the council at Surat realized the extreme instability of Phaulkon's position, a foreign adventurer in an oriental court. But they wanted the Japan trade and they still thought the king might grant it to them. It would be better to hold on till the inevitable fall of Phaulkon. Strangh had been too touchy, they thought, Thomas Yale, who, as I have remarked, had himself done a little business with Phaulkon, advised them that more tact might accomplish wonders.

While the directors in London were being given time to receive and digest the news from Siam and pass such orders as they might deem fit, the council of Surat decided to make feelers again at Ayudhya, in case Strangh's failure was chiefly due to his irascible temperament, and on 13th May 1685 they sent back Thomas Yale assisted by two other factors, with letters to Phra Narai. In their instructions to these gentlemen they say:

'Let not any little Punctillio cause any difference between you and any in Siam. The Right Honble Company have suffered by the folly of some of their servants that have been there, chiefly from peevishness etcetera, giving dislike to Mr. Constant Faukcon, thinking mean of him, because he came out in one of the Company's ships in a mean employment. . . . We would have you give him all fitting respect and treat him with all handsomeness, for gaining on him we do understand to be the only way to secure a settlement at Siam.'

The letter then continues significantly: 'Use all fair means first for a settlement; if it cannot be effected, we shall hereafter see to let the King and his ministers know that we will not be abused and that we have power and force enough to right our Masters, but keep this private to yourselves, we adjure you.'

It was at this date that the Company's affairs in Siam were transferred by order of the Court of Directors from the council of Surat to the independent charge of Madras. The letter quoted above is therefore the last from Surat where instructions are directly given to factors at Ayudhya. From this onwards the president of the Madras Council becomes solely responsible, first William Gyfford and then Elihu Yale.

So far the correspondence quoted has revealed anger in Ayudhya and patience in Surat. London now began to react. By June 1685 letters had reached England which roused the forceful Sir Josiah Childe. Though he disbelieved in Siam as a paying proposition, he was not going to be insulted by a Greek and he wanted damages.

On the 17th of that month he wrote out to Madras:

'We have received articles against Constant Faulcon of Siam, containing such notorious abuses of our servants there . . . that we are resolved not to put up with them. . . . Damages may amount in the whole to about 10 or 15 thousand pounds sterling, which we are resolved to reprise ourselves for upon the said King of Siam in case he makes us not satisfaction. . . . We do not think it advisable to tell you where or when we intend to reprise ourselves.'

Sir Josiah was making his preparations, not only for a move on Siam, but also on the Mogul, whose proceedings against the Company had also inflicted heavy loss, It must be remembered that the East India Company had under their charter the power of making war on the governments of the East. They hired frigates from the Admiralty, when required. But though free to make war, they were careful to obtain the king's full concurrence, as that gave a national colour to their projects.

During the summer of 1685 Sir Josiah Childe continued his reading of the Siam correspondence, and on August the 12th wrote to Surat to recall any factors who might have stayed behind at Ayudhya. It was to be a complete breach pending settlement. In that letter he described Phaulkon as 'a wicked fellow'. During the year he obtained James II's sanction for sending out a fleet, which was to chastise both the Mogul and the King of Siam. The expedition consisted of six companies of infantry and ten ships of twelve to seventy guns, and its programme on the Indian side alone was ludicrously beyond its power, for it had to evacuate the English from Bengal, seize the Mogul's ships at sea, capture and fortify Chittagong, a strong walled city in eastern Bengal, march on and besiege Dacca and extort a favourable peace. As Aurangzebe had an army at the time of 700,000 men, Childe 's project was fantastic. Those ships intended for the Indian operations reached Bengal at the end of 1686. The expedition was a complete fiasco and, had it not been for the fact that Aurangzebe hardly regarded the matter as a serious attempt against him, the Company would not have survived. But so insignificant did this war seem to him, that his historians do not mention it.

Returning now to the Siamese side of the operations, I will note the steps leading up to the sending of a man-of-war to Mergui.

Early in 1686 letters began to arrive in India from Childe, making it clear what he had meant by the reference to reprisals in his letter of the previous June. In January, before he had heard of the depredations of Coates, he ordered the Agent in Bengal and the council at Madras to seize any Siamese ships they could find and sell them, in that way indemnifying themselves for the losses they had sustained in Ayudhya, real or fancied. In June 1586 the council at Madras received a copy of a proclamation which Childe had induced James II. to issue, also before the fact of Coates's seizures were known to him. This proclamation not only forbade the king's subjects to take office or employment under princes in the East, but also recalled any who had done so, on. October the 15th Childe gave Captain William Perse of the *Bengal Merchant* letters of marque to seize any Siamese ships on the Bombay coast. Finally on 22nd October 1686 he sent a secret letter to the President of Madras, which disclosed in full his intentions towards Siam. By this time lie had received information about Coates and also about White's outrageous behaviour and he was carried away by his anger. The letter begins:

'We . . . require you to pursue the King of Siam with open war until he has satisfied us for the injuries formerly done us and those lately at Metchlepatam by Captain Coates, then in his service . . . and we require you, according to his Majesty's late proclamation, to try all the English by martial law whom you shall find in the said King of Siam's service, or otherwise detain them in close imprisonment . . . until our Judge Advocate shall arrive.'

White, of course, had had no information that so drastic a course would be taken but, with an intuition of something dangerous of the sort, we have seen how he attempted to regularize his position at law. Had the Judge Advocate got hold of him, he would have been hanged. The letter continued that the Madras council was to send a ship to seize Mergui and erect a fort there:

'We are well informed that there is no power at Mergui to resist one ships company and that the people there are a sheepish, cowardly people who will not fight. However, we think it necessary, for the greater certainty of keeping what we get, that you should send 50 soldiers, English and Portuguese. . . . We can promise ourselves no great trade from that place at present for Europe, which is our principal business, but we think it may be an excellent place for raising a revenue of customs etcetera upon the Moors and Natives that frequent that place, and most especially no pan of India like it for fitting and repairing of ships in time of peace or war, and plenty of provisions, and how much we shall want such a place of resort for our ships, if we should hereafter happen to fall into a war, you are best able to judge.'

This is a somewhat important letter in the history of the East India Company in the seventeenth century. It goes a certain distance to blunt the argument elaborately documented by Shafaad Ahmed Khan in his *The East India Trade in the Seventeenth Century*, that the Court of Directors never for a moment contemplated during that century the foundation of an English dominion in India, Here is a definite case where, disregarding their old guiding principle of trade and security, they desired to conquer and occupy a town with its adjacent territory. True, Mergui was not in India, but the project shows a state of mind. At the dates admittedly, it was a preposterous notion, as the sequel will show.

But there is an explanation. Childe had recently come to the alarming conclusion that if the English did not take Mergui, the French would do so. Though England was at peace with France, that would enormously increase the embarrassments of the East India Company in the bay.

To establish the fact that it was his preoccupation with French designs in Siam that drove Childe to the issue of the above rash letter, I must make a few further extracts from the correspondence. It will be recalled that French interest in Siam was missionary at first. The laborious journeys of eminent ecclesiastics have already been mentioned. All that, of course, was quite harmless and excited no interest in England. But in 1683, the year White was appointed Shāhhandar, the King of Siam sent an embassy to Louis XIV to discuss reciprocal trade arrangements. This was actually the beginning of Phaulkon's policy to strengthen himself against the multifarious dangers of his position as a foreign adventurer in an oriental court.

Observers of eastern affairs in England began to scent the wind, in the autumn of 1684 Lord Preston wrote from Paris to the Earl of Sunderland: 'The Mandarins of Siam saw the day before yesterday, in passing by, his most Christian Majesty in the gallery of Versailles. When he was about 10 paces from them they threw themselves upon the floor and covered their faces, and being bid three or four times to rise they would scarce do it.'

The same diplomat continued to keep his government

informed of what he noticed in this palavering. 'The Ambassadors from Siam . . . have been highly treated by Monsieur at St. Cloud and by the Prince de Condé at Chantilly and by the Premier President at dinner after they had assisted the other clay at the opening of this Parliament.'

Then there were the presents, a cabinet of china, consisting of many pieces of K'ang Hsi Ware, screens from Japan, filagree work in gold and silver. Lastly, most important, he sends the information: This King hath named the Chevalier de Chaumont, a man of quality and a Captain of a man-of-war for his Ambassador to the King of Siam; he hath assigned him a vessel to transport himself and the Ambassador of Siam thither with very considerable presents.'

This was the famous de Chaumont embassy which arrived at Ayudhya in September 1685, with the Abbé choisy, a member of the Paris smart set, Père Tachard a learned Jesuit, numerous fine gentlemen, two warships and with what the Siamese considered most vital of all, a royal letter from the Roi Soleil himself. The French had a tremendous social success in Siam. They were the first European gentlemen of quality the Siamese had ever seen. The mandarins were fascinated. They liked the French so much that for the moment they did not see the danger which threatened themselves. Phaulkon, who had organized the affair from first to last and was chief showman, had a triumph. When White was called in about his accounts the following year, everyone was still talking of the French and Phaulkon was at the height of his power. It WAS currently known that the Chevalier de Chaumont had returned to France with Phra Narai's request for troops. These events account for the ease with which Phaulkon was able to protect White from the mandarins.

During 1686 Childe watched the alarmingly rapid progress the French were making in Siam. A letter addressed by him early in 1687 to Surat is indicative of what was already in his mind when in the previous October he had ordered the occupation of Mergui. He writes to warn the Company in India that Phra Narai's request for French troops had been granted and sums up the directors' view of the situation. He begins: 'Faulcon's villainy . . . we long since foresaw and early lamented the misfortune you were drawn into by our too mild president Gyfford.'

Childe had the habit of fulminating from the safety of London to the unfortunate council in India, who were supposed, without adequate resources, to accomplish prodigies in the face of overwhelming forces and in a heat wave temperature.

Sir Josiah goes on; 'Faulcon's way is to bribe and flatter our chief servants in India and corrupt any of our factors in Siam who are corruptible . . . while his drift is evidently to destroy the Company's interest . . . and this he has perpetrated to such a degree that he justly fears the revenge deserved by him from us . . . which has forced him in his master's name to the craving of succour from the King of France and upon what secret terms we know not.'

He then gives details of the troops and ships which France is sending out, three great men-of-war with four other vessels well armed, 1,600 soldiers and 300 engineers; and adds: 'We verily believe Faulcon will endeavour to engage them against us.'

Phaulkon's intention certainly was to impose his policy and will on Siam by the help of French troops and, with French men-of-war based on Mergui, to overwhelm the Company in the Bay of Bengal. These extracts, I hope, explain why Childe wished to occupy Mergui.

I must now turn to the practical effect which was given to Childe's orders by the President and council of Madras, The distance between London and Madras and the length of time it took to communicate by sailing ships makes the sequence of events a trifle confusing. It was in the middle of 1686 that Madras had its orders to take prizes from Siam and to publish the proclamation withdrawing Englishmen from foreign employ. During the months which followed they strove to put these orders into effect. In the matter of prizes they had considerable success for they took four ships White had out, the *Satisfaction* at Mocha in the Red Sea, the *Derrea Dowlat* at Achin in Sumatra and the *Mary* and the *Revenge* in the bay. In regard to the proclamation, they served printed copies on interlopers in the vicinity, who, it was reported, paid not the slightest attention. There was no vessel handy during 1686 to carry it to Mergui, and not until 24th March 1687 had they available a ship. The *Curtana*, a frigate of about twenty-four guns, under the command of Captain Anthony Weltden, which had sailed from England in the middle of the previous year, was deemed suitable. It must be pointed out that Childe's letter of October 1686, directing the seizure of Mergui, had not yet reached them. It came to hand only in August 1687.

This Captain Weltden was a young gentleman of some twenty-nine years of age, about eight years White's junior. He came of excellent family, for his father, Henry Weltden of Thornby, traced his descent directly to Bertram dc Waltden, who came over with the Conqueror. Anthony was the youngest son and though his crest was a demi-lion rampant arg. gutté-de-sang, he had not a penny. Indeed, his appearance was so ragged that the first resolution in his regard passed by the council of Madras was as follows: 'To encourage Captain Weltden in this present design of the Siam business, it is ordered that three yards of Scarlet be given him to make a Coat.'

The *Curtana,* also, was rather a ragged affair to our eyes accustomed to the Grand Fleet, I have said that the East India Company hired frigates, as you might hire a motor car nowadays, and they did not always hire them from the Admiralty. The *Curtana* was owned by an English private firm. She was an ordinary merchantman armed as a frigate. Inasmuch as she was commanded by Captain Weltden, who had a commission from the crown to serve the East India Company against the Mogul or any other eastern king, she became a man-of-war and a unit of the overseas naval forces of England. But she was not a smart vessel. indeed, she had not altogether put off her mercantile character, for though she brought out the mail, soldiers and military stores, she had two merchants on board, called Mr. Far well and Mr. Olindo. Her owners intended that, when she had finished her contract with the East India Company, she should take a cargo and come home. Though she was actually bound for Bengal, the Madras council took the liberty of detaining her for the Mergui expeditio, for it was felt there could be no more delay in complying with Childe's orders to recall White.

Not that the council liked the business nor thought the means at their disposal were adequate. They knew far better than Childe how risky it was, They had to send the *Curtana* (which they proposed to support with a sloop called the *James*) right into a port belonging to a foreign power against which they had already taken reprisals. Weltden had never been there before and he had no chart of the harbour, Apart from what White might do, it was quite impossible to foretell what the attitude of the Siamese would be when they found a man-of-war in their port. How the defences stood, whether there were armed men there, in what manner the *Curtana*, if she succeeded in entering the harbour, would get out of it—these were all moot points. And that White would leave all his property and tamely obey—other interlopers, with permits sanctioned by the Mogul, had refused—was by no means certain. Then there were the frigates which White had sent out under Leslie and Cropley, the *Resolution* and the *Dorothy*, which were Siamese men-of-war and which they knew to be in the bay. They knew it to their cost, for there was a famine in India that year and they had to provision themselves by sea. The provisions were 'delayed by the domineering of one of the King of Siam's ships here upon this coast, Alexander Lessly Commander', as was reported to them in April by one of their captains, and in March they had had news that Cropley, with a ship of war and three sloops: 'had done us some, but this country very great injury by taking, burning and sinking great numbers of vessels with grain bound to this and other places,' Altogether the bay was most unsafe.

It was one of those fluid situations, of which it was extremely difficult to take a precise view. Into it, blindly obeying general orders from the other side of the globe, the council plunged. Their orders to Captain Weltden, dated the 31st May 1687 were as follows:

They began by recapitulating his position in law. He was an officer of King James's navy lent to them under a special commission signed by His Majesty, empowering him to fight the Mogul and further enjoining him to obey all orders given to him by the East India Company.

'We, therefore, the President and Council of Fort St. George for the said Right Honble East India Company do order you to repair aboard your ship the "Curtana" Frigate, and the first opportunity of wind and weather presenting to weigh anchor and set sail, bending your course for the speediest attaining of the Fort of Mergen in the Kingdom of Syam as near as you can out of Command of their guns.'

The first sentence is sufficiently informative. The council knew well Mergui was a fort, had shore batteries and that the *Curtana* could not expose herself to their shot. From what follows it is clear that they wanted to give the *Curtana's* visit the look of a diplomatic mission. It was not such a mission, could not be regarded so, on account of the reprisals, which were still to continue, but the reader shall judge himself from the documents what name to call it. Weltden's orders went on: 'You are first to secure all the King of Syam's or his servants' or subjects' ships in that port for hostages for the present.'

How he was to do this, if they resisted, is not clear, but presumably in his barge with soldiers of whom he had forty, as the *Curtana* was to lie off. He was also—this was thrown in—to take any Mogul or interloper ships he might see. When one reads instructions of this kind, it is brought home that the English character has always been the same, They act first and, if still alive, think afterwards. The procedure has had marvellous results, but it does not always come off.

When Weltden had seized what ships he could as hostages, he was to go, if possible, in his barge, with a flag of truce at her bow, and deliver the king's proclamation to White and Burnaby, getting their signatures and remarks on a certified true copy of the original, and then; 'Charge them (in the name of his Majesty of England, King James the 2nd and by virtue of said Majesty's Royal Proclamation and charter) to leave the King of Siam's service and come aboard your ship for Fort St. George.'

The proclamation was further to be given to all other subjects of King James in Mer gui, who also were to leave their employ, taking what wages were due to them from the funds of the King of Siam in their hands and crediting the balance of those funds to the East India Company towards satisfaction of the Company's claims.

Supporting Weltden's letter of instructions were four documents which had been signed by Gyfford, Yale and the council on April the 25th, over a month earlier. The first was a personal letter to White and Burnaby, drawing their attention to the proclamation and containing a list of twenty-five Englishmen in Mergui and twenty-seven in Ayudhya on whom it was to be served. It called upon client to assist Weltden to obtain satisfaction for the damage caused to the East India Company by Phaulkon.

If White, Burnaby and the others refused to obey the proclamation within thirty days, they were to be adjudged guilty of contempt of the king's orders, 'for which they are to be prosecuted in his Majesty's Courts of Judicature as interlopers and rebellious persons, staying and trading in India contrary to his Said Majesty's Royal Proclamation . . . besides giving his Majesty high displeasure for the same.'

Weltden might not be able to force them to accompany him; but, if they did not obey, one day they would be taken, either in eastern waters or when they returned home to spend the money they were now amassing. That was the threat. But there had been interlopers for many years and against very few had the law been set in motion. Yet there began to be a difference here. The king was operating against Siam; to side with that country placed you in the category of rebellious persons. The resulting trial might be for high treason. There had already been other unpleasant suggestions going about. On February 16th of this year Surat had written to Madras; 'We hope you may meet with some of his brother rogues [Captain Coatcs's colleagues] and punish them for their robberies. . . . That is piracy, we think, and hanging some of those that served the King of Siam may clearly do great good.'

So much for the proclamation and the letter of recall to be served on White and Burnaby. The next document was a bill of damages addressed to the Honble Constant Faulcon, chief minister of state to His Majesty of Siam. The total came to £65,000. Most of the items had to do with Coates's activities in 1685-6, the details of which we have already given. The paper ends with a statement that the Company proposed to reimburse themselves by reprisals on Siamese ships, a true account being kept.

The third document was a letter to the king himself, phrased in a milder manner, wherein it was further explained that the *Curtana*, supported by the sloop *James*, would blockade Mergui and secure its shipping pending a settlement of the bill of damages. A time limit of sixty days was laid down. The letter continued that the Company was convinced that this pass would never have been reached had His Majesty been fully informed of the mismanagement of his affairs by Phaulkon and of the intolerable injuries and indignities suffered at that minister's hands. It concluded with an expression of regret that the Company, in default of any other method of winning his majesty's ear, should have been obliged to secure Ms ships as a security for payment. Attached was a note to a Siamese member of the council for Mergui and Tenasserim, requesting him to forward the Company's letter to the king. It is germane at this point to wonder whether Phra Narai had really been kept in ignorance of essentials by Phaulkon. It is a well-known trick of oriental statecraft to pretend or let it be supposed that a policy, likely to cause trouble, is the work of a subordinate, who is represented as difficult to control,

Such were Captain Anthony Weltden's orders. When he had carried them out, he was to wait in the archipelago till the monsoon was over and seize any Siamese ships making for the port, especially the *Derrea Dowlat* and the *Satisfaction*, news of the capture of which had not yet reached Madras. The *Curtana*, accompanied by the sloop *James*, weighed front Madras road on June 5th and, as we have seen, reached Mergui on June 23rd. But before continuing the internal narrative of events there, I must set out what Madras did when Childe's further letter, which ordered the seizure of Mergui, was received in August.

It is clear from the correspondence that the council were not happy about Childe's more extended plan. They had already written to London saying that it was too much for them to have a war with the Mogul and Siam at the same time. In a consultation on August 3rd they recapitulated their difficulties, The Mogul war had gone disastrously. The emperor's governors had seized or were about to seize the factories at Surat, Masulipatam and Hugli. Madras was in the territory of the King of Golconda or it would have gone the same way, and it still might be taken, for the Mogul was in process of defeating the King of Golconda in another war. Heavy French

reinforcements of ships and men they knew were on their
way to Ayudhya, while a separate French frigate was reported
to be designed for Mergui, However, Childe's letter was so
peremptory that they had to obey it. They decided to rein-
force Weltden by sending at once another frigate, the *Pearl*,
with nineteen soldiers. They had no more than nineteen to
send without dangerously weakening their own defences.

On August the 22nd—though by that day, unknown to
him, all was over in Mergui—Yale, who had now succeeded
Gyfford, drew up a commission of instructions for Captain
James Perriman, commander of the *Pearl*, and for a Mr.
Hodges and a Mr. Hill of their council, whom they had
selected to accompany the frigate and take over the civil administration of Mergui, after it had been seized. This document began by explaining that, since their late commission to
Captain Weltden, fresh and more positive orders had arrived
from London to press the war against Siam. Accordingly the
Pearl was to make Mergui as soon as possible, on arrival Captain Perriman and Mr. Hodges were to reissue the proclamation, if White and Burnaby had not already obeyed it, and
they were to strengthen the demand for the withdrawal of
these men by informing them, that King James had, in addition
to the proclamation, issued a personal letter to them—the
letter itself being unfortunately not available, only an abstract
of its contents having arrived. This 'express letter' called upon
White and Burnaby to deliver Mergui to the English. It was
to be impressed upon them that their duty was to comply, for
otherwise the French would take the place, to the vast detri-
ment of the East India Company. If White agreed, he was to
be made deputy governor under Mr. Hodges. Thanks to
Davenport's diary, we know White better than did Elihu Yale.
The surrender of Mergui was one of the alternatives which he
had considered and rejected. Yet it is important to note it, in
contrast to Childe's threat of the judge advocate. Yale knew
his own weakness and realized that to take Mergui without

White's assistance was impossible. If White were unaffected by their arguments about 'sense of loyalty to our King, love to our country or honour to himself 'perhaps this bait of a promise to be kept on as second in council, his irregularities overlooked, would attract him. In a personal letter to White and Burnaby, Yale repeated all these arguments and inducements at length, adding this solemn caution; 'For know that disobedience to his Majesty's summons from the country of any Prince at war with him is made treason by Act of Parliament. Therefore consider and resolve well lest you plunge yourselves into that heinous crime.'

Indeed, so solemn and fraught with difficulty and doubt did the council consider the occasion to be, that departing from their usual dry practice they concluded with these heartfelt words to Perriman and his ship's company: 'And since it is the inexcusable duty of Christians, and the success of all things solely depend upon Providence, we strictly recommend and require your due and daily observance of divine worship, imploring the Almighty's blessing upon your endeavours and protection of your persons and affairs, and that your deportment and conversation be so virtuous and exemplary as may win to a respectful, willing submission.' The *Pearl* sailed on August the 29th. Its fate will be related when the narrative of events at Mergui is brought to that point.

XXXV. H.M.S. *CURTANA* (CAPTAIN WELTDEN)

I return now to the main narrative. The *Curtana*, as I have stated, left Madras on June 5th with the sloop *James*. On the early morning of June 22nd she passed through iron Passage and entered that inner sheet of water, which leads down to Mergui, still about forty miles away, Weltden had no proper chart and by taking an easterly, instead of a south-easterly course, he ran into shoal water. This alarmed him and he dropped his anchor. To ascertain his position and find out how to cross the bar into Mergui harbour, he launched the ship's yawl and in the afternoon sent her off to explore under the command of the second and third mates, Joseph Weld and Arthur Hoddy. The sloop *James* had fallen behind and was not to arrive for some days.

The yawl had a very long pull before her. It was not until the following afternoon at 4 o'clock that she crossed the bar. The mates saw the *Resolution* under English colours just inside and went aboard her. They and the men, much exhausted by their exposure in the heat, were very glad to accept the refreshments set before them.

White's scouting boats, observing the yawl's arrival, for the *Curtana* was under the horizon, hastened to inform him. He immediately sent Captain Leslie to the *Resolution*. When that officer arrived and was apprised that the yawl belonged to an English frigate, he told the mates that they must accompany him on shore forthwith to see Mr. White, The mates hesitated. They had no notion whether to land was foolhardy. But there seemed no alternative and they set out with Leslie.

On reaching the wharf, they were conducted to White's house, where Burnaby was also waiting. White received them with the affability he knew how to command and began asking questions. They answered readily enough that they had been sent to explore the bar by their captain, Anthony Weltden of the frigate *Curtona*, but to pressing inquiries as to his intentions, when he reached Mergui, they were silent.

As it was of much importance to obtain some information, Burnaby, to frighten them, said that Mergui was a Siamese port, that foreigners could not enter it without giving an account of themselves to the local authorities and that they would have to go before one of the mandarins and explain their presence. They were accordingly taken to the police court. The magistrate, however, failed to elicit more than the general statement that an English man-of-war lay outside and wanted to enter the port. Of Captain Weltden's intentions the mates professed complete ignorance.

When their examination was concluded, they were taken back to White's house and invited to stay the night They protested that they ought to return at once and inform the captain of their doings, but White pointed out that there was no moon and that squalls were flying in, so that to attempt to leave at that hour would be foolish. He would send them back next morning. Reassured, they sat down to supper.

During the meal, after the wine had gone round, White attempted again to get the mates to talk. When he failed to draw any information from them, he was much put out, muttering: 'I would rather go quick to Hell than go to Fort St. George to be under the lash of that same Yale. For me to go to Madras would be like a man making a good Voyage and on his return homewards falling into the hands of the Andemanners.'[1]

Next morning early, before sending the mates back along with a pilot, to bring in the *Curtana*, White took Weld aside to a window away from the rest of the company and said to him: 'If Captain Weltden comes in a friendly manner, no man shall be more kindly treated or more honourably received than he shall be in Mergen, but if he comes in a hostile manner, I myself will come at the head of two or three thousand men to oppose him and defend the place, for I am the King of Siam's servant and will serve him faithfully.'

With that message he dismissed the mates, who immediately embarked.

White was now face to face with the situation which he

---

[1] The savages of the Andaman islands further out in the bay, who at that time were cannibals.

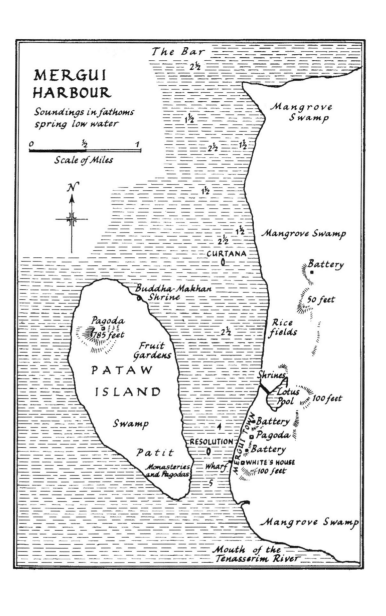

had thought to circumvent by Ms flight. He had told Daven-port that he did not believe a man-of-war would arrive till October; he had also made it abundantly clear that if one did appear before he left and threatened his liberty and his fortune, he would fight, treason or no treason. So fixed, how-ever, had been his conviction that he would be gone before a warship came, that he had hesitated to spend the money required to strengthen Mer gui enough to resist. He now decided to make up for this. There was time to do something and, in point of fact, one warship could accomplish little in the face of even moderate fortifications. The evening the mates arrived he sent out an urgent order to impress as many men as possible from the villages round the town. This was promulgated and hardly had those officers departed when crowds of Siamese began to pour into Mergui. They were set to work at once to improve the fortifications. A new battery of fifteen guns was erected on a platform beneath, and, slightly north, of the main battery on the ridge. Working all day and by night with torches, White himself visiting the men and encouraging them, the corps of labourers had the place in some state of defence by the morning of June 26th. There were altogether three batteries—on the ridge, on the platform below and by White's wharf—and these were now supplied with ammunition. The *Resolution* was recalled from the bar and anchored in front of White's house.

Meanwhile the mates, who had left on the 24th, had reached the *Curtana.* on the 25th she began to come in, piloted by the man sent by White. It may seem extraordinary that he should have encouraged her to come in and at the same time have prepared to resist her, but it must be borne in mind that he hoped even yet to avoid a clash. In his sober moments of reflection it was clear to him that while he might without much difficulty destroy the *Curtana* or any small expedition of the kind sent against him, it would not be to his ultimate interest to do so, as his money was in England. If in some way or other he could get the better of Weltden without resorting to force, the victory was his. Therefore he had received the mates with hospitality and had sent his pilot to help, at the same time increasing his defences in case diplomacy failed.

During the whole of the 25th the *Curtana* continued to beat in against the S. W. wind. At one time the pilot ran her into 2¼ fathoms, she drawing about twelve feet. Weltden was very nervous and, when he found himself in danger of going aground, he threatened 'to hang or kill' the pilot, unless he took the ship at once into deep water. At last, on the 26th at 8 a.m., she crossed the bar and continuing into the harbour, anchored short of the town and out of range of all the batteries. It was remarked that the *Resolution*, in her new position at the top of the harbour, was now flying Siamese colours.

As we have seen, Davenport had gone to stay at Tenasserim early in May, but had kept himself informed of the course of events in Mergui, During this period of inaction and reflection no doubt he had considered the best line to adopt in all eventualities. He had dissociated himself from White, and his only chance of safety was boldly to range himself against his former master, when the events he foresaw closed in. On receiving the information, therefore, that a man-of-war was in the offing, he hurriedly left Tenasserim, and when the *Curtana* dropped her anchor on the morning of June 26th, he was in Mergui, unknown to White.

It was essential for him to get first on board. Accompanied by three of White's men, namely Threder, Grant and Barnes. whose position was as delicate as his own, he embarked on a country boat and was alongside the *Curtana* before White had stirred. Weltden received him at once.

When the two were seated together privately, Davenport, after explaining that he was in the employment of the Company in Bengal, but had been captured by White and obliged to act AS his secretary for a year, began to sketch how matters stood on shore. He said that White, fearing that he might be summoned to Madras under royal proclamation to give an explanation of the injuries he had inflicted upon the Company, had made every preparation to flee the country, and he repeated to Weltden, what that officer must already have learnt from the second mate, Joseph Weld, that White had sworn he would resist if Weltden tried to force him. A description of the hurried fortification of the town was also given. In conclusion, he told Weltden that White, violent of temper though he was, would not fight except at the last resort, but that he would attempt one way or another to manipulate the situation so as to be able to leave on the *Resolution* for home.

Weltden thanked him for this warning: 'I shall make use of it in my proceeding ashore to the avoiding and preventing of all Mr. White's subtilties,' he said.

This snatched conversation was hardly finished when it was announced that the Shāhbandar's barge had arrived, with Don Joseph de Heredia on board. The Don stepped on to the quarter-deck and reported that Mr. White had sent the barge and that he hoped Captain Weltden would make use of it for his coming ashore.

It was now nearly three o'clock. Weltden gave orders to prepare his yawl and to muster his guard. He himself, attended by Lieutenant Mason, who commanded the guard, and by Mr. John Farwell and Mr. Joseph Olindo, the two merchants who had come with him from England, entered White's barge and took a seat under the awning with the Don. Into the yawl climbed Davenport and Grant. The country boat, in which Davenport had rowed out, was occupied by the guard, ten men being taken armed with blunderbusses.

The Union flag was run up on the barge and, as the procession started, the *Curtana* fired a salute of eleven guns shotted with stones 'though the ship rode not much more than ¼ of a mile from the Eastern shore and several boats were passing within shot to the westward'. Rowing down on the flood they rapidly covered the two miles which separated them from White's wharf.

There were assembled White and Burnaby with all the English. As Captain Weltden stepped ashore in his new scarlet coat, he was handsomely saluted by White, who presented him to the rest and invited him to ascend the steps leading up the hill to his house.

When they were all seated in the dining-room, Weltden produced his papers and explained his mission. His instructions were, he said, to call upon all present to repair on board his ship, when he might appoint the time, and proceed to Madras, leaving the service of the King of Siam, who had inflicted injuries upon the East India Company. In proof of his authority to make these demands, he called upon Mr. Farwell to read His Majesty King James II's royal proclamation. This was done, Mr. Farwell concluding with the words, 'God save the King', to which the assembled company said 'Amen'.

Captain Weltden then asked them all to acknowledge service of the proclamation by signing their names at the foot, There was no hesitation to comply. The smaller fry, having made some money and feeling very uncertain about their future in Siam, were satisfied to go with what they had, especially as no blame would be attached to them when they reached Madras. Those who could sign did so; those who could not write affixed their marks. White signed as part of his present policy of feeling his way. Burnaby signed, though we do not know how he viewed the future. only 'Captain Leslie seemed somewhat loth to sign'. That is not surprising, but, of course, Captain Leslie with his piratical record had no more intention than had White of going to Madras.

After this business was over, White entertained Weltden and his officers to supper. They left at 9 p.m. and returned to the *Curtana*. It is not known what talk White and Weltden had together that first evening, but it is clear that White set himself to charm the captain by his hospitality and easy manners.

Next afternoon Weltden went ashore again and calling the English together told them that, if they were owed any wages by the King of Siam, they should recoup themselves front what royal property might be in their trust. But White did not fancy this at all. The following conversation ensued:

WHITE: 'I hope not so, Captain, the King of Siam owes these men nothing. I am responsible for their Sallaries and several of them are in places of trust and have considerable stores of the Goods of the Kings in their hands and 'twill be very unreasonable that they should have such a latitude given them to play the Rogue. What is due to any of them lie see paid them.'

WELTDEN: "Tis very well: Gentlemen, you hear what Mr. White says.'

WHITE: 'Ay, ay, Gentlemen, the Captain has summoned you all out of the King of Siam's service, therefore from this moment take notice that I dismiss you. You may come when you will and I will pay you what is due to you. And you that have any charge of the Kings in your hands, bring in your Accounts of Disburstments and surrender up to me the remains, as you ought to do.'

It is evident that White intended to stay master. While these men still looked to him for money, he had a hold over them.

Weltden now felt the need of a further conversation with Davenport, and he despatched a message to him by Mr. Olindo that the more often he came on board, the more welcome he would be, Davenport sent back answer:

'The Captains desires bear with me the force of a Command. At the Captains going off to-night, I will attend me at the yawl, for no person at present is to go off in any country boat without express order from the Shabander.'

White's intention was to isolate Weltden and as far as

possible oblige him to look for his information to him alone. There could be no traffic behind his back, if he was to carry through his plans to circumvent the captain.

That evening, just as Davenport was preparing to board the yawl, a messenger asked him to come to White's dining-room, where Burnaby wanted a word with him. He complied and found White and Burnaby there.

WHITE: 'Where were you going?'

DAVENPORT: 'On board the "Curtana" to observe the Captains Commands in the service of the King and the Right Honourable Company.'

WHITE: 'I will prevent that.'

He then ordered the lascars to make fast Davenport's hands and to take his rapier from his side. With that, he sent him back to Tenasserim, manacled like a felon, where he was flung into the common gaol.

But the situation had changed; Davenport was no longer the helpless man in White's power. Indeed, as he was lying in the heat and filth of his dungeon, he may have reflected that his imprisonment was not altogether inconvenient, for it would prove to Weltden and afterwards to the Madras council, provided he emerged alive, that he was not White's accomplice.

The news reached Weltden next day, June the 28th, for Threder went aboard early and told him. The captain Came ashore and had a talk with White, On his return to the *Cur tana* he observed to his officers; 'I did not spare to use such harsh language, as I thought the occasion did require. I have made demand for the said Davenport to be surrendered within five days.'

On July 4th Davenport was brought to the *Curtana*, 'disentangled from his irons', and entertained to a good dinner. We must suppose that White had come to the conclusion that it would do him more harm to resist Weltden over this matter than to let Davenport talk. He believed that he could counterbalance in Weltden's mind whatever Davenport might say against him. In fact, during the seven days of Davenport's absence, he had made great progress with Weltden, as will appear.

XXXVI. THE SEIZURE OF THE *RESOLUTION*

B esides serving the proclamation on English residents of Mergui and embarking them for Madras, Weltden had also, as I have shown, to send on letters to the court of Ayudhya, demanding compensation within sixty days, and to make meanwhile what seizure of Siamese vessels he could, holding the same as surety until satisfaction was received. The sixty days were to be regarded as a truce. This programme covered more or less the period of the monsoon, at the close of which he would return to Madras. Accordingly, on June 30th he went ashore with the letters and engaged with one of the mandarins to despatch, them to Ayudhya. In the matter of taking prizes he had made no advance. Beyond the *Resolution*, there were no Siamese ships in harbour. We know that White had sent them all up to Tenasserim. As to that ship, White had told him that she was his own property, It was a question what he should do. If White would come quietly to Madras in her along with the *Curtana*, it was obviously preferable to the hazards of a seizure. So far White had appeared amenable. But there was his defiant message by Weld and Davenport's warning.

Meanwhile the sloop *James* had arrived under the command of Captain Armiger Gostlin. Weltden ordered him to ride with the *Resolution* opposite White's house. The idea was to prevent White's ship from leaving the harbour by the south entrance and escaping out 'o sea that way. Weltden was unaware that shoal water made escape in that direction impracticable. The *James* was to fire on her if she stirred. But as the *Resolution* had twenty-two guns and there were eleven gum on White's wharf 'with shot lying by ready to clap into them', the posting of the sloop with her ten guns at that place was tantamount to making a present of her to White, if he intended to fight. A certain Johnson and the Barnes, already mentioned having decided their interests lay with Weltden, went aboard her when they saw where she proposed to ride, and expostulated with Gostlin, pointing out that not only was he completely dominated by the shore battery and the *Resolutions* broadside, but that White was preparing a little further up a fleet of fireboats and platforms, which if loosed on the ebb would burn him out. To this Gostlin replied that he must obey orders. He dropped his anchor as he had been directed.

Such was the state of affairs on July 1st. Weltden tended to think that White was not going to give trouble; White (with Davenport out of the way till the 4th) had begun to manoeuvre Weltden, while he secretly continued to make his preparations to resist, if it became necessary to do so. He had invited the captain to sleep ashore in his house, an invitation which was accepted. On July 3rd we have a glimpse of them going about together. At 1 p.m. with Burnaby and Farwell they boarded the *Curtana* and later dinner was served. In the middle of the afternoon they rowed ashore, eleven guns being fired as they left the ship. Weltden was still with them. He returned on board at midnight after some entertainment at White's house. on the 4th Weltden slept ashore. What transpired that night we do not know, but we may assume that White had a heart-to-heart talk with him. On the 5th morning White went up to Tenasserim accompanied by Farwell, Olindo and the *Curtana's* surgeon, William Westbrook. His business there has not been recorded, but it must have been of an urgent nature. What it was will be suggested later. Farwell and Olindo went as merchants, to buy goods. When Weltden returned on board, he found Davenport, who, as explained, had arrived the night before from prison.

Davenport immediately began to give him an account of what was happening on shore. He assured him that White was not sincere. Had not Weltden seen the preparations that were going forward, did he not realize that White was at the back of everything which was being done and that an attack on the *Curtana* was being made ready? White's escape having been prevented, he will attack you, expostulated Davenport:

'What else should mean the Natives going about to stake up the River, what else the making of Great Cables, the building of the Platform, planting in it fifteen great Guns, whole and demy-culvening,[1] for the forwarding of which he himself attended in person on the 24th, encouraging the Natives to their despatch of it? What else should mean Ms summoning so vast a number of Natives into the Town by written order, of which I saw two, shown me by the Queens of two several villages? When I asked the reason, I was always answered that the Oluang Chomoung[2] had summoned the men to work on the fortifications and man the boats because an English Man of War was come to destroy Mergeu. Lastly what else could mean his imprisonment of me, but to prevent the discovery of his projected Treacheries?'

WELTDEN: 'I have promised Mr. White and Mr. White has promised me so fairly that I do much doubt being over-reached by him.'

Davenport perceived that during his absence something had been arranged between the two, but what precisely it was he could not guess. He continued to remonstrate, saying that there was not a man in the villages all down the Tenasserim river, In the rice fields, ploughing and sowing, were only

[1] Eighteen-and nine-pounders; 5½ and 4½ inch bore.
[2] Luang Chao müang=Lord Governor.

women and boys; behind the stakes and cables, designed to block the entrance into the river, White was mustering war-canoes and fire-boats. But nothing he could say at the moment was able to shake Weltden's faith.

Next day, the 6th, Weltden's complacency received a slight shock. The reader will remember the two rich ships which White had out, the *Satisfaction* and the *Derrea Dowlat*. Actually as we know these had been captured by the East India Company's men-of-war in April-May at Mocha and Achin, but neither White nor Weltden was aware of their seizure. Madras, as I have mentioned, had ordered Weltden to look out for them. White was expecting them daily, and before he left for Tenasserim had sent out two of his men, Nat Carter and Gammen, to keep a watch beyond the harbour and, if they saw the ships, to warn them not to come in, but to hide in the islands, Gold, which they carried, was to be secretly unloaded and stowed on the *Resolution*.

News that he had sent these men was carried to Weltden. He directed Davenport, as he knew the islands, to go with a boat of soldiers and seize them. They were brought in without difficulty. Weltden arrived on board very late and forthwith began questioning them, but he could get no information. This made him feel something was going on behind his back, and he said to Davenport: 'Mr. White has broken his promise and shall never more be trusted on his smooth words.'

We do not know exactly what White had promised nor is it of much importance, for it is clear in general that up to this episode Weltden believed that he had White's confidence.

on July 8th, White being still away at Tenasserim, Weltden, who had been thinking over Davenport's words and who now noticed that 'the stoccado thwart the River', to the existence of which Davenport had repeatedly drawn his attention, had grown very strong, proposed to pull tip the stakes and destroy the cables. He discussed the idea with Davenport, who opposed it on the ground that it would alarm and excite the mandarins and the native population. There was supposed to be a truce for sixty days pending a reply to the East India Company's letters to Ayudhya. If during that time Weltden took any action to interfere with the Mergui defences, even if those defences were being improved, the local people would have reason to think that he had intentions upon Mergui itself and there might be an outburst of popular indignation. Weltden said that everyone knew that Ms business was simply to recall the Europeans and submit to Ayudhya a diplomatic protest. He had no instructions, nor indeed the force, to attack Mergui If he pulled up the stakes, it was solely in self-defence. Davenport replied that it would not be interpreted in that light and that it would excite the people. Had not White published the report that he had come to burn Mergui?

Weltden had no means of judging whether Davenport was right. He had no experience of oriental peoples, he had not the slightest idea how he was regarded by the natives, who appeared to be going about their ordinary avocations ashore as if nothing unusual was happening. He did not know anything of the subterranean and crooked working of the eastern mind. But as a captain in His Majesty's navy his training told him that his position was most precarious. Though out of range of the batteries, he was right inside the harbour. An attack on him by fire-boats and native galleys from behind the stockade on a fast ebb might take him by surprise and before he could weigh his anchors and manoeuvre under sail, he might be surrounded, boarded or set on fire. He replied accordingly to Davenport that he intended to pull up the stakes. He coold not trust White any more.

Davenport then asked him why he slept in White's house nearly every night, it was most dangerous for him to be ashore after dark.

Weltden replied, that he had his guard, that it was cooler and pleasanter ashore and far more amusing. Besides, it was diplomatic, it made White less suspicious.

Davenport said that it was not Weltden who was deceiving White, but exactly the reverse. At that home truth Weltden became more obstinate, saying that not only would he pull up the stakes, but that he would spike the guns on White's wharf, yes, and on the platform below the big fort also.

DAVENPORT: 'They could soon drill the vents again.'

WELTDEN: 'Ay, but I'll order the English Smith on shoar to harden the heads of the spikes and then no drill they have can touch them.'

He then ordered his boatswain, Thomas Johnson, to take out the barge with a crew of lascars and pull up the stakes, They pulled up a good many, but they did not touch the guns. There appeared to be no excitement on shore. No one made any protest.

This encouraged Weltden, and he began to think that a bold policy was the thing, It always worked best with natives. It would work well with White, too. Accordingly, next morning at seven o'clock, after taking a turn or two on the quarter-deck, he sat down and said to Davenport and some others who were present: 'Gentlemen, I am resolved to fetch down the ship "Resolution", I cannot answer the letting her He there under command of the Enemies Guns. I think it would be better to do it now than to defer it until Mr. White comes down.'

DAVENPORT: 'Sir, you know best what you can answer, but you may be sure 'twill not be long before he has News of it and will be much exasperated to hear it. And it is farther to be considered, your Frieads, Mr. Farwell, Mr. Olindo and the Doctor, are there along with him and whether they might not suffer by his passionate resentment of such News, God only knows.'

WELTDEN: 'That's true. Mr. Farwell and they are there, but I'll write both to Mr. White and Mr. Farwell and I doubt not that Mr. Farwell will manage things so discreetely as to prevent any passionate transport of Mr. White.'

He immediately sent for the boatswain and the gunner, telling them to serve out small arms and man the boats. He would take some of his force of forty men with him. While these orders were being executed, he and the rest went to breakfast.

During the meal Threder, with three other Englishmen, namely Highoe, Salter and Whittamore, came aboard. Weltden, invited them to join him at table. They declined, saying: 'Unless you take some course to prevent what is going on ashore, in a short time you shall have nothing to make a breakfast of.'

They then reported that the mandarins had driven all cattle from the town and forbidden any to sell provisions to the *Curtana* or the *James*. They continued: 'If the Captain gives too much credit to Mr. White's fair words, he will certainly find himself abused; for 'tis most certain that these things cannot be acted but by Mr. White's directions; and therefore we advise the Captain to be very careful how he sleeps any more ashore or stays there until unseasonable hours.'

THREDER (interposing): 'The Devil could not be falser than Mr. White.'

WELTDEN: 'It does not become you to use such terms. But (he continued) I'll take such measures as my own reason shall dictate to me, I am going now, as soon as I have ate a little, to fetch down the' 'Resolution'' to Ride under my command, and if yon Gentlemen in the meantime will stay on board my ship, you shall be welcome.'

They offered to go with him against the *Resolution*, but he said there was no need.

The boats and men being all in readiness with the soldiers aboard, and a Union flag at each bow, Captain Weltden entered his barge and rowed up on the flood. At nine o'clock he boarded the *Resolution*, a pistol in both hands, at the head of his men, But there was no resistance of any kind. He accordingly addressed the crew with politeness, saying: 'Gentlemen, I do seize this ship in the name of the King of England.'

He then ordered the anchors to be weighed and sail to be bent on her, meanwhile transferring her gunner, Floate, to the *James*, which was riding beside her, and ordering his own gunner, Beck, to see all the guns drawn and laden again with round shot and grape, in case the batteries should oppose the carrying of her down. But there was not a sign from the batteries as she sailed past them and came to anchor between the *Curtana* and the eastern shore.

After coming aboard his own ship again, Weltden was asked by Davenport whether he proposed to set a prize crew on the *Resolution*. But he said not, that he did not want to take undue advantage of Mr. White, The ship was safe enough, He would now be able to force him to do whatever was necessary. But if White tried to unload her he would place a crew.

Next morning, the 10th, Weltden went ashore and had an interview with Burnaby and with the Siamese mandarins. He explained his action, pointing out that as his instructions were to bring White to Madras, he was obliged to move the *Resolution* to a position where he could control her. Nothing was said in reply, no objection was taken. The mandarins bowed him out politely. It was rather disconcerting, particularly as news was received shortly after that a new battery was being erected in a wood opposite the *Curtana*, which lay, as will be remembered, only a quarter of a mile from the eastern shore.

There was also a rumour that White had supplied the Siamese with a thousand glass bottles which, filled with powder, would serve as grenades and could be thrown by men attacking the frigate from boats. Far more boats than usually lay there were observed to be congregated at the top of the harbour.

At this moment (July 11th) White returned from Tenasserim where he had been for six days. He had no doubt heard that the *Resolution* had been moved from her moorings; at least he immediately perceived it and in a great rage wrote a note to Weltden, asking him to come ashore. 'To prevent the worst', Weltden decided to go, for he feared that in his first transport White might do some desperate act. With a strong guard he disembarked at the wharf.

White was truly half mad with anger. Before Weltden reached him, he had pulled down and set fire to the outbuildings round the square behind his house. As Weltden came up he was ripping with an axe the banisters and rails enclosing a brick platform in front of the hall door, where he had a gun mounted, Weltden advanced, his guard on the alert. White looked up with a terrible expression and said: 'What, Captain, now you have taken my ship and a rich Cargo, you think you are sure of me, but you shall be damned first.'

He then ram on at an extravagant rate, cursing and swearing. What with the smoke, the crackle of the flames and White's roaring voice, the quarter was roused and the Siamese officials arrived in a fluster, White shouted at them: 'The English Captain is coming to burn the Town, but I am resolved that he shall not have the honour of burning my house.'

He spoke with great passion, vowing that he would now set fire to his house. 'Captain Weltden thought best to let him run himself almost out of breath and then calmly took him up and work'd him into a better humor.' When he was rather more calm, he went into the house with Weltden and Farwell. 'After a short stay there they came to a right understanding of each other' and 'now were stricter friends than ever.'

XXXVII. WHITE'S PLOT AND
THE WIZARDS

I must attempt some explanation of these occurrences. Though White's original intention had been to fight Weltden if he was cornered, it seems tolerably clear that he improved upon that bold plan as the situation developed. To fight Weltden openly Was high treason, a desperate course. But what if the Siamese fought Weltden and he could prove that he was not a consenting party, that he was on the best of terms with Weltden, was ready to go with him to Madras? I advance this explanation, I suggest that White plotted to organize the Siamese until they were strong enough to take and burn the *Curtana*. He would then leave Mergui and, in his subsequent account of the passages there, would have little difficulty in making it seem that the mandarins of the Tenasserim council, acting on instructions from Ayudhya, attacked Weltden, who moreover had foolishly exposed himself to such a danger by lying inside so strong an enemy port. I suggest that he went to Tenasserim for the purpose of arranging his coup. In consultation with the mandarins there, he impressed more men and boats and procured more ordnance. The guns for the new battery in the wood may have come from that place. After playing on the *Curtana* with those guns, he would launch unexpectedly an overwhelming attack on her from small galleys and with fire-boats. The *Resolution*, riding two miles farther up the harbour by his house, would, of course, be unable to get to her assistance in time. His subsequent departure on his ship could be represented as a flight from the infuriated natives.

On his return from Tenasserim and finding the *Resolution* moored near the *Curtana*, he perceived that his plan would not now be so easy to put into effect. The *Resolution* lay between the *Curtana* and the battery in the wood. Moreover, if the attack were made on the *Curtana* alone, how was he going to explain that Ms ship was spared or in the alternative that she abandoned the *Curtana* to her fate? He had to count on the possibility of there being survivors among the frigate's crew. Their evidence might be very dangerous afterwards.

But there was no alternative; he most go on with his plan. When he had spent his rage, the necessity of an even closer apparent friendship with Weltden was borne in upon him. He would think of a way to stage the destruction of the *Curtana* so as to divert all suspicions. Meanwhile, the more he could pretend to like Weltden, the better.

The narrative of the next few days shows how he developed this technique.

When Weltden returned to his quarter-deck, congratulating himself that he had handled White with great tact and saying to those about him that there was now no doubt that he would go quietly to Madras, Davenport interjected that to believe he would voluntarily go was to believe a thing against reason, But Weltden replied that he was satisfied with his sincerity and friendship and 'that they had now unbosomed themselves to one another and that he knew White would be ruled by him in everything proposed to him'. He added that he did not believe half the stories that were told him. For instance, Salter and Highoe had said a few days back that provisions would be stopped. But this was untrue; White had assured him that it was nonsense. Davenport retorted that if Weltden was so indiscreet as to tell White the names of his informers, no one in future would dare to give him news and that 'perhaps the want of advice may be a matter of ill consequence'. Weltden to this stated that he did not believe there would be any plots about which he would require warning. 'Mr. White, I am sure, will be very plain and faithful with me.' Davenport then suggested with a sneer that perhaps there was a private arrangement between them, as Weltden was deliberately shutting his eyes to facts, 'which construction seemed to startle the Captain and put an end to that Night's Discourse'.

Davenport had touched on the truth, for White had now discovered that the best way to blind Weltden to his intentions and to win his confidence and regard was to tempt him by offers which would fill his pocket. There is definite reference to this on the following day. Weltden said he Was going ashore to treat with the Shāhbandar about his taking certain goods on the *Curtana* off their hands and putting his own money, plate, jewels and the most considerable part of his effects into safe custody with them for transport to Madras and concealment there; for, added the captain, 'we have promised to give him such assistance of our fidelity to him in that point as himself shall seem good to demand from us'.

Now I take this to mean that White had offered to find a market for some cargo or other on the *Curtana*, which belonged to Weltden. By placing or pretending to place and secrete some valuables on the *Curtana*, he tempted Weltden by a share in them.

The captain went cheerfully over the side to see about his affairs. He was a poor man and it looked as if he might enrich himself and at the same time carry out his instructions to bring White to Madras.

When he was on shore, Captain Armiger Gostlin came aboard. With the removal of the *Resolution*, the *James* had been ordered to lie opposite the battery on the platform. Gostlin now complained that his position was most unsafe. Far from overawing the foit, his little ship with its few light guns was completely dominated. He said that he had explained this to Weltden, who would listen to no arguments.

The afternoon and evening passed; Weltden remained on in White's house, supping and drinking. His lieutenant of marines, Mason, was with him. At 11 p.m. they left the Shāhbandar's dining-room and descended the steps to the wharf. There they were again struck by the menacing appearance of the upper harbour, which was teeming with galleys and men-of-war boats full of natives.

WELTDEN (to Mason): 'Step up the Stairs to the Shabander and acquaint Win that though we arc not afraid of any Treachery, yet these unaccustomary numbers of armed boats spreading quite over the River before his house are no arguments of any friendly design,'

White, who had been undressing to go to bed, came out in his night things when Mason reappeared at his door. To the lieutenant's protest, he said: 'In these boats are nobody but a parcel of poor harmless fellows come to sell a little Betel-nut.'

When Mason said he could not believe that so many men would come selling nuts at eleven o'clock at night, he provoked White, An altercation between them started at the top of the steps. White, his anger rising rapidly, began complaining of the unwarranted suspicions to which he was subjected. It is a curious fact that men of a certain type become genuinely indignant at a true accusation, Mason, who did not share Weltden's faith in White's honesty, told him his mind. At last White 'with more execrable oaths and curses swore that as they apprehended danger where there was none, he would go along with the captain aboard ship and be his Guard'.

Saying this, he ran down the steps like one distracted, 'without Hat, slippers or anything but his Nightgown and a pair of Drawers'. In this posture on the wharf, raving, swearing, protesting and 'pawning his Soul', he shouted that not the smallest harm would come to any of them and that they could search the boats if they liked.

Weltden remained quite calm according to his wont. He declined to search the boats and in a few minutes White got a grip of himself again. They all entered Weltden's barge, White just as he was, half dressed. Don Joseph de Heredia was also of the party.

They reached the *Curtana* near midnight. Weltden immediately called for drinks. After a toast or two, White found his spirits rising as rapidly as had before his anger. He proposed to Weltden that at each toast a gun should be fired.

Davenport, listening in Ms cabin, wrote in his diary:' Accordingly that night 64 guns were fired shotted with bullets or stone and that more were not fired was owing to the raininess of the weather.'

So with furious downpours and squalls sweeping in from the S. W. they drank on till dawn, firing their balls at random over the harbour. We shall see later what sort of an interpretation the local inhabitants placed upon this conviviality, wherein their Shāhbandar and the captain of the frigate, who was said to have come to burn Mergui, mingled toasts.

White did not go ashore until the following afternoon. Indeed, none of them showed up until late in the day. When Weltden climbed on to the quarter-deck at last, he found Davenport there. He began at once saying what an obliging man was White, for he had offered to bring down the *Dorothy* from Tenasserim and load her with timber on his account and, when they all went to Madras together, sell the timber for him there. He had proposed, too, that the lead ballast in the *Curtana* should be exchanged for tin blocks, a metal worth ten times as much. It could be changed back in Madras, making an excellent profit. There had been no end to his affability. He was even prepared to careen the *Curtana* in the dock near his house; he had promised beef; he had promised to give him the *New Jerusalem* and load another cargo for him on that ship.

At this mention of careening his frigate in the enemy's port, Davenport thought Weltden had taken leave of his senses. The offers of money had evidently dazzled him. He no longer understood where he was or with what manner of man he had to deal. He was bemused with greed. Davenport reflected that any influence he had had with him was now gone. But again he solemnly warned him. Weltden listened with only half his attention. Davenport then repeated to him a strange rumour which he had been told by the Don. It was said that certain of the mandarins were planning an attack on the

Curtana. quite apart from any project of White's of the like nature. The Don had significantly added: 'The Wizards have made offer of a Tryal of their Skill to lull the Captain and his Company into such security that they should not be able to fire a gun or resist.'

Now it may be taken as axiomatic in Indo-China that, when there is talk of magic, some kind of a popular rising is in contemplation. That the wizards had been Called in struck the clever Davenport as sinister, though he did not fathom the meaning of the rumour nor guess that the news which the Don had given him was of the greatest importance and that it constituted a new factor in the situation. Up to that the machinations of White had occupied the field; the danger had been a treacherous onslaught by him, disguised as an official Siamese offensive. But the Don's story suggested that unknown to White some mandarins were making independent preparations. As I say, Davenport had not the experience of Indo-China to grasp the full import of the rumour, but he repeated it as something strange and, with a brilliant flash of insight, told Weltden that he should take the English on board for safety. But Weltden brushed all that aside. There was enough work already without having to give attention to wizards. He could not possibly take the English on board; he had not the provisions. When White sent him down the *New Jerusalem* they might go aboard that ship. There Was plenty of time; he had to wait for the reply to the letters sent to Ayudhya. They had only been gone fifteen days out of the sixty allowed. They were hardly in Phaulkon's hands yet.

Davenport saw that it was useless to argue with Weltden on the general situation, so he introduced the purely tactical matter of Gostlin's position near the lower fort, a subject upon which the captain should have been fully competent to form a sound view. But even there Weltden refused to see reason.

WELTDEN: 'I suppose Captain Gostlin has been relating his fears. He told me all the guns on shore were fresh primed and all the shot laid by them in baskets. But I find he's a faint-hearted fellow.'

DAVENPORT: 'I can say nothing to Mr. Gostlin's timorousness; he's a stranger to me. But I think he has a great deal of Reason on his side. A battery of fifteen guns of such size as those are, are far more likely to awe the sloop than she the battery.'

WELTDEN: 'If men would but consider the tye Mr. White is under by bringing down his ship, they would not be so fearful. I cannot imagine the reason of their bad opinion of Mr. White.'

There was clearly nothing more to be said, and Davenport returned to his cabin.

XXXVIII. THE MASSACRE

It was now July the 14th. The *Curtana* had been in Mergui a little over a fortnight. Events had been gathering to a climax and it was on this day that the climax was reached, Our eyes have been fixed upon White and Weltden, the chief protagonists. We have observed White's subterranean preparations; the suspicion and fear which they engendered in the minds of some; how they were discounted by Weltden. But, except for the hint in the last section, we have made no attempt to understand the attitude of the mandarins and the native population.

I must recapitulate. The Province of Tcnasserism, as we have seen, was governed, under the court of Ayudhya, by a council of seven. Besides White and Burnaby, there were five mandarins, three of whom lived in Tenasserim city. In effect, as we know, the council did not function as a body. White and Burnaby were uncontrolled by it within their respective departments. For those conversant with oriental officialdom, this is what might have been expected to happen. The mandarins, though they certainly kept themselves fully informed of White's activities and no doubt did not think it beneath their dignity to join in anonymous protests against him on occasion, never attempted openly to oppose or to use their majority in the council to bring pressure. The port, the ships, the seizures in the bay, those were his affairs. Besides, he was Phaulkon's favourite. They had no mandate to interfere.

But with the arrival of the *Curtana*, the situation changed. In the first place that event was a great blow to White's prestige. The powerful Shāhbandar, the man who by his filibustering had taken prizes in all parts of the bay from Golconda and the Mogul, and had dared to flout the Honourable the East India Company, was now ordered by a man-of-war of his own nation to go to Madras and stand his trial. It was not necessary to be afraid of him any longer.

Or rather it was necessary to be afraid of him, but in a different way, The *Curtana* had come, not only to effect his recall, but to demand damages from the court of Ayudhya. for the injuries he had inflicted. The mandarins were experienced enough to know that the king would never pay any damages. He would repudiate White, They concluded that White was equally aware of this. On these premises, when they proceeded to reflect what would happen, they arrived at the inevitable conclusion that White would hand over Mergui to Weltden. For him to fight and drive off the *Curtana* would not rehabilitate him in the eyes of the king, who would never forgive the embarrassment caused by the presentation of the bill of damages and who would have reason to anticipate an English revenge. But if White handed over Mergui, his compatriots would forgive him. We know that this view was sound. We have already seen that the *Pearl* was shortly to be sent to Mergui with that very offer; if White would

hand over the place, all his misdemeanours would be condoned and he would be kept on as second in council. The
mandarins could not know that White had already in general
considered this course among three or four others and had
rejected it, nor, had they known his reason, could they have
understood it. They were pliant and subtle; the pride and
independence of White were beyond their experience. Had
his character been explained to them, it would have remained
a mystery. But we, his fellow countrymen, can understand,
with the help of Davenport. What he once said in privacy to
his secretary reveals him: 'If I was sure going to Madras
would keep me from going to Hell, I would choose to be
damned rather than go thither to be laugh'd at by Yale and
Freeman.'

That is the point—to be laughed at by Yale and Freeman,
White would never surrender Mergui, because there was that
in his character which made it impossible for him to swallow
the mockery to which he knew that action would expose
him. He had stood against the Company as a free adventurer.
No interest could balance for him the intolerable humiliation
of having to seek favours from persons he hated. This stub-
born independence was intensely English; it had animated
half his countrymen during the civil wars just over; even now
we should think less of him, if he had bowed to Yale and
purchased his immunity. The surrender of Mergui would
have mortally wounded his conception of himself as a free
man of England making a fortune in the whirligig of eastern
politics, In his heart he felt that the manipulation to his advantage of all the perils of his strange life was ultimately to his
race's renown. But if he became afraid of anybody, of the
Company, of men like Yale and Freeman, then he was no
longer what he had thought himself to be, the man who had
said to Davenport: 'You are not wholly unacquainted with
those Salvoes, which I reserve as yet in my own Breast for
whatsoever exigence or emergency.'

But, I repeat, how could the mandarins understand all this? They had not read English history. They judged him on their experience of the world. In his place they would happily have traded Mergui.

Thus they were certain that he would surrender the place. His preparations to overwhelm Weltden they did not believe to be genuine. Did he intend this, he could already have accomplished it ten times over. The Captain was taking no precautions; he and his officers, while drinking ashore, could easily have been seized; an elementary stratagem would then have disposed of the *Curtana*. White had the *Resolutions* her equal; he had the *Dorothy*, quite a fair frigate, the sloop *Robin*, and hundreds of galleys, thousands of armed men. If a trick failed, Weltden's destruction by force presented no difficulties. For him to have anchored his ship inside an enemy port as strong as Mergui, he must have had reason to believe from the start that White was his man.

So the mandarins argued. The right explanation did not occur to them—that White was preparing to direct from behind the scenes a Siamese attack. That with his clandestine advice and organization they were going to rout Weltden, that White later would stage an imaginary escape from them, never crossed their minds, because the facts did not suggest it since he had so comfortable an alternative,

If they had had any doubt as to his intentions, it was dissipated as they observed his apparent friendship for Weltden. When he was not dining on the *Curtana*, Weltden was ashore, confabulating with him until midnight. The drinking party of July 12th was so well advertised by the multiple discharge of ordnance that it cannot have escaped their notice. Beyond question the two were celebrating together in advance the surrender of Mergui. If anything more was required to confirm their interpretation, it was provided by the closure of the route to Ayudhya.

With this verdict on the situation the mandarins opined

that all the English were involved in White's project. The whole of them had signed or approved of the proclamation, signifying their loyalty to the English throne. Without their assistance White could hardly bring off his coup. At a given signal—perhaps the arrival of reinforcements from Madras, for rumour had it that more men-of-war were coming—they would help White to seize the forts and other strategic points. On that supposition the mandarins laid their plans. Lethargic and timid though they were, they possessed as strongly as anyone else a dislike for foreign dominance. The policy inaugurated by Phaulkon of putting Europeans into administrative posts had always been unpopular. With no press or articulate public opinion to shout disagreement, with a patient race accustomed to autocracy, such measures were accepted for a time without viable indignation. But below the surface there was grave discontent. When it seemed imminent chat these foreigners were about to betray the country, anger burst up and, because it had been suppressed for so long, it was all the more deadly.

I will now return to the narrative and let it unfold the mandarins' solution to this complexity.

On this fatal day, 14th July 1687, Lieutenant Mason was early on the *Curtana's* quarter-deck. As he paced up and down, he began complaining to Davenport, who had joined him, of his commander's folly and uttered the gravest suspicions of White: 'We go every day ashore to be gulled by that sharper and stay on shore until such unseasonable hours every night. If no mischief comes on it in the end, I'll e'en proclaim Mr. White a very honest man. But I like not the mustering of so many Men of War boats about the Shabanders House every night.'

But these views were already out of date. Danger, pressing danger, there was, but from another quarter. That night Mason was doomed to die, to be hacked to pieces and to be cast into the sea, but not by White's instrumentality.

A little later Weltden came up. There had been a persistent rumour chat the *Derrea Dcwlat* from Achin was outside the port. He asked Davenport to take a guard-boat, which had been placed at their disposal by White, and with six soldiers to drive off any country boats, which might appear to be waiting below the bar for the merchantman. The crew of the guard-boat was Burmese. When they received their orders they refused to obey, saying that the Shāhbandar had instructed them to remain on guard alongside the *Curtana*. It crossed the mind of some of those present that the Burmans were spies. The thought increased the general uneasiness.

Later on Weltden decided to go ashore as usual. He took Lieutenant Mason and his guard. Joseph Olindo also seems to have been of the party, Davenport remained on boards the vessel being left in charge of Mr. Stilgo, the first mate.

Weltden wended his way to White's house and in due course, after an uneventful day, for there seemed unusually little happening, they sat down to supper. Comparatively early, about nine o'clock, Weltden rose to go. Word was sent to the guard to go ahead down to the wharf and wait there in their own boat till the captain came down and embarked on his barge.

White decided to see Weltden to the wharfside and presently they were descending the water-steps together, accompanied by Aires, a second gunner of the *Curtana*, and, I think, by Mason, It was a dark night, overcast with the monsoon cloud and without moon. For some unaccountable reason the usual torchmen were not to be found, though even on moonlight nights their practice had been to light the captain down.

When White and Weltden reached the wharf and 'were passing to each other the parting Courtesie', there was a sudden shriek and a skurry of naked feet as a large number of natives—Siamese, Burmans, a riff-raff maddened with raw spirit—rushed out of the warehouses by the wharf, in which they had been concealed, and flung themselves sword in hand upon the Englishmen, one of them struck Weltden a furious blow on the head and he fell unconscious, Aires filing the man down before he could finish his work. A general mêlée ensued and somebody unknown pushed White out of danger iato the surrounding blackness. The guard from their boat poured in a random volley,

White, who had no idea what this attack amounted to, turned back an instant towards his house, but seeing a crowd at the gate, a threatening rabble, realized that something extraordinary had happened and made a rush towards Weltden's barge. He jumped on board and ordered John Cogshill, the manner in charge, to push off at once and take him on board the *Dorothy* which was riding close by in the pool, Cogshill obeyed, though it meant leaving his commander. But they both thought Weltden was dead and they themselves were in the greatest danger, for it seems that Mason and Aires had been killed and that the whole guard, before they could load again, had been overwhelmed in their boat and despatched to a man. The neap flood was still running up and the barge for the first minute or so drifted close to the edge of the mud, a stretch of which, quite twenty yards wide, separated the water from the rising ground.

But Weltden was not dead. When he received the blow, he was wearing one of the thick wide-brimmed beaver hats of the period, and this had turned the blade. He quickly recovered consciousness and during the diversion caused by the guard's volley, rendered invisible by the black clothes he was wearing, escaped into the darkness. He, too, turned back towards the house and, avoiding the crowd at the gate, tried to go round behind and enter that way. There he met an Indian, probably one of White's servants, who pointed out to him the shadowy line of his barge 'as she was driving up along shore with the flood'. It was evidently the moment after White had pushed off. Weltden realized that his one chance of life was to get on board her. Avoiding the steps and the wharf, he ran down a side way to cut her off, plunging into the swamp between the bank and the edge. In this he sank almost to his knees. After a struggle, covered with mud and sweat, bleeding freely, he reached the sea and plunged in. By this time the barge had passed him and he was alone in the water. But the trumpeter had noticed a figure in the mud and they put back, Weltden was pulled up half dead.

White, who by now had realized that his plans had gone wrong, and that he was forestalled by an independent rising against all the English, decided that the only safe course was to make for the *Resolution*, He had always intended chat his frigate should be his floating protection against an infuriated populace. But suddenly the batteries opened fire upon the *James*, which lay between him and his ship, and there seemed to be a movement of men-of-war *prahus* right across the harbour. He was afraid to go down, particularly as the tide was against him and his progress would be slow. He therefore resolved to make for the south end of Pataw island (called Patit) and, if possible, work right round it and come at the *Resolution* that way. But, on reaching the south point, he saw two large armed boats, and ordered Cogshill to put into the mangrove. They lay concealed there, hearing in the distance a furious cannonade.

In two or three hours it blew up very thick from the south-west, a blinding squall sweeping over. Covered by this, they crept out of the mangrove and decided to make down the harbour on the ebb, which had now set in. Rowing hard, they first saw White's house and the shipyard in flames. When they were abreast of the *Dorothy* and the sloop *Robin*, which lay close by her, they noticed movement on board, as though the Siamese had seized them. A little farther on they saw the *James*, dismasted and smoking. Still protected by the heavy squall, they hastened down the harbour, on reaching the anchorage of the *Resolution* and the *Curtana*, they found nothing. Both ships had disappeared. As they could hardly have been sunk, White concluded that they had dropped down below the bar for safety. He gave the order to row on. In a mile and a half they reached the bar. Right on it, in three fathoms, they perceived the *Resolution* looming over them. They hailed her and were taken on deck at once. They could dimly see the *Curtana* just ahead over the bar in seven fathoms.

The first tiling White did was to send one of his seamen, Harris, to inform them on the *Curtana* of the death of Mason and the guard, but to say that Weltden and he were safe and to ask for the doctor. While waiting for Westbrook, the *Curtana's* surgeon, he took his ship over the bar and dropped anchor in deep water near the other frigate. It seems that Mr. Smith, his first mate, had been obliged to anchor on the bar in Spite of the ebb on account of the violent squall, which had threatened to drive his ship on to the shoals to the eastward.

When the officers of the *Curtana* received the message brought by Harris, they could not believe that their commander was alive. It seemed impossible to think 'that all his guard should be cut off and only himself escaped'. They seat the doctor, but asked Harris to return with written word from Weltden that he was really safe. There was reason for their apprehension. They had had an alarming night Between nine and ten o'clock they had heard a discharge of firearms near, as they thought, White's house. This was the volley fired by the guard. Soon after that they heard and saw the battery on the ridge and that on the platform below firing as fast as the guns could be reloaded. The hidden battery in the wood, 'not much above the place where the "Curtana" rid', opened upon them, but the balls went wide. In alarm they then saw the Shāhbandar's house and shipyard in flames. Shortly afterwards a vessel—some insisted it was the *James*—appeared to be on fire, for they perceived her masts plainly in the middle of the flames; and they heard an explosion. They had been at first not certain what was wrong, if anything was wrong. As they crowded the rail, straining their eyes up the harbour, a few suggested that White was only giving a party in return for the entertainment of a few nights earlier on the *Curtana*, that he was firing cannon and burning an old vessel 'in Civility and Compliment to the Captain'.

But about midnight Captain Gostlin, accompanied by his mate, M oil ins, and four other men, had arrived with a dreadful story. He said that suddenly both forts had opened upon him, the forts which Weltden insisted he could overawe, He had immediately cut his cables and tried to stand out, but at the moment the wind was insufficient and he had failed to stem the flood. He was held in front of the batteries. The thirty guns had pounded him; his main mast had been fractured, his crew had begun to fall. With the survivors he had launched one of his boats and, abandoning the ship, had rowed down to the *Curtana*. The most appalling rumours were current, he said. All the English on shore were reported to have been massacred.

When this news was received a council of war was summoned. There were present the three mates, Stilgo, Weld and Hoddy, Westbrook the surgeon, Long the carpenter, with Johnson the boatswain and Beck the chief gunner. Farwell and Olindo, the two merchants, were ashore; but Davenport was on board. After a hurried discussion, they had decided to take the ship out of danger. She was in no state to resist an attack. A quantity of stores was lying in confusion about the deck, several of the gun-carriages were unserviceable and none of the guns were clear. The ebb had just set in and it was the moment to get over the bar. Davenport volunteered to act as pilot. To get away the ship and bring her head round from the ebb, they hoisted a foretopsail. The capstan bars were manned, but the litter on deck delaying them, they had not got in the small bow-anchor before they saw fire-boats coming down on the tide. In this distraction they had to cut both their cables and launch the boats to bring the ship's head

round. They got weigh on her at last, just escaping the fire-
boats. Gostlin went on to the *Resolution* to warn and help
Smith, her first mate, for Captain Leslie, her commander, was
on shore. Together both ships had made for the bar and
anchored where they were later found by White and
Weltden.

Next day in the afternoon Weltden was sufficiently recovered to go aboard his ship, which had dropped down a
little further, otherwise nothing was done on that day.

On July 16th, 'with the morning flood, the Captain ordered
to weigh and stand up towards the "Resolution" into 6
fathoms of water, short of the Bar'. White then rowed over
to the *Curtana* and a consultation took place. They had to
come to some decision. There was no precise information
about the upshot of the rising. The assumption was that the
council of mandarins now held charge and that all the English residents had been murdered. It was also assumed that the
council, not content with routing the *Curtana* from the harbour, would pursue her. on the other hand, it was a dreadful
course to abandon Mergui without an effort to take off any
survivors there might be. They were just debating whether at
least they might not slip up the harbour in the long boat and
recover the two anchors they had lost and a topsail, which had
previously been left at the north point of Pataw, when 'the
miserably mangled Corpse of Mr. Olindo driving by the
ship's side' alarmed them so much that they abandoned the
project.

The next day—it was now three days after the massacre—
they returned to the debate. White was very anxious to go
back, if he could get the others to follow, Was Leslie killed
and what about Mary, his Mary, and her little children?
Weltden agreed to go with him. They would take the boats
and the remainder of the soldiers, doubly or trebly armed.
They would row round the west side of Pata Pataw Island and,
approaching the harbour from the south, they would be able

to perceive from there whether White's house was still standing. If it was and appeared to be maintained by any remnant of the English against the natives, they would land, fight their way to it and carry the beleaguered down to the boats.

But this proposal was strongly opposed by the officers as too daogeroos. If they sallied from the boats, these would be destroyed and their retreat cut off. It was a forlorn hope; the house had been observed in flames. Yet, in spite of these arguments, White and Weltden were preparing to go, 'when there was taken up near the Ships side another dead English man, worse mangled and hacked than the former'. That settled the matter. But they drew up a letter in Dutch, Portuguese and English addressed to the mandarins, in which an offer was made to redeem any English left alive. This letter was sent ashore under a flag of truce by the hands of two of White's lascars in Gostlin's small boat. Davenport docs not state what answer, if any, was returned to this letter, but I think we may at least assume that the lascars, when they came back, gave an account of the situation on shore. We know from other sources what this was. Not less than sixty Englishmen were killed in Mergui on the night of the massacre. Burnaby was slaughtered in his house, though as governor he might have expected a warning, had his informers been any good. Captain Leslie was killed, though it appears that Mary Leslie[1] and her children, and with them all the other English women and children in Mergui, were not touched. Captain Cropley escaped, either because he was in Tenasserim, whither we know he removed with Davenport, or because, if he was on board his ship the *Dorothy* he bought his life by her surrender. We shall End him later commanding her

---

[1] There is reason to think that Mary Leslie and her children were never repatriated and that they lived on in Mergui till their deaths. A son of hers appears to have in arried there and his descendants, now mixed with the local blood, Portuguese and oriental, still live in Mergui and still are called Leslie.

against the English. Of the *Curtana's* company, Farwell, Olindo and Mason were dead, besides the guard.

So much for the massacre of Mergui. The mandarins struck after their manner and the English had to go. Next year they were to strike again and to deliver the land from the French.

XXXIX. WHITE AND WELTDEN FACE TO FACE

Werpe have now arrived at a new conjuncture in this peculiar story. White, who before the massacre had planned to set the Siamese on Weltden, now found him self with Weltden outside the bar, possessed of the *Resolution* and all his property safe. It was clear that he could now escape home to England at any moment. Weltden could not hold him. A dark night was all he required. But he saw at once that immediate flight would throw the strongest suspicion upon him. He might be accused of the massacre. Flight for the moment was out of the question.

Even as it was, the officers of the *Curtana* suspected him of having had some hand in it. It was indisputable, they said, that he had helped the Siamese to organize their attack. That was common knowledge; they had warned their captain again and again of his preparations. There was nothing surprising in the fact that the attack began by a massacre of the English on shore. Those men were no friends of White; Salter, Barnes and the others, now all dead, had frequently informed them of White's secret plans. What more natural than that he should have agreed to their despatch? He was not above such a crime.

On July 18th the officers waited on Captain Weltden and

asked hint to detain White, who had been on board the *Curtana* since the 16th. He should be taken to Madras as soon as possible, with the *Resolution* as a prize, and there the true cause of the massacre should be examined before competent judges.

Weltden, who had been with him when the massacre began, knew from, what his own eyes had seen that White had been intended as a victim like the rest, and he declared to them that it was impossible to suppose that he had had any part in the bloodshed. One should note that Davenport never associated himself with that allegation. He had too penetrating an understanding to be misled by appearances, He knew the East well enough to guess what had happened.

The officers were not satisfied with Weltden's declaration. Their captain's friendship with White had already made him suspect. They declared that White must be arrested. Weltden replied that he had no power to do this. His written orders from Madras directed him to serve the notice of recall upon him and to warn him that, if he disobeyed, he was liable to be treated thereafter as a rebellious person. They said nothing about arresting him, particularly as White had signed as having received the proclamation and declared his willingness to go to Madras. To arrest him in those circumstances would give White the power to ruin him when they reached England. He had no authority.

THOMAS JOHNSON (the boatswain): 'Sir, there's the King's Colours at the top Mast head and the Boltsplit end will bear you out for carrying him to Madras. There's nobody desires to put an affront upon Mr. White, but if you do let him go, we must needs say that you yourself and nobody but you does put an affront upon the King of England, by whom you are commissioned to observe the Honourable Companies Orders, and upon the Honourable Company themselves that employed you hither; and if you do let Mr. White and that ship go, I suppose the Company will never thank you for it. However you shall never have our consent. And if you plead a want of power, I wonder you do not take down the King's Colours and not disgrace them by only using them for private interest.'

At this insubordinate speech, which suggested that his leniency to White was due to a private understanding, Captain Weltden flew into a great rage and 'called the Boatswain a parcel of foul names', adding: 'Mr, White is a very worthy gentleman and if I hear any man presume to speak a word more about carrying him or his ship to Fort St. George, I will make an example of him to all the Rogues in the world, I mill vindicate Mr. White with my life.'

THOMAS JOHNSON: 'Sir, I value not your threats. All the world shall never force me to believe that Mr. White had not a hand in this Murther; and you shall never have my consent either to let him or the ship "Resolution" go before they come to Madras.'

MR. WELD (2nd Mate): 'I do own you for my Commander, but I will and must needs declare that you shall never have my consent to let cither Mr. White or that ship go, and if you will not carry him to Madras, you must expect to answer for it.'

CAPTAIN WELTDEN: 'Sirrah, then hold your prating or I'll let you make me see who dares hinder him for going out of my ship.'

White was in the *Curtana's* great cabin duriug this hot exchange. Shortly after, it was about 4 p.m., he came on deck and went directly on board the *Resolution*. He was confirmed in his view that he must now act with the greatest restraint and caution.

---

* But see Welteden's orders on pp. 197, 198. He had authority to seize the *Resohition* and oblige Wkite to travel to Madras on the *Curtana*.

XL. HIDING IN THE ISLANDS

With the ebb both ships weighed and dropped down to a large bay on the north-east of King Island, now called French Bay, where they were well away from all danger of fire-boats. There they lay until July 24th. White had renewed his propositions to Weltden about a substantial share in the cargoes of the *Derrea Dowlat* and the *Satisfaction*, if they could intercept them. As Weltden had missed his chance of profiting by White's previous offers of a timber cargo on the *Dorothy* and the ballast for the *Curtana,* he agreed eagerly to wait for the overdue merchantmen. There was plenty of time, moreover, for during the monsoon he could not cross to Madras. This suited White perfectly. If the ships arrived, he would give Weltden enough to make that poor gentleman very grateful and he would distribute sums among the officers and crew, which would shut their mouths for ever.

On July 24th they moved from French Bay to an anchorage on the east side of Iron Island, for it was rumoured that the Siamese were preparing to make a sortie from Mergui in force. If they were caught in French Bay, they would be unable to manoeuvre and might be boarded. They had hardly reached Iron Island before a Siamese fleet was seen approaching. They recognized the *Dorothy* and the *Robin* and were surprised to observe the *James* also; she had been repaired. Another small ship called the *Faulkon* was included, together with fourteen boats full of armed men. It is likely that Cropley was in command. White wanted to stand and fight, and suggested cutting off the Siamese from their base, but Weltden would not face them and turned out through Iron passage into the rough water west of Iron Island, where nearly the full force of the monsoon is felt. They anchored to windward of Canister Island, The Siamese boats could not follow them into such a sea.

Next day with the freshening of the monsoon Weltden

found his position too much exposed- The question of whether to fight or not was again raised. The officers were summoned and a council of war was held in the great Cabin. The fact was that the *Curtana* was in such a disgraceful condition that she was unfit to engage. The officers in a body protested.

MR. STILGO (1st Mate): 'You know the fitness of the ship for such an undertaking as well as we do. None of the guns on deck will house and to load them, the men will be forced to expose themselves. That will be hot work, when they come to pistol shot.'

CAPTAIN WELTDEN: 'I will go on board the "Resolution" and consult Mr. White.'

Later a note came off addressed to Mr. Stilgo, ordering him to follow the *Resolution*, which weighed in the afternoon and stood in with the north end of Tavoy Island, about sixty miles north of Mergui. There both ships anchored in six fathoms of smooth water with good holding ground. The *Curtana* was running short of provisions and White sent her stores from the *Resolution*. They saw no more of the Siamese fleet. No doubt the mandarins concluded that their enemies were now in full retreat.

They stayed at this anchorage till August 10th. It was then resolved to stand out towards the edge of the archipelago, to the island called Tenasserim, which has been described in an earlier part of this book as the first land sighted on the Madras-Mergui run after leaving the Andamans. They made for the deep sheltered bay on the north end of it and there anchored. It is one of the most lovely spots in the archipelago when the weather is fine, but in August, with overcast skies and the monsoon roaring outside, the dripping jungle and the utter loneliness, it is no amusing place for a ship's company or any mortal man. How they amused themselves there, I cannot think. As it lay on the route White's merchantmen must take if they came back, he kept a sharp look-out. He borrowed Weltden's long boat, with its mast and sails, and sent her off with Nat Carter and others of his men to points of vantage from which they might watch the southern approaches, None of the *Curtana's* men accompanied them. This gave rise to more talk, though by this time, as it was clear to the officers and crew that White was making no attempt to escape, suspicion of him had rather abated. But the boatswain, Mr. Johnson, was heard to observe that it was a great shame that the captain 'should juggle with the Honourable Companies known enemy'. If he himself had been in the long boat and they had met the ships 'neither Mr. White nor the Captain would have been a farthing the better for them,' said he, 'for I should venture to pilot them into Madras Road and surrender them to the President and Council there'. After ten days the long boat returned to report no success, which, as we know, was not surprising.

On August 29th, when they had been on the island over a fortnight, Weltden sent for Davenport one evening, after returning from supper on the *Resolution* with White. When they were in the great cabin alone, Weltden said that the *Curtana* would have to be careened. She was very foul and slow. Could she be careened on the island which White had selected as a hiding-place for the *Resolution* at the time when he thought to leave before the *Curtana's* arrival? That was Mergui Island, as I have stated, some twenty-seven miles south of Mergui, where there was a hard shelving beach of fine sand and a rise of twenty feet. Davenport, who had evidently changed his original view, replied that it would be dangerous. The island was too near the inhabited zone. They would be discovered. When the *Curtana* lay on the beach unrigged, she might be burned. Even if White guarded her in the *Resolution* (and Davenport, who now began to understand White's subtle policy, believed he would guard her) she might not be safe from a boat attack; indeed, once inside that maze of islands, the Siamese *prahus* could overwhelm them both, Davenport's vivid description of the chances of two frigates

243

in such waters against native craft is interesting. He said to Weltden:

'The Tides running so contrariant round every small island, they [the frigates] would be often forced to Anchor in their going and coming, and perhaps many times be necessitated to have the Ship's boat out a head of the ship, to keep her clear of a Point, or an Eddy, which would be hazardous when surrounded by a vast number of Enemies boats, that could take or leave by the benefit of their Oars, as themselves should see convenient.'

But as the careening had now become a necessity, Weltden replied that he would have to take the *Curtana* as far as Negrais on the Burmese coast, 300 miles north. It could be done there. The question of the *Resolution* then arose. Should she go to Negrais also?

Weltden had already discussed this matter with White, who had no intention of going to Negrais. It was on the beat of the East India Company's men-of-war. He might fall in with one commanded by a very different type of man from Weltden and by being forced to fight and flee, like a pirate, would undo all the careful nursing he had given the situation, He also had to watch for his two ships. Davenport now said to Weltden he supposed the *Resolution* would accompany him, to which Weltden replied that White had objected and that he could not force him. If one studies Weltden's instructions, there is no point-blank order that he was to seize White. As he certainly did not wish to do so, he stood on the letter of his orders, saying now to Davenport: 'I am certain that Mr. White will go on his own accord to Madras, for his interest leads him to do so.'

There on be no doubt that White had shown Weltden his papers, had persuaded him that all his actions in Mergui were done under orders from the King of Siam, to whose service he had been lent by the East India Company, and had said that he could and would justify himself at Madras.

If he could do so, it was certainly to his interest to go there.

Weltden went on to say that he would be back at Tenasserim island on October 20th; the *Resolution* would wait till then, when together they would make one last effort to trace the *Derrea Dowlat* by dropping down to Achin on the N. E. wind, which begins to set in from about that date. From Achin they would cross to Madras.

Davenport raised a further point. Weltden's instructions contained a particular order for him to seize the *Derrea Dow lat* and the *Satisfaction*, if he could. There was still a possibility that White would meet them while Weltden was at Negrais. His orders would cover the transfer of some of his officers to the *Resolution* and of her officers to the *Curtana*, 'by which means . . . neither could there be any juggling with the Prize . . . nor should you need to fear Mr. White being gone before you return to this place'.

CAPTAIN WELTDEN: 'I cannot answer to do it.'

On September 1st the *Curtana* accordingly weighed for Negrais. leaving the *Resolution* behind. We must interpret these occurrences as indicating that Weltden believed White had nothing to fear from Madras and that he could fully be trusted to go there. That Weltden put so favourable an interpretation on White's intentions was partly due to the personal liking he had for the man and partly because his interest was engaged in the offers of gain which White had made to him.

I need not interrupt the narrative by a description of Weltden at Negrais. Coming upon that coast on September 5th in dark rainy weather, with twenty-three fathoms and a soft mud bottom, he had to ask the invaluable Davenport to pilot him into the harbour on a course between Alguada shoal and Diamond Island. They removed Captain Cropley's flagstaff and Siamese inscription, which they found on the west point of Deer island, substituting their own. The place was uninhabited. Davenport, always competent, surveyed and mapped the harbour; the *Curtana* was successfully laid on the beach' scraped and refloated; the crew shot deer, collected turtles and so provisioned her. She sailed on October 13th for her rendezvous at Tenasserim island with White on October 20th. But the N.E. wind, though blowing, was weak and they did not reach the island till November 2nd. White was gone.

This was something of a shock for Weltden, and some of his men were beginning to make slighting remarks, when a party which had gone ashore reported a bottle on the beach, in which was a letter addressed to the captain. It was from White to say that as soon as the north-east wind blew, he had thought it best to hasten down to Achin, for at that port they must know what had happened to the *Derrea Dawlat*, and that he would wait for Weltden there. The *Curtana* immediately set off after him and covered the distance to Achin, some 500 miles south, in seven days. The *Resolution* was in the road and Weltden went straight on board. He was delighted to see White again. It made him feel justified in his appreciation of his character. As for White, it was all part of his plan to give the impression that everything was straightforward and above board. There was a drinking party on the *Resolution* that night.

XLI. TREASON

They stayed on at Achin for a month, as the wind was not yet suitable for crossing to Madras, The full story of the *Derrea Dowlat* was then disclosed. Her seizure on behalf of the Company by Captain Consett of the *Berkeley Castle* as far back as April meant a loss of £1,838 to White in the values of that day.

White, having now quite dashed his critics on the *Curtana* by not running away when he had the opportunity, thought it a good opportunity to clear himself of all suspicion in regard to the massacre. He put the matter to Weltden, who agreed and called his officers together. Speaking directly to Davenport, he said:

'I am heartily glad to have met with Mr. White again in this Road. You and my officers were so earnest to have him detained when we made our escape from. Mergen, now I am resolved to have a meeting of the Commanders in the Road, Then, if under your hands any of you point blank charge him with Treason against the King of England, I will make him a Prisoner aboard my Ship, otherwise he is at his own liberty to go when or whither himself pleaseth, both with his Person and his Ship.'

DAVENPORT: 'I am no competent Judge to determine what is Treason and what's not, but before ever you set foot on shore at Mergen (as you may very well remember), I informed you of so many of Mr. White's expressions, designs and practices, as might very well oblige you to carry the said White to Madras.'

it is clear from this that Davenport did not think White had had a hand in the massacre and that none of the others felt very sure about it. Davenport's point was that White's conduct of naval operations in the bay had been such as to cause the Company to send the *Curtana*, and that White should be called upon to explain his actions in Madras. Apart from any animosity, he was obliged still to press that view, if he wished to protect himself afterwards from a charge of abetment. When Weltden found that nobody was prepared to swear treason against White, he dropped the matter. White himself was now satisfied that he had little to fear. He was back again in the position he had occupied before Weltden appeared in Mergui. If he thought then that he could sail home to England on the *Resolution* and make his peace, with the help of his money, when he got there, he had now the same conviction. His papers were good enough for an English court of law; he could point to having obeyed the King's order to leave Mergui; he could make it appear that he had been largely instrumental in saving Weltden and the *Curtana* from the fury of the Siamese. Not putting into Madras would be a mere peccadillo. Now that the treason charge was wiped off, he would slip away at a convenient moment.

Such Was the position when they weighed front Achin on November 20th.

XLII. WHITE AND WELTDEN ARRANGE DAVENPORT'S MURDER

D avenport was one of those tiresome men who are always right. On December 9th he irritated Welt den unbearably. They had sighted the Indian coast 200 miles north of Madras near Madapollam, the scene of Captain Coates's exploits, which had started all the trouble. It is not explained why they overshot Madras, whether it was unfavourable wind or business, but it seems to have been intentional, Weltden, who had no knowledge of those waters, took the ship into 6½ fathoms off Corango shoal against Davenport's advice. It was a lee shore. Davenport pressed him to get into the other tack. They hardly got her round in time. The rest of the watch saw this little scene, Weltden was angry, but he could say nothing as Davenport was tight. Moreover, the officers and crew were behind him.

On the 11th they were safely anchored in an outer roadstead. Weltden dined on the *Resolution* and at midnight he and White came aboard the *Curtana*, both the worse for drink and very quarrelsome. They began by sending for the second mate, Mr. Weld, and hectoring him about nothing. 'That fit being over with them,' they decided to get Davenport out of bed, He was woken up and called on to the quarter-deck, where the captain met him with a blast of the most filthy language. White heartily seconded the abuse, adding: 'Hang him up at the Yard-Arm immediately. I will bear you harmless for five pound.'

CAPTAIN WELTDEN: 'I won't do that, but I'd give a hundred the Admiral of India was here and he would have a Council of War, to hang all the mutinous Rogues in the Ship.'

DAVENPORT: 'I do not believe there is one mutineer in your ship. There has never been disturbance in your ship but what would be found to owe its rise merely to your own promoting, by acting as you have done with Mr. White.'

on this, 'with many curses and oaths,' the captain replied; 'What have you to say against Mr. White? I charge you to say it to his face before this company. Mr. White is a civil worthy gentleman and I'll venture my life in his Vindication. By God, do all of you what you can, he shall not go to Madras.'

DAVENPORT: 'You know very well I have somewhat to say to Mr. White if ever he comes to Madras.'

CAPTAIN WELTDEN: 'I charge you forthwith to declare it. You shall not stir off Quarter Deck until you have done it or I'll clap you in Irons and carry you to the Fort in Irons.'

Davenport replied that he would write his allegations. Weltden swore bitterly that write them he should, there and then, and repeated that he should not stir off the quarter-deck 'till he had writ what he could say against Mr. White'. A sailor was told to bring pen, ink mud a lantern and Davenport was ordered to begin.

It was some time past midnight and the wind was blowing very fresh, making it difficult to write on the fluttering paper.

The light flickered; but Davenport set to work. 'About four o'clock in the morning he gave notice to the Captain, who all that while was in the Cabin a-drinking with Mr. White,' that he had finished. Weltden emerged and Davenport put the writing in his hands. He read it over twice and after some pause said: 'I little expected any paper of that nature from you. What made you give me that Protest? For not carrying Mr. White to the fort?'

DAVENPORT: 'You ordered me to write what I had to say against Mr. White, but I thought what I have here written and given you is more proper.'

He had written a considered charge against Weltden himself, which he proposed to lay before the council of Madras, when he got there. Weltden, who was too drunk to see the danger of the threat, swore bitterly he would clap him in irons before sunrise. As Davenport remained cool, Weltden, parsing to bathos in the manner of men in his condition, said:

'I once thought not to ask you a Farthing for your Passage or the Freight of your Chest or anything else, but now you shall go ashore at Madras in your bare shirt. You shall not carry with you a Rag of Cloaths or Penny of Money or your Boy [Lazarus] nor an Inch of Paper out of this Ship till you have paid me Sixty Pagodoes (£27).'

DAVENPORT: 'As for the Irons, you may put me in them if you please, but you will do it at your Peril to answer for it, And as for the Pagodoes, if you had threatened to demand six hundred, 'twould be as reasonable and probable to be recovered.'

Davenport was pretty bold because he knew that, if Weltden touched him, there would be a mutiny. So they parted, White and Weltden to sleep off the punch. Not till noon did White return to the *Resolution*, when both ships entered the inner road of Madapollam.

Weltden had now leisure to think out his position. On sober reflection he was alarmed by Davenport's draft charges.

He talked it over with White, who suggested that an accident might be arranged. There was a ruffian on board the *Resolu tion* Called John Noleman. The idea was to send him over to the *Curtana*, fully armed, and get him to spit in Davenport's face. When Davenport drew, Noleman should be able to pistol him, in self-defence or by mistake. However he did it was of no consequence, so long as he killed him. They could hang Noleman afterwards, if necessary. He was suspected of other crimes.

On December 17th Noleman arrived. But there was one difficulty. He did not know Davenport by sight. He asked the others which of them he was. But they, suspecting something, put him off. He left the ship without accomplishing his purpose.

Weltden then thought the best course would be to get Davenport murdered ashore. It was easy to arrange an assassination in India. Such things did not cost much. There were plenty of professional murderers for hire. Arrangements were made and two days later Weltden sent for Davenport, in 'a fine starched Prologue' he began: 'I have permitted you to eat in your own Mess, never denied you a glass of wine or a dram of the bottle or a Pipe of Tobacco.' He then referred to Davenport's unbearable manner when the ship was off Corango shoal, on top of that were the charges which he had said he would bring against: him at Madras. The captain continued: 'I shall carry you on this Ship no further. You may prepare to go ashore. There is at Mr. White's stern a country boat. As for your things, be what they may, you can seal up your Chests and I shall put them safe into the Fort at Madras till you have paid your passage thus far.'

In this way Weltden planned to rifle the chests and extract Davenport's notes, papers and particularly the diary, which he knew he had been keeping and which he suspected incriminated him, Noleman would go in the country boat and superintend Davenport's murder on land. But Davenport saw through the stratagem and, relying upon the solid backing he had among the officers, replied with a smile: 'I am unwilling to go ashore or, if I do to leave anything behind me. . . . Nor will this project answer your Expectations, for you need not much doubt that most of your Intreagucs with Mr. White will by one means or other be unravelled by some other hands.'

As Weltden was afraid forcibly to put Davenport ashore against the wish of his officers, he fell back on cajolery. Withdrawing, he sent Surgeon Westbrook twice to induce him to go. But Davenport was unmoved. He knew that to go ashore, beyond the protection of his friends on the *Curtana*, was madness.

Weltden thereafter called him again to the cabin and said very gravely: 'You may carry your things with you, for I have considered on't and would rather lose a small matter than Carry a man with me to the Fort that perhaps might ruin me.'

He offered to give him a letter to an Indian in Madapollam attached to the local factory, who would secure him a passage to Madras. He then tried to make out that far from having tried to get Noleman to murder him, he had refused to countenance that scoundrel: 'you are not for all that my Enemy, Noleman offered me fifty Pagodoes to deliver you into his boat, but I would not do it for a hundred, for I know Noleman is a desperate fellow.'

Davenport answered most of this nonsense with a smile. but made no preparation to go on shore in the boat 'which Captain Weltden out of pure love had provided for him'.

Weltden was desperately anxious to get him off the ship. To know that if he took hint to Madras he would go straight to the President and council with his diary and cleverly written charges was appalling. He must be stopped. It then occurred to him that if in the presence of the ship's company he made him attractive Offers, their objection to his departure would be withdrawn. So he Called all hands aft and promised

Davenport to make it worth his while, if he would go. But Davenport remained unshaken. He did not dare to step off the ship.

CAPTAIN WELTDEN: 'What are you afraid of?'

DAVENPORT: 'Mr. White's treachery and perhaps your own.'

At this the attitude of the officers and men became unmistakable. They were clearly prepared to protect Davenport, if the captain tried force. Weltden, seeing the game was up, changed his tone.

CAPTAIN WELTDEN: 'Will you believe me when I tell you the Truth?'

DAVENPORT: 'Yes, why should I not believe the Truth?'

CAPTAIN WELTDEN: 'As I have a Soul to be saved, I never intended you to go out of the ship. I only did this to sound the Inclinations of my Men. If you will believe me still your friend, all is well.'

Davenport, having at last won the battle, had no objection to leaving the matter at that. Weltden immediately went over the side and was rowed to the *Resolution*, where he confabulated with White.

on his return at night, both ships set sail for Madras. Weltden had decided that his only chance now was to get round Davenport by kindness and affability. He sent for him privately to his cabin, opening the conversation by saying that he had come to the conclusion that it was unfair to ask him for any passage money and that he did not propose to do so. He said a number of other agreeable things. Davenport had never seen him so charming. He concluded by explaining that his 'rashness' the other night, when he had threatened to put him in irons, was 'due to his being in Ale'. At the mention of liquor, he took the occasion to condemn all strong drink, the ruin of many a fine man, he said. He himself would never indulge again. Davenport, 'tired with such romancing, betook himself to his lodging'.

XLIII. WHITE GIVES WELTDEN
THE SLIP

W hite now felt that the time had arrived to end the farce. True, he had become such a friend of Weltden's that that gentleman had declared, in his cups, he need not go to Madras; but he knew that Weltden, sober, expected him to go, believed he wished to go. The time had come to give him the slip.

Yet White did not propose to run for it like a malefactor. He would arrange a departure to which Weltden would agree. So on their way south towards Madras he told him of a wish he had to call in at Pulicat on private business of an urgent nature. Pulicat is only thirty miles north of Madras, practically within sight of it. He would stay there only a day or so, he said, and would then follow on. It would be just as well for the captain to arrive first, have time to see the council and smooth the way for him.

Weltden suspected nothing and agreed. White filled out the little comedy by handing him a letter addressed to Elihu Yale, the president, his most deadly enemy. I give the letter nearly in full, though slightly modernised; it is highly di verting.

From on board the 'Resolution',
December 24th 1687

'RIGHT HONOURABLE AND WORTHY SIR

'Yours to Mr. Richard Burnaby and myself came safely to hand by the "Curtana" and the dismal fate since attending us has left me alone to answer it, wherein I should have been more particular could I recollect the contents. The originall, with all other of my papers, with other more momentary concerns, being then lost. The most materiall as I remember in it was to demand us in his Majesty Our Royall Sovereign and the Right Honourable East India Companies names from the King of Siams Service; with which and all other your mands, how readily they were complied with, none can better informe you than the bearer Captain Anthony Weltden, not only from ourselves but all Ms Majesties subjects under our commands; since which all that has befell us Captain Weltden will not be wanting to render you a faithful accompt of; whereto please to be referred.

'Since our comeing from Mergen, haveing notice from Captain Weltden that to secure such ships of the King of Siams as was then supposed to be come from Acheen and gone to Mergen, the better to prevent his encountering them,[1] he resolved thither and, as I believed my self obliged, made him tender of my ship for the Honourable Companies Service, as he should see good to appoint her. . . .

'Some urgent occasions requiring my appearance at Pollicatt will detain me here some days, but not that I intend with all possible speed to wayte on you at Madras, when if in person or not else I may be capable of doing the Right Honourable Company any acceptable service, I shall not fail to embrace the proposition as the greatest honour which can be conferred on

'Right Honourable and Worshipful Sir
'Your most obedient Servant
SAMUEL WHITE.'

This letter, rather confused and poorly composed though it is, sadly lacking the polished touch of his former secretary, has yet craft enough. The careful reader will notice with amusement that the only material point White pretends to remember is the Company's demand for his withdrawal from Siam. This he has loyally complied with, he says. The little matter of presenting himself at Madras he turns into a voluntary visit with the object of placing his services at the President's disposal, as they had already been placed at Weltden's.

---

[1] This phrase means' to anticipate them', i.e. to get to Achin before they left for Mergui.

Innocence, obedience, duty, sacrifice—the letter breathes them all, but the writer's eye is on his papers and on an English court in London.

With this precious missive aboard the *Curtana*, Weltden parted with White near Armagaon shoal, about forty miles north of Pulicat. The last scene is given in the ultimate sentence of the Davenport Papers, a sentence which shows that the writer, who did not know of the existence of the letter, believed that Weltden was privy to White's escape. Weltden may have shut his eyes, but I do not think the evidence points that way, for it was so easy for White to escape, that I hardly imagine he would have risked taking Weltden into his confidence. Moreover, a trick was cheaper. But I will quote the sentence for its literary value and its atmosphere of distant seas.

'Captain Weltden was as good as his word not to bring Mr. White of the ship Resolution into Madras Road, for on the 24th December he drop'd him on the edge of Armagon Sand, Mr. White handing all his sails, and Captain Weltden making all the sail he could from him.'

White did enter Pulicat, where he remained some days, either adding provisions to his ship or disposing of some of his cargo more suited to the coast trade than to England. He thought it prudent to send from there further letters to Yale, assuring him of his early arrival.

On leaving Pulicat, he passed Madras unobserved and put into Pondicherry, the French settlement sixty miles south, where he had business connections. Previously he had remitted money home that way and, no doubt, had affairs to wind up and debts to collect.

Weltden reported himself to Yale on December 25th. The President at first believed that White would arrive in a day or so, but when he heard what Davenport had to say, he realized that he would never come of his own accord and that he was as big a rascal as they had always supposed. The *Resolution* herself was not even his property, but the King of Siam's and, as such, the Company's lawful prize. Weltden had captured her in Mergui under his instructions and for White to take her now was a crime, which, with his other crimes, amounted to intolerable effrontery. As for Weltden, Yale was very angry with him. He later wrote to Sir Josiah Childe in London describing his mismanagement of the commission entrusted to him and saying that he would be court martialled. His eventual fate I shall mention further on.

News was now brought that White was in Pondicherry. Yale decided to pursue him. Ou January 20th he ordered the *Curtana* to sail to the French factory. Captain Weltden was left in command, but William Fraser, a member of the council, was detailed to sail with him and supervise his actions. They were given a letter addressed to Monsieur Martin, Director General of the French East India Company, in which he was asked to deliver up White 'to be examined before our Court of Admiralty'. But just as the frigate was about to start, news was received that White had sailed for home.

So he got away safe at last and with a wonderful harvest. We gather roughly that he had some £30,000 invested in land near Bath; he had the good ship *Resolution* and her rich cargo; he had cash, plate, rubies and his papers in perfect order, If he knew his du Bellay, he may well have hummed as he rolled down towards the Cape:

> *Heureux qui, comme Ulysse, a fait un beau voyage*
> *Ou comme cestuy là qui conquit la toison*
> *Et puis at retourné.*

PART THREE

CONCLUSION

XLIV. THE FATE OF THE PEARL

The reader will want to know what happened in the end. The spread of this book has been unavoidably wide, embracing Ayudhya, Mergui, Madras, Paris and London; the characters have been so various with King Narai, Phaulkon, White and James II, that a number of points remain outstanding. But the massacre of Mergui forms part of a round drama and it is possible in a series of concluding scenes to give an impression of finality. This I propose to attempt in chronological sequence, describing in turn what occurred at Mergui after White's departure; the strange events which supervened in Ayudhya, when Phaulkon was reinforced with French troops; what White did when he reached England.

After the fatal 14th July 1687, the Mergui mandarins found themselves masters of the situation. The measures they had taken to ensure their own safety and the inviolability of the port had been completely successful. But on reflection these now appeared very bold, perhaps too bold, as they had not been authorized in advance by the king. That had been impossible, of course, as the road to the capital had been closed; but the mandarins felt uneasy, for the Siamese system did not encourage independent action. The Lord Phaulkon, moreover, was a friend of their late Shāhbandar.

They had a difficult report to write to headquarters. The bare truth could hardly be baldly stated. When they sat down to draft their letter, they soon saw that they were able to make out no sort of case for the massacre by talking of Suspicious drinking parties on the *Curtana*. They must improve the story. Beginning truthfully enough with a recital of Weltden's tampering with the defences and his seizure of the *Resolution* during the truce, they went on to say that White and Burnaby, backed by the English residents, had at midnight on July 14th opened fire from the gun or two in White's compound upon the residence of the leading mandarin, the

Viceroy of the province, which was 180 feet distant, their object being to overawe subordinate officers and pave the Way for a surrender of the place to the English, The letter then gave a suitable description of the gallant resistance offered by the Siamese, ending in their victory and the death of many of the English.

That this fanciful report was at first believed at court is proved by a letter from the King of Siam to the East India Company, dated August 1687, in which he recapitulates the mandarins' story, thereafter declaring formal war upon the Company, the war to take the form of the seizure of their ships on any waters east of the Cape of Good Hope and the complete closure of the country to their trade, English interlopers were exempted. Phaulkon, who was responsible for the letter, believed that the French, who were due to arrive at Ayudhya the following month with considerable forces, would enable him to put these threats into execution. in anticipation, he sent down a Frenchman to fill Burnaby's place, a man whose name has not been recorded, but who was probably one of those left behind by the de Chaumont embassy of 1685.

It was to this changed Mergui that the frigate *Pearl* headed on 22nd September 1687, with Captain Perriman, the commander, Messrs. Hodges and Hill, the civil officers, quite in the dark as to the massacre and the retreat of the *Curtana*. They passed Tenasserim Island, where White lay hidden on the *Resolution* awaiting the return of the *Curtana* from Negrais. That gentleman may have seen them; he certainly gave them no warning. He may well have laughed heartily at the surprise that was awaiting them farther on.

Captain Perriman took his ship through Iron passage and when off King Island, with a distant prospect of the bar of Mergui, he saw two men-of-war. These were probably the *Dorothy* and the *Robin*. Sailing closer he perceived that the larger ship had an English flag dyed red. When within hail he was told that the vessels were Siamese men-of-war and that Captain Cropley was in command. We have already seen that there had been something peculiar about Cropley's behaviour during the massacre.

Perriman then ordered Cropley to come aboard the *Pearl*, Cropley replied that he could not come, but that he would be glad to see Perriman on his ship. By this time some doubts had begun to find their way into Perriman's mind. The more he studied the appearance of the Siamese vessels, with their cut-throat crews leaning over the bulwarks, the less he liked them. His conclusion was that they were pirates, for there were reputed to be many buccaneers on the coast. Cropley himself looked like a pirate, As we know, he had been one, though at the moment, unguessed by Pcrriman, he was a Siamese admiral, like poor Coates before him. Accordingly the offer to go aboard his ship was declined and Perriman, hearing up closer, gave him a broadside, to which he replied with another. After this exchange, Cropley tacked and taking the sloop in tow, for she was slower, made for the bar. He was pursued by Perriman, who was entirely oblivious that he was running into a trap. Cropley outsailed him and, night falling before the harbour was reached, Perriman was forced to anchor.

Next morning he weighed at daylight. As the harbour came into view, he expected to see the *Curtana* riding inside. Instead, he perceived Cropley bearing down on him supported by thirteen sail of men-of-war galleys. There was no sign of the *Curtana*. It was a decidedly awkward moment. With orders to take Mergui and put Mr. Hodges and Mr. Hill into possession of the administration, he found himself hopelessly outnumbered, without the smallest idea what to do next. His 'victuals were stinking and water almost spent'. If he turned tail, he did not know where to make for, how to provision himself, in what way to pass the rest of the monsoon before he could return to Madras. There was nothing for it but to hoist a flag of truce. This was hardly done before the Siamese came up with him. Without much hope, he tried a last bluff and called again upon Cropley to come aboard the *Pearl*. This did him credit, but Cropley only told him to hurry and send a boat, which he accordingly did, with a flag of truce at her bow. The men in the boat were detained, but a pilot was sent to the *Pearl* and she was escorted into the pool as a prize.

Petriman then asked for news. He was not sure yet what had happened to him. But they soon put him in possession of the facts—the massacre, Burnaby's death, the rout of the *Cur-tana* by fire-boats, White and Weltden's flight. But all was quiet now, they said. The new Raja, a Frenchman, was in command, a French frigate was farther up the harbour, but there was war between Siam and the Company and he must regard himself as a prisoner. Shortly afterwards, on receipt of orders from Ayudhya, Hodges and Hill were taken there in chains and flung into a dungeon.

So ended Sir Josiah Childe's ill-considered, ill-organized and unfortunate project of taking Mer gui.

XLV. THE TORTURE AND DEATH OF PHAULKON

As this book concerns White, Phaulkon perforce has less space, though of the two he was far the greater adventurer. White was content to eat Mer gui and what he could get in the Bay of Bengal. His takings were comparatively modest, say a quarter of a million sterling in modern values. Phaulkon intended to eat the whole of Siam. By the end of 1687 he was already a millionaire several times over. But he did not possess White's sense of the practical. It is true that in

1685 he sent a message to Louis XIV to say that, if things went ill in Siam, he hoped to find asylum in France, De Chaumont, the ambassador, assured him of a welcome there, It also appears that he remitted to England considerable sums. But he left his escape too late, for he had a side to his character which White did not possess. He took himself seriously as a statesman and an administrator, a fancy which never entered White's head for a moment.

Phaulkon aspired to make Siam a rich and powerful country, He wanted to see her utilize to the full her geographical position, with one port, Mergui, opening on the trade of India and the other, Ayudhya, receiving the trade of the Far East. To carry out his plans, he required competent instruments, men who were equipped to move in the world beyond Siam. He saw that the mandarinate was too ignorant and old-fashioned, The Siamese had neither the energy nor the inclination for such a policy. The Mahomedan business class was certainly more able, but it was not sufficiently amenable or up to date. The East India Company, too uncongenial, poor and tame, too little a believer in his star, was no use to him, but the free-trading Englishmen outside the Company were the kind of people he wanted. Men like White could help him to found an armed trade. But these people were not enough. He must have the support of a foreign state.

For years France had taken a religious interest in Siam. By flattering the French prelates in that country, by turning Catholic himself and suggesting, what was an absurdity, that King Narai might do the same, Phaulkon had led the French on step by step till he induced the cabinet at Versailles to believe for a time that under his protection French commercial influence could be spread in Indo-China to the supplanting of the Dutch and the arrest of English ambitions. Having once interested the French in Siam. he planned to use them for his own purpose. As I have suggested, this had two aspects, the maintenance of his position as executive of the state and the strengthening, and enrichment of the royal monopoly trade.

In plain words, with the help of French troops Phaulkon sought to maintain himself in power and by French technicians to forge the means of putting his wide plans into execution.

It was a fortunate coincidence that in Phra Narai he had a master of remarkable imagination. The king was stimulated and excited by Phaulkon's vision of the future. With the royal monopolies, which were the pick of Siamese products, properly organized, lie saw himself the richest potentate in Indo-China. A modernized army and navy, led by English and French officers, would enable him to exploit his trade to the full, a trade which, turning on the exchange of commodities between India and China, was unlimited. He therefore supported Phaulkon, whose great abilities he recognized, against the gathering storm of protest which such a policy was bound to rouse in an oriental court, with its approved way of transacting business and its complicated vested interests.

To the mandarinate at Ayudhya the phenomenon of Phaulkon had the same dry clear outline as had White for the Mergui council. He was a European and he was planning with the help of other Europeans, his co-religionists, to hand over Siam to the French, his reward being the throne. Attaching the greatest importance to two matters, their money and their religion, they came to the conclusion that both were seriously threatened. Had they been more intelligent, they could have derived great benefits from Phaulkon's policy. A general enrichment all round was implicit in his ideas. But they knew their weakness and their limitations. They knew that once the French got a footing they could never hold their own. It would be a matter of time only before the country was swallowed. They would be driven down, no longer masters in their own house.

Their rage and horror had boiled over in the Macassar

rising of August 1686; the same sentiments had been more effective in Mergui in July 1687. They were now in 1688 to gather strength and sweep all before them in the capital.

It is strange that Phaulkon did not realize that he was attempting the impossible. The French men of letters and of the world who studied him at close quarters in 1685 and 1687 all testify to the penetration of his mind, his enormous abilities. It is evident that he believed himself strong enough to carry the day and that to the many warnings he must have received he shut his ears. Others did not share his optimism. As far back as 1684 Surat had written that he would not stand long; White thought he stood but in a slippery place. He could so easily have got away. As a Count of France, a Chevalier of St. Michael and St. Peter—titles bestowed upon him by Louis XIV—fantastically rich, clever, witty, a position awaited him at Versailles. But ambition, excitement, honour held him in his place.

At the time when the *Pearl* lay a prize in Mergui harbour and Hodges and Hill were trudging painfully as captives to Ayudhya, the last French embassy arrived with the troops and engineers upon which Phaulkon depended for the furtherance of his plans. Fourteen hundred men and several warships —he no longer doubted his ability to hold down malcontents.

The two key positions in the country were Bangkok. commanding the approach to Ayudhya, and Mergui, the head of the Indian trade route. There he sent the troops, placing M. des Farges, who was commandcr-in-chief, at Bangkok with the largest contingent and Major Debrüan at Mergui with the rest. Thus the English fear that Mergui would go to France was realized for a time early in 1688.

With des Farges at Bangkok, Phaulkon felt that he commanded the capital. He had a dazzling position. His wife, the Lady Phaulkon, was a picturesque woman of twenty-two, Japanese, or partly Japanese, for it is not quite clear who she was, Their way of life was magnificent. He had two palaces, one at the capital and one at Louvo. The private chapel attached to the latter was the finest the French had seen anywhere, faced with marble, gilded, and decorated inside with biblical pictures by Japanese artists of ability. He had a bodyguard of twenty Europeans, who accompanied him when he went out. He had an English secretary called Mr. Bashpool. His table was lavish; forty covers were laid for dinner daily; it was calculated that he spent every year on wine alone fourteen thousand crowns. He gave audience like the king, everyone, except the French noblemen of the embassy, having to crawl before him. No check was now exercised by Phra Narai, who was old and afflicted with dropsy. Phaulkon had become dictator.

We must admit that the mandarinate had ground for their suspicions. The posting of the French troops to Bangkok and Mergui was the last provocation. In February and March 1688, as White was sailing home to safety, the crash he had foreseen to be inevitable was rapidly approaching.

It would be outside the scope of my book to attempt a description of the revolution which followed. The object of this part is to inform the reader what eventually happened to White's old friend and patron. The causes of Phaulkon's downfall illuminate White's history and demonstrate how fortunate he was to reach England alive; the narrative of his death shows the frightful dangers from which White escaped.

It is sufficient here to say that Phaulkon's French legions failed him when the call came in May 1688. Des Farges was not competent to meet the emergency. Unsupported against the mandarinate, who had found an energetic leader in a general called Phetraja, and deserted by the allies on whom he counted, Phaulkon was seized and flung into prison.

In the East it is the custom that when a great minister falls he is treated with exaggerated indignity and insult. Manacled heavily in a filthy prison and without food, he is brought forth from time to time to be tortured. The object of this first stage is to force him to reveal his hidden wealth. Phaulkon suffered all this for fourteen days. The Reverend Father Marcel le Blanc, a Jesuit, who was in Ayudhya at the time and wrote a book about the revolution afterwards, states that no one will ever know exactly what Phaulkon endured, because he was confined in a prison within the palace enclosure. The Father was told by some that the soles of his feet were burnt off to prevent his escaping, that his head was pressed in a vice and that he was flogged till his flesh was in ribbons. There is no doubt that terrible cruelties were practised upon him. But if, said the Father, it was uncertain what were the precise torments which he suffered in prison, the manner of his death was generally known.

On 5th June 1688, after they had found his valuables, he Was formally condemned to death for having introduced French troops into Siam with a view to a *coup d' état*. At nightfall his executioners placed him on an elephant and took him to a lonely jungle outside the city. It was remarked by those who saw him pass that though his face was pale sad drawn, as from the prolonged sufferings he had undergone, his eyes were lit up and the voice in which he repeated the prayers for the dying was firm. He had a gentle tranquil air as he went by, without a sign of fear or despair.

On arrival at the place of execution, he dismounted from the elephant and is said to have handed over to the mandarin in charge of the execution a crucifix, which the Pope had sent him, asking that it be given to his little son. He then prayed for a time, protesting at the close that he was not guilty of any crime against the state; his object had always been the greater glory of Siam. He ended with a plea for his wife and children, that they might at least have life and liberty. Then making the sign of the cross, he abandoned himself to the executioners, still in ignorance of what kind of death was awaiting him. One of them struck him a backhanded blow with a sword in the middle of the body. He fell on his face and they hacked him to pieces. He was only forty years of age.

Had White been at Ayudhya at the time as Phaulkon's right-hand man—and we know he might very well have been there—he would certainly have shared his master's fate or at least have suffered like Mr. Bashpool, the secretary. That unfortunate man was arrested and confined in prison for years with a plank round his neck, being taken out from time to rime to be tortured and forced to disclose the names of rich men supposed to have hidden wealth,

It is interesting to note that Phaulkon did not die in the belief that White had intended to surrender Mergui to the Company. Before his death, some of the truth came out, for he discovered that the report from the mandarins at Mergui was a fabrication. The Viceroy was summoned to Ayudhya and there tortured with hot irons in an attempt to arrive at the true story. Cropley was so strongly suspected of complicity in the massacre that he was seized and imprisoned at Louvo. His subsequent fate is unknown.

With Phaulkon's execution the mandarins under Phra Phetraja proceeded to make a clean sweep. They imprisoned everybody, they tortured everybody; French missionaries, French gentlemen, the English, all foreigners were treated with the greatest cruelty, except the Dutch, who, there is reason to think, surreptitiously helped the mandarins from the first. Princes of the blood were executed; the king died, either from his disease or by a hidden hand. Des Farges was beleaguered at Bangkok and Debrüan at Mergui. Against a large army of Siamese, Chinese and Malays, des Farges held out until they let him take ship for France; Debrüan made a sortie, slid down the hill at Mergui on a wet day, losing many men, seized and embarked on the *Dorothy* after a rearguard action and cleared the port with the survivors.

Like all successful palace revolutionaries, the mandarins terminated the dynasty and enthroned their own leader. Not until they had put the country back into the position it occupied before Phaulkon's rise to power did they rest. Trade with Europe except through the Dutch was at an end. The Mahomedans resumed their position at Mergui. We must admit that according to their lights the Siamese achieved what they had set out to do, which was to keep the exploitation of their country to themselves.

There is one last touch before we leave Siam—the hill for £65,000 which Weltden had sent up from Mergui. Eventually Phra Phetraja, the new king, when reminded of that account, replied with pretty sarcasm that he advised the Company to collect the sum from the estates of Phaulkon and White, which he understood were in England, as both those persons had acquired their wealth by robbing the Siamese, This king must be given credit for an act of clemency. He spared the life of the Lady Phaulkon. After she had been tortured, robbed of all she possessed, and imprisoned, she was liberated and appointed controller of the royal confectionery, in the best tradition of the oriental kaleidoscope.

XLVI. WHITE IN LONDON

We have seen that White left Pondicherry on 20th January 1688. In those times a voyage home occupied about eight months. He cannot have reached England much before October 1st, when William of Orange was heading for Torbay. The news he received on landing will have seemed both welcome and strangely familiar. It was familiar because it seemed to be the history of Siam all over again. King James, having surrounded himself with advisers who were either in the pay of Louis XIV or, as

Catholics, strongly pro-French, had threatened with their support to subvert the country's religion and independence. The Whig lords, corresponding to the Siamese mandarinate, seeing that all they valued was in jeopardy, had conspired to overthrow him and place their man, William of Orange, on the throne.

It is true that White had not the latest news from Siam; but, as he had clearly foreseen what was to happen in that country, he must now have found himself watching an analogous situation. There was some resemblance, even in details, between the Siamese and the English revolutions. Just as Phra Narai had imported Catholic troops from France, posting them at Bangkok to overawe the capital, so King James had brought over Catholic troops from Ireland which, encamped at Hounslow, threatened London. The flight of James in November, his deposition and the coronation of a man who had no blood relationship with the royal house, were events which may well have made White eventually reflect that after all there was not much essential difference between politics in East and West.

The news which greeted White on his arrival was also welcome, for the revolution represented the triumph of Whig principles and of those men who had always opposed royal monopolies, the greatest of which was the East India Company. The day of the free traders had dawned at last. They had never admitted that the Stuarts were acting within their rights, when they had granted monopoly charters to the Company; they believed that Judge Jeffreys's judgment had been given to please the crown; and they had continued to trade in the East. With James II, the greatest supporter of the Company, in flight; with Jeffreys, its legal champion, dragged disguised as a common seaman from an alehouse in Wapping and thrown into the Tower; with every tradesman rejoicing at the extinction of despotic authority; the influence of the Company in London fell very low. Its humiliation by the

Mogul was represented, not as a blow to the prestige of the English nation, but as proving that the management of the India trade was in the hands of incompetent persons. As for the Siamese war, people did not know what it was all about, but there was a shrewd suspicion, which was partly justified, that the councils in India had been more moved by considerations of private trade than by any advantage to commerce in general. The massacre at Mergui was also thrown in their teeth.

As soon as White had seen his daughters, Susan and Mary, who were now girls of twelve and ten years of age, he discussed his situation with George, his brother. Legal advice was taken and the opinion expressed that, no matter what despatches were received from Madras, the Court of Directors in London would never proceed against him at so inopportune a moment. In the then state of public feeling they could not secure a verdict in their favour. There was, in point of fact, no flagrant matter upon which to found an indictment They could not prove piracy—his papers were too sound for that, There was no treason—he had obeyed the late king's order, and even if there had been, no one was going to be prosecuted now for treason against James. A charge of interloping was out of the question at the moment. As for the ship *Resolution*, if they claimed it was their prize, they would have to prove that it belonged to the King of Siam. That could not be proved in London. In short, counsel held that White was safe.

Public opinion was so very much against the East India Company that many merchants felt that now was the time for another test case on the question whether a subject of His Majesty had an inherent right to trade freely in any part of the world. As the law had been interpreted by Jeffreys, he had not that right in areas outside the realm, in which the king had granted under his prerogative a monopoly charter to a joint-stock company. White decided to test the validity of that ruling by petitioning the House of Commons, in which there was a Whig majority, to find that the East India Company's seizure of his goods on the *Derrea Dowlat* and of his ship the *Satisfaction* with her cargo had no warrant at law. The House of Commons was selected because, had he gone to the courts, they would have been bound by Jefreys's ruling, while the legislature had the power of clearing the point by a statutory declaration. White's decision to take up again at this favourable conjuncture a legal point of the greatest interest to merchants in London and Bristol must have made him a popular figure. For himself, if he won, not only might he expect heavy damages and a most satisfying revenge upon Yale, but there was the chance of becoming one of the leading people in the city, a man who had rendered an eminent service to the mercantile community.

His legal advisers accordingly drew up his petition, a copy of which is preserved in the Record Office. It may be studied in Anderson's invaluable book. For those who know White's true history, this document is amusing enough in parts. It begins by a sketch of his life, how he went out to India in 1675 as mate on the East Indiaman *Loyal Subject*, joined the establishment at Madras, visited Ayudhya, where his brother lived, and, on the King of Siam asking for a pilot for one of his ships plying between Masulipatam and Mergui, was recommended for that appointment by the Company itself. It continues with a note on Phaulkon's rise to power in Siam and on his own elevation to the Shāhbandarship of Mergui, how Madras congratulated him upon his promotion, how he promised to advance both the public interest of the Company and the private trade of its members and how he carried out that promise. It then gives his version of the Golconda war, namely that at the command of the King of Siam he was ordered to fit out ships against that country. It alleges, as indeed was the case, that the Company at first accommodated him with ammunition and men, as they too had found the

King of Golconda's officials rapacious and dishonest. He took the greatest care, it is argued, in the course of this war not to damage the Company or those under its protection and if, as sometimes unavoidably happened, a Company ship was taken, it was immediately discharged on producing English passports.

The petition then pretended that suddenly, in April 1687, without any warning of a change of front, the Company's ships of war seized the King of Siam's frigate, the *Revenge*, and the sloop *Mary*. Private advices were received to the effect that the Company had ordered their captains to make those seizures without the declaration of formal war.

The petition then proceeds to state, what has no shadow of truth, that the King of Siam appointed White to proceed to England as his Ambassador Extraordinary to put the Siamese case against the high-handed action of Madras before King James II; that he was to sail on the *Resolution*, his own property, with presents from the King of Siam; and that when he was on the point of embarking, the presents being on the way, the *Curtana* suddenly appeared in the harbour of Mergui,

The reader will admire the agility of this argument. The House of Commons would have no way of determining whether the King of Siam had ever contemplated such an embassy except from such papers as White himself might submit.

White then alleges that the arrival of Captain Weltden not only prevented his proceeding to England as Siamese ambassador, 'but occasioned the Massacre of about 60 of my Country Men on the Place; I only by a Miracle of Mercy being left to bring the sad account of that bloudy Tragedy.'

The petition thereafter comes to the point. White introduces it by speaking of 'that unhappy Period when those heavy Calamities began to fall upon me, which have brought me to ruin and desolation.' He had to flee from Mergui in an empty ship, leaving effects to the value of £21,877 on shore.

His private ventures afloat were seized upon by the Company's men-of-war. Though no war had been declared with Siam, the Siamese sloop *Mary* with £400 worth of copper belonging to him was taken. They had no colour of right to his property in such circumstances. The *Derrea Dowlat*, a Siamese merchantman, with property to the value of £1,838 on board belonging to him, was also seized. Least excusable of all, his own ship, the *Satisfaction*, with a cargo upon which he expected a gross return of £15,800, had been captured and all his goods confiscated on the ground that he had been granted no permission to trade by the East India Company, That plea, said White, was ridiculous, When trading backwards and forwards between Mergui and Madras in the first years of his Shāhbandarship, carrying his own cargoes and the private ventures of the Madras establishment, there had never been any talk of passes; the gentlemen then had only been too delighted to make use of his ships for the convenience of transporting their own goods for the coast trade. But when it suited their convenience, they invoked their alleged power to prevent anyone trading in the East except themselves and took possession of his private property. Was the House of Commons ready to endorse the delegation of such despotic power to a Company in the face of the Common Law of England and the statutory liberties of her people? He claimed £40,000 damages.

Now the judicious reader will perceive that there is one point, and one point only, in this petition. Was White within the law of England when he traded without the East India Company's permission? That was the sole point because, when the seizures were made, no declared state of war existed between the Company and Siam, and it could not be argued that he, an English subject, was trading with the enemy.

In this manner the case raised the old question of Free Trade versus Monopoly Trade.

The petition was presented to the House of Commons on 18th April 1689, when it was referred to a committee, which had already been appointed to go into the whole matter of the East India Company and the renewal of its charter, with the examination of other complaints which had been made against it. White supported his petition with a document called *A True Accompt of the Passages at Mergen*. This document has been lost, but it was, beyond question, a digest of his Mer gui papers in a more detailed form than was possible in the petition.

A week later a totally unexpected event occurred. White suddenly died at Bath. There is no information on record as to the cause of his death. It may be that he had never completely rid himself of the malaria, which he contracted in 1686 when crossing the forest between Tenasserim and Ayudhya or that after twelve years' continuous residence in the tropics the rigours of an English winter were too much for him. That it was a particularly cold winter we know, for Evelyn notes under the date 7th January 1689, 'A long frost and deepe snow; the Thames almost frozen over.' Whatever was the reason, he was unfortunate in enjoying only for six months the fruits of his depredations.

With his death the prosecution of his case remained in the hands of his executors, George White and Francis Heath.

In due course the East India Company submitted an answer to White's petition. This document was supported by the Davenport Papers with which we are now so familiar. Davenport had succeeded in convincing Yale and the council of Madras that his account of White at work in Mergui and of Weltden's behaviour was true. The council adopted this as their official view of the whole matter and that view was in turn accepted by the Court of Directors in London. The answer itself was a summary of the main allegations contained in the Davenport Papers.

It began by the statement that White was 'a very ill man

and a great Interloper and a great Enemy of this Kingdom in general'. At his door, not at the Company's, must be laid the blame for the massacre at Mergui. This was going beyond Davenport but, as it was unsupported by evidence, it may be taken as a legal *tu quoque*. The document then proceeded to cite the more disreputable incidents in White's conduct of affairs at Mergui, expressing astonishment and indignation that such a person should have the effrontery to go to the House of Commons as an upholder of the rights and liberties of Englishmen. As his practice had been to make little or no distinction between the property of his master, the King of Siam, and his own, it was impossible to say to which of them belonged the cargoes on the *Derrea Dowlat* and the *Satisfaction*. He was a man who had not hesitated to forge a commission authorizing him to go to war with Golconda; he had made slaves of Indians living under the Company's protection at Madras; he had inflicted damages estimated at £30,000; he had employed English deserters to further him in his lawless and injurious Attempts'. So ill a man was he, that consorting with Papists and Heathens he had attempted to destroy the regulated English interest in India.

The answer then pointed out that the Company, damaged and provoked though it was, had confined itself to legal remedies of a mild type. The Dutch Company had the power (and exercised it) to hang interlopers, while the English Company, dealing with an arch-interloper like White, had only resorted to confiscation. In doing that, they were acting strictly within their powers granted by charter.

If they were not to take action of the kind, how were they going to continue in business? They had enormous overhead expenses to meet. Their establishment alone cost them £200,000 a year. If interlopers, besides poaching on the trade, were to be let conspire with oriental princes against the Company, inducing these to maltreat the Company's servants or alternatively, corrupt them with money and lucrative employment; if they were allowed to carry confusion into settled commerce and turn filibuster, then honest merchants would have to look elsewhere for their rightful profits. The India trade would be dead.

More arguments of this kind were advanced, arguments which had been used over the course of the century to justify the privileged position of the Ease India Company, and which were perfectly sound, except that they neglected to take account of the chief characteristic of the English people, the importance they attach to individual liberty.

So much for the Company's answer. Here, again, the judicious reader will observe that there was but one point. Though White was attacked to shake his credit and alienate the sympathies of members of Parliament, the Company was chiefly preoccupied to give grounds for the retention and renewal of its chartered rights, which were now felt to be threatened by the new régime.

Such was the case upon which the committee of the House Was asked to report. To find for White, they would be obliged to advise the Commons that the charter upon which the Company depended for their seizure of his property was repugnant to law. If they found for the Company and held that the charter was good, there would be an outcry, for the abuse of the royal prerogative, which gave validity to the charter, had been the chief cause of the revolution.

As the decision was likely to be of great importance to the future of English trade in the East, any rapid decision was to be deprecated, It was desirable to watch how public opinion would develop. The East India Company was not without following. No action was therefore taken to report at once, Months passed. A war of pamphlets began. Each side bombarded the other in the scurrilous style of the century. During this exchange, George White published an attack upon Davenport, whose papers on Mergui must have been read by those interested in the case, For a short time the latter became one of the best-known names in London, one side shouting that he was a perjured villain, the other maintaining that his narrative was convincing and well written. This is the last we heat of him. No doubt the Company rewarded him by promotion. He was a very able man.

But the times were in favour of the opponents of monopoly trading. The set against the Company increased. It seems that about December 1690 the Court of Directors thought it safer to settle with George White out of court. What the terms were are not known, but no doubt the trustees were able to add some more thousands to Samuel White's estate.

The agitation against chartered trading, of which White's petition was a part, continued unabated. When, by 1694, there was no longer any doubt about public opinion, the Commons passed a resolution 'that all subjects of England have equal right to trade in the East Indies, unless prohibited by Act of Parliament'. Had White's petition been still outstanding, this statutory declaration might have given him authority to recover the £40,000 he claimed, but I think it unlikely that it bad retrospective effect At all events it would have thrown over him a mantle of respectability. He would have appeared to many a much wronged man. His robberies and his filibustering, his cheating and his embezzlements, would have been condoned. As a rich country gentleman he might have stood for Parliament. He might have founded a great family. That these speculations are not without some warrant is shown by the history of Diamond Pitt, as great an interloper as White, called by Hedges 'no better than a Pyrott, a fellow of haughty, huffing, daring temper', who became an M. P., succeeded Yale at Madras and was the grandfather of Lord Chatham.

One last paragraph is required to round off this matter of monopoly versus free trade in India and bring out the underlying truth. With the declaration that the trade was open, the old interlopers founded a rival Company. The result was precisely what had always been contended by the old Company —confusion, a divided policy toward oriental princes, danger from European competitors, a fall in prices and loss of money. Experience proved Sir Josiah Childe right; trade in India could only successfully be carried on in the circumstances of that period by one Company, under one management and with one policy, These hard facts were too strong for the new Company, and in 1708 it became fused with the old Company under the name of the United East India Company. This arrangement worked well and satisfied the London and Bristol merchants, thereby demonstrating that the real objection to the old Company had lain in the small number of Its shareholders.

XLVII. THE LAST OF WELTDEN

There have been very heavy casualties in this book, Besides the death of the two great protagonists, Phaulkon and White, whose fortunes were interwoven in a manner reminiscent of classical drama, we have lost Burnaby and Leslie, butchered after supper at Mergui, Coates despatched in the mud of the Menam by the drug-maddened Macassars and Phra Narai mysteriously departing this life within the recesses of his Forbidden City. Many others of lesser note, too, have gone the way of all flesh, poor Mrs. White, disgruntled Mason, Cropley, the pirate, though here we pause in doubt, Udall, resurrected twice, and Olindo driving by, a mangled corpse, on the ebb. If we except the common crowd, who gave background to the story—and many of them too have become casualties—only Davenport and Weltden are left on our hands.

It is a matter of the keenest disappointment to me that I cannot add to the names of these two that of Mary Leslie, The relegation, for want of historical data, of her after-fate to a vague footnote leaves unanswered romantic surmises. Was she White's mistress, what did she think of him when he left her unprotected and in danger at Mergui, did she miss him or her murdered husband most, what sort of a chequered life was hers thereafter?—these are all questions which, if I could answer them, would add enormously to the appeal of this book. I disentangle myself from them with regret, hoping that some day a novelist or film producer will take the matter in hand.

Reflecting on Davenport, I see that my position is the Same. In his case also the data have given out. I do not know what happened to him, though I argue that a man, so collected and methodical, is unlikely to have continued to meet vicissitudes at all comparable to his sojourn with White, I can see him settling to the routine of his profession and when I pass the Horse Guards and remember that a map by him of the Hugh river reposes there, I feel that that is the sort of fame he would have chosen. But if thwarted in his regard, I am in a position to round off this book with a surprising tale about his brother actor, Anthony Weltden.

Yale, as I have said, was very angry when White got away, The Mergui affair had certainly been unfortunate from first to last. But there was no way of retrieving the situation and the best course was to cut expenses. At an early consultation it was decided to discharge the *Curtana* from her contract to serve the Company, Captain Weltden was told that he was free to take her anywhere he liked. They were not prepared to pay him or for his ship any more. He was given a pass to trade in the bay, The idea of a court-martial was abandoned, though Weltden was informed that when he returned to England the

Court of Directors would certainly hold an inquiry before settling accounts with him and the firm who owned the ship.

For two years—from January 1688 to December 1689—Weltden hacked round the East in the *Curtana*. He was associated for a short time with so distinguished a navigator as Dampier, but his adventures, which are unrecorded, were probably no more than what might have befallen any merchant captain of that date engaged in the coast trade. He made a little money and selling the *Curtana* to an Indian subject of the Mogul, he returned home to take up the position, to which he Was born, of country gentleman. He purchased an estate at Wellen in Lincolnshire, marrying, bringing up a family and hunting like all his equals. His differences with the Court of Directors were eventually composed. Mergui and the extraordinary drama there, in which he had taken the part of dupe, receded into the mist.

Twenty years passed. His eldest son grew up. He himself was now a man of over fifty. Suddenly he was seized with an unaccountable nostalgia to revisit the seas where as a young man he had commanded the *Curtana*. In the autumn of 1709 he heard that the Court of Directors had decided to depart from their usual practice of appointment by rotation from the council to the Governorship of Fort William in Bengal. A Mr. Sheldon, the second of council, was due to get the post, but for some reason the directors wanted an outsider. Captain Weltden, as he still called himself, wrote in and applied. His name came up before the board on November 11th; voting was by balls in a box; it was found that he had the majority of balls.

As governor-elect of Fort William in Calcutta he left England on 7th February 1710. He cook his family with him, Mrs. Weltden, his sister, his son and daughter, two of the maids and a footman. Though he had promised Davenport in December 1687 never to touch liquor again, in his luggage were ten hogsheads of wine and sixteen chests of bottled beers, etc. One of the ladies had a harpsichord, for by 1710 even the small county families were getting sophisticated, He took also £4,000 in cash, for he intended to do some business.

In this posture, as they used to say in the good old days when White was there, the family in July reached the great bay, the main of the Mergui shore well to the eastward, and came to the Hugli, up which they were piloted by one of Davenport's successors, but by means of his chart. The usual crowd of notabilities were on the wharf at Calcutta. Weltden was received by them with the same courtesy with which White had received him on Mergui wharf twenty-three years before and the same number organs were fired, as he left the ship. It was all rather similar, but there was going to be one big difference. He had made nothing out of the Mergui expedition. That must not happen again.

He got to work at once. 'His term of office,' wrote Hamilton soon afterwards, 'was very short, but he took as short a way to be enriched by it.' His method was the well-worn device of allowing it to be known that he expected to be paid for every grant or concession through his wife or daughter, who interviewed and bargained with the applicants. That the women demanded large sums is made evident by an entry in the court minutes of 19th December 1711, where reference is made to a 50,000 rupee bribe he had taken from an Indian called Jonardaun Seat.

But he was to be duped again, for four months after he left England, when he was just entering that bay, which had been so unpropitious to him, the Court of Directors decided without recording any reasons that they had made a mistake in appointing him governor. They revoked their order and elected Mr. Sheldon instead. The letter conveying these instructions reached Calcutta on 4th March 1711, seven months and a half after he had taken over charge. He had the mortification of having to hand over to one of his council, Mr.

Sheldon being dead, and sailed for England with only a fraction of the fortune he had expected to make. His last trip east was no more successful than his first, and if he left Mergui in panic, Ms departure from Calcutta was hardly more dignified, As a last blow, he was captured by the French on his way home arid lost what money he had made, the Company voting him, when he eventually reached England, only a miserable £1,200 compensation. He returned to Wellen and with the bottle, and its attendant, the gout, passed the rest of his days.

So much for the persons of this narrative. But I am forgetting—there is still one character left, Mergui itself. What happened there in the end? Has it had a history since? In a sense, it has had a history, for in 1765 the Burmese conqueror, Alauagpaya, descended upon it, slaughtered its inhabitants and incorporated it in Burma; and in 1824 the English frigates arrived again, this time to take and keep it. But in the sense of an important or dramatic history, it has had none. its severance from Siam ruined it commercially. It became and has remained a little coast port. The ordinary people there are the same as ever they were; there is plenty to eat and drink in that little paradise; but no more do personages from overseas pass through it and no one like White has sat on the ridge.

APPENDIX I. THE DAVENPORT
PAPERS

What I here call the Davenport Papers consist of two primed pamphlets contained in a volume catalogued in the India Office Library as 'E.I.C. Charters and Pamphlets. M.S.S. Eur, D.300.' The titles of the two pamphlets are:

(1) *'An Historical Abstract of Mr. Samuel White, in his Shabander Ship of Tenassery and Mergen, during Francis Davenports stay with him, in Quality as Secretary: Collected out of the said Davenports own Private Memoirs: for the clearer Discovery of whatsoever may have Relation to the Right Honourable English East India Company themselves, or others our Country Men in India, through his proceedings, in pretence of his Ministration of that Publick Office Under the King of Syam.'*

There are thirty-six large pages of this 'Abstract'. It covers the period from the arrival of Francis Davenport at Mergui in March 1686 to the appearance in that port of the frigate *Curtana* in June 1687, It is in diary form, and purports to have been written by Davenport from day to day. The above tide was given to it by the East India Company when they printed it as one of the papers supporting their case against White.

(2) *'A True and impartial Narrative of Captain Anthony Weltden, Commander of the "Curtana" Frigate; his Management of affairs in his late Mergen expedition, so far as it came under the Cognizance of the Subscribers: Divided into the subsequent several articles, to the end that both the matter may be related in an unintermitted Series, as it past or was acted, and also each respective Subscriber may Attest the Truth of those particular distinct Articles, which according to their best knowledge, and with clear Consciences, they are ready to maintain upon their Oaths, when Lawfully thereunto required.'*

This 'Narrative' of ten pages and thirty-seven articles,

carries the story from the arrival of the *Curtana* to Christmas Eve 1687, when White was dropped at Armagaon Sand. Internal evidence of style shows beyond question that it was also written by Francis Davenport. Though composed partly in diary form, as if founded on a diary, it differs from the previous 'Abstract' in its division into articles.

The first paper is signed by Davenport alone, while the second is signed, in addition, by Joseph Weld, second mate, and Thomas Johnson, boatswain, of the *Curtana* as well as by three others, probably seamen of that vessel, namely Robert Reay, Edward Gray and Robert Mansell. Each of these persons testify that certain articles are within their particular knowledge as eye-witnesses. The reason for constructing the 'Narrative' in this consecutive manner, in lieu of the usual method of a separate testimony by each person, is to give the events described an uninterrupted sequence, thus making them easier to follow.

These two Papers both drawn, largely verbatim, from Davenport's private diaries, were composed in Madras during 1688, immediately after the transactions they describe took place. The 'Narrative' was signed on January 30th by the above-mentioned parties, who made oath before Elihu Yale, President of the council of Madras, of the truth of all the articles. The 'Abstract' was signed by Davenport on February 21st, he taking a similar oath. Though these Papers were used in 1689 by the Company to document their defence before the House of Commons in the case of *Samuel White* v. *The East India Company,* in the first instance they were not written for that purpose. They owed their origin, in my opinion, to Davenport's desire to clear himself of the imputation of having abetted White and to a similar desire of certain persons on the *Curtana* to dissociate themselves from Captain Weltden. They constituted part of Yale's inquiry into the affair of the Mergui massacre.

The only historian who has made use of these papers, to

my knowledge, is John Anderson, who published in 1890 a book called *English Intercourse with Siam in the Seventeenth Century*. The scheme of Anderson's scholarly work was such that he could not find room for a full exploitation of this material, Samuel White is not his central figure, and receives in consequence a limited attention. A perusal of his work provides the reader with only a hint of what the Papers contain nor does it give sufficiently detailed information to permit of a full judgment upon White.

In Anderson's view the Davenport Papers, where they denounce White's malpractices, are not wholly to be trusted. But Anderson was not free from bias against Davenport, for, as a free-trader, his sympathies were with White against the monopoly system of the East India Company, and he was shocked by Davenport 's betrayal of White's secrets to that Company. This feeling for White led him to attach great importance to the pamphlet by White's brother, George, which was published in 1689 to rebut the Davenport Papers, and wherein an effort was made to discredit the truth of their contents by blackening the character of their author. These *Reflections*, as George White called his diatribe, are couched in the style of other scurrilous pamphlets of the seventeenth century and substitute for any reasoned refutation of what Davenport had written a frantic abuse of Davenport himself, He is termed a 'treacherous Cheating Villain' and a 'Profligate Scandalous Person' and the like. Several witnesses were produced to testify to his iniquities, but some of them were either White's friends, like Mr. Heath, his agent, or Mr. Smith, the mate of his ship, or were persons of little weight and whose testimony might have been, but was not, supported by official documents. Moreover, though some of these witnesses had a full personal knowledge of all the events described by Davenport, not one of them attempted to say in what particular he lied. Their case against his veracity rests entirely upon allegations against his character. But a dispassionate perusal of George White's 'Reflections' is their surest refutation in Davenport's favour, for, in truth, they are nonsensical. I have read other pamphlets in the India Office, wherein the stupidity of George White's vociferous publication is demonstrated. Of these, that published the same year by Nathaniel Tench, on the Court of Directors of the East India Company, is very sound. He points out with great truth that the nature of the Davenport Papers is such that they could not have been forged. It would be impossible, he says, to fabricate so long a narrative, dealing in detail with so many people, without some of those people being able to prove false statements; all the substantial parts of the second paper. which supports and dovetails into the first, are attested by five witnesses whose veracity has not been impugned; there is such a vividness of description, such a coherence in a maze of unusual facts, that both narratives are entirely convincing.

These arguments of Mr. Tench appear to me conclusive, He might have added that where, as is often the case, it is possible to check the Papers against outside authorities, their fidelity is confirmed.

Part II of this book is almost entirely founded upon the Papers. The transcriptions of conversations are taken verbatim from the original, except that in some cases indirect has been turned into direct speech. The Papers in their entirety are obscure and tedious in places, but I think that those extracts, which I have given, show that Davenport possessed a power of style and characterization quite unusual among adventurers over sea.

APPENDIX II. OTHER AUTHORITIES

After the Davenport Papers I found the most essential and useful authority for the period to be a publication of the council of the Vajirañana National Library, Bangkok, called *Records and Relations between Siam and Foreign Countries in the Seventeenth Century*, 1921, 5 vols, It is a printed collection of letters and reports, preserved in MS. in the India office, which were written chiefly by agents of the East India Company in India or Siam and by the directors in London.

John Anderson's *English Intercourse with Siam in the Seventeenth Century*, published in 1890, has almost the value of a collection of original documents for, although it is a history, it contains many verbatim transcriptions, such as Samuel White's petition to Parliament, his letter about the Macassar rising, the Madapollam Diary of 1685, which gives an account of Captain Coates's depredations, and Strangh's Diary, together with a large number of other letters and papers. As a book of reference it is invaluable.

Another book of great worth is L. Lanier's *Étude Historique sur les Relations de la France et du Royaume de Siam de 1662 à 1703*, published in 1883. This work is founded on a masterly study of unpublished papers in the Ministry of Marine in Paris, from which it largely quotes. It provided me with a sound basis upon which to construct that part of my book which deals with Phaulkon, As I have stated in the text, I have not gone further into the history of Phaulkon than was necessary to illuminate White's career. It remains for some future historian to give the world a definitive picture of that extraordinary man.

Besides the above three publications I have read and quoted from the following early writers and papers:

John Fryer, *A New Account of East India and Persia*. (1672–1681). Edited by the Hakluyt Society in 1919.
Dampier, *A New Voyage Round the World*. 1690.

Thomas Bowrey, *Countries Round the Bay of Bengal.* (1669–1679). Edited by the Hakluyt Society in 1905.

Alexander Hamilton, *A New Account of the East Indies.* 1727.

William Hedges, *Diary.* Edited by the Hakluyt Society, 1888.

Duarte Barbosa, The Book of. Edited by the Hakluyt Society, 1921.

Caron and Schouten, *A True Description of the Mighty Kingdams of Japan and Siam.* 1636. Edited by C.R.Boxer, 1935. A most valuable book.

Kämpfer, *History of Japan*, vol.i. 1728.

John Struys, *The Perrillous and most Unhappy Voyages of*, in the 1683 English edition.

Royal Charters and Pamphlets preserved in the India Office.

Anonymous, *A Full and True Relation of the Great and Wonderful Revolution which hapend lately in the Kingdom of Siam.* 1690: given on p. 95 of Thomas Osborne's *Collection of Travels* in the library of the Earl of Oxford, published in 1745.

de La Loubère, *Du Royaume de Siam.* Paris, 1691.

Père Tachard, *Voyage de Siam des Pères Jésuites.* Paris, 1688.

Père Tachard, *Second Voyage.* Paris, 1689.

de Chaumont, *Relation de l' Ambassade de M. le Chevalier de Chaumont à la cour du Roy de Siam.* Paris, 1687.

Nicolas Gervaise, *Histoire naturelle et politique du Royaume de Siam.* 1684, (Seen in a recent Bangkok edition, trans.).

Père Marcel le Blanc, *Histoire de la Revolution du Roiaume de Siam.* Paris,1693.

Le Père d'Orléans, *Histoire de M. Constance*, Tours, 1690.

de Bourges, *Relation du Voyage de Mons: de Béryte, Vicaire Apostolique.* 1683.

L'Abbé de Choisy, *Journal du Voyage de Siam.* 1687.

Later writers consulted include:

Mgr. Pallegoix, *Description du Royaume Tai ou Siam.* Paris, 1854.

Turpin. *Royaume de Siam.* Paris, 1771.

H. D. Love, *Vestiges of Old Madras.* 1913.

Sir William Hunter, *History of British India*, 1899.

Sir William Foster, *John Company*. 1926.

S. A. Khan, *The East India Trade in the Seventeenth Century*. 1923.

D. G. E. Hall, *Early English Intercourse with Burma*. 1928.

W. A. R. Wood, *History of Siam*. 1926.

H. G. Quaritch Wales, *Ancient Government and Administration of Siam*. 1934.

R. S. le May, *Coinage of Siam*. Siam Society, 1932.

J.S.Furnivall, 'Samuel White', *Journal of the Burma Research Society*, vol. 7, part 3.

C. R.Wilson, *The Early Annals of the English in Bengal* 1900.

APPENDIX III. NOTES

PART ONE

Where I quote from books, I give sufficient infor formation in the text to enable the reader to find in Appendix II the full ride of the work. Where I cite letters, the reader may assume that if he consults *Records and Relations* under the date shown he will generally be able to find the reference. If a letter is not included in *Records and Relations* I give its separate source.

White s birthplace (p. 18): This may have been Bristol or some place in its vicinity. It cannot have been Bath, since in the burials register of Bath Abbey he is described as a stranger.

White's date of birth (p. 18): As we know that in 1675 he went east as a 'young mate' [Masulipatam Diary] he cannot have been more than twenty-five years old in that year. He may have been less; it is quite possible that he was not more than twenty-two. Yale, to cite one case, was appointed to the Company at twenty-two.

Mary Povey (p. 18): The source here is the Masulipatam Diary, It is not quite clear whether Mary Povey travelled out from England with Samuel White or whether she was already at Masulipatam and went thence to Madras with him. I have adopted what I think is the more likely story.

Company Finance (p. 23): The figures I give about the East India Company stock and profits are taken from Shafaad Ahmed Khan's *East India Trade in the Seventeenth Century*, The book is full of detailed information of the kind. One of the arguments which the author seeks to substantiate is that trade and security, not conquests was the Company's aim in the seventeenth century. He will not allow that Sir Josiah Childe, the President of the Court of Directors in London, even *thought* of conquest, and urges that his famous dictum about founding a dominion in India, which is often quoted from one of his despatches, cannot bear the modern meaning of the words. As I have pointed out later in this book, Childe's orders to Madras to take Mergui and found a settlement there show that he did entertain a specific idea of dominion of a sort. But in 1675, when White arrived in India, it may be taken that trade and security were the sole aims of the Company.

Interloper (p. 25): In saying that an English merchant, unless he was a stockholder in the East India Company, could not trade anywhere in Indian or Far Eastern waters, I have stated the broad fact. It appears, however, that there was a system of passes, which were issued by the Company to certain free merchants, and which gave them authority to trade. The method and extent of the issue of such passes remains to be worked out. There is evidence to show that interlopers who helped the factors in their private trade received passes.

Salons (p. 33): The sea gypsies of the Mergui archipelago are an interesting race, about whom much has been written.

In appearance they are strong, dark, with brutal features which belie their timid character. They have a language of their own. Some of them live in Mergui town in circumstances of unnecessary squalor. Those who keep to their boats remain excellent seamen. They seem to be one of those races which cannot fit themselves into the modern world. But the psychological explanation of vagabondage, on land or sea, remains in debate.

Mahomedans (p. 39): The Indian Mahomedans who settled in Mergui to develop trade across the bay were a class of people called Chulias. They were never much liked. The Siamese of Siam proper were not the only people who detested them. About the year of White's arrival in the East the inhabitants of Junkceylon rose against their governor, who was a Chulia, killing him and many of his sect. Bowrey, who was lying off the island at the time, was delighted when he heard of their massacre.

The Overland Route (p. 41): It has been argued by some writers that the overland route from Mergui to Ayudhya was connected with the fact that a transcontinental route from the Mediterranean ended at Masulipatam. That, of course, is the case, Some people travelled from Rome to Ayudhya via Persia, Surat, Masulipatam and Mergui. Goods also went by that route. But the Mergui-Ayudhya trade did not hinge entirely upon the transcontinental road. As my narrative shows, a great part of the trade was direct by ship to Persia and the Red Sea.

In a paper called 'Fresh light on the route taken by export porcelains from China to India and the Near East during the Ming period', read by me before the Oriental Ceramic Society on 9th October 1935, I have gone very fully into the age and significance of the Mergui-Ayudhya cut. The paper is published in the *Transactions of the Oriental Ceramic Society*, vol. 13.

Phaulkon's appearance (p. 50): My sketch is founded closely on that given by Père Marcel de Blanc on p. 20 of his *Histoire de la Revolution du Roiaume de Siam.*

Phaulkon's statement of policy In 1680 (p. 64): The remarks which I suppose Phaulkou to make to the Barcalong in 1680 on the necessities of the situation are, of course, without direct warrant. But that he formulated about that time such a policy is certain enough, Barcalong was as near as the seventeenth century could get to 'Phra-klang'.

The Siamese Administration (p. 66): Those who wish to know more about the Siamese mandarinate to which White was appointed in 1683 should study Dr. Quaritch Wales's *Ancient Government and Administration of Siam*, bearing in mind, however, that White's appointment was a special one and that the ordinary rules hardly applied to him.

Potts (p. 70): No one had a good word for Potts, though they were shocked when Phaulkon had him beaten. That he burnt the factory down was believed by Captain Hamilton, who visited Ayudhya after the revolution and made inquiries, Chapter XV generally is founded on Strangh's Diary, as given in Anderson.

Part Two

The source for everything in Part Two is the Davenport Papers, unless a particular reference is given either here or in the text.

Coates at Madapollam (p. 85): The whole episode is constructed from the Madapollam Diary, given in *extenso* by Anderson, and from Davenport's Abstract. Without the Abstract the Diary is not fully intelligible. The bill of damages at the end can be deduced front the bill ultimately handed to the Siamese government by Weltden (*Records and Relations*, vol. iv, p. 138).

The 'Traja Raja' (p. 96): This affair has plenty of documentary support outside Davenport, There is correspondence in

Records and Relations, and the original petition of the imprisoned merchants is preserved in the India office.

Siamese Money: In the values of the seventeenth century, the following table may be taken as approximately correct.

1 tical	= 2 shillings and 6 pence
1 teal	= 10 shillings
1 cattee	= £10
1 rupee	= 2 shillings and 3 pence
1 pagoda	= 9 shillings

(see le May, *Coinage of Siam*. Siam Society, 1932).

The Macassars (p. 128): White's letter about the Macassar rising is quoted in full by Anderson on p. 289 front a copy preserved in the British Museum. The circumstances of their torture may be compared with a note by Thoreau, in his *Walden*, on the American Indians, 'The Jesuits were quite baulked by those Indians who, being burned at the stake, suggested new modes of torture to their tormentors. Being superior to physical suffering, it sometimes chanced that they were superior to any consolation which the missionaries could offer.'

Prime *Minister* (p. 136): The expression 'Prime Minister' to describe Phaulkon's position is used by White in his petition to Parliament.

The exasperation of Elihu Yale (p. 156): It should be noted that Yale was not President of the Madras council until July 1687. But he was a man of far stronger character than Gyfford, his chief. Davenport never even mentions Gyfford. When there is question what Madras may do, it is always Yale that White is afraid of. The jewel affair had infuriated him, for he was officially called on to explain his conduct in that matter by Gyfford.

The 'startling letter' (p. 158): This letter about the *Traja Raja* merchants had been signed in Madras exactly a year previously, 22nd March 1686 (*Records and Relations*, vol. iv, p. 10). Why delivery had been delayed is unknown.

'*Behind the scence in London and Madras*' (p,183): The source here is the correspondence collected in vols. iii and iv of *Records and Relations*.

Barren (p. 187): That he joined Phaulkon is proved by an entry in Hedges's *Diary* (vol. ii, p. clxxxv, Hakluyt Society edition).

Aurangzebe's Army (p. 190): For the statement that he had 700,000 men under arms see Hunter's *History of British India*, p. 247.

Letter from on board the 'Resolution' dated 24th December 1687 (p. 254): This document is transcribed by Anderson (p. 350) from Inv. Off. Rec, (J.J.C. 13.)

If it is not quite clear why White had not left Weltden before this, a summary of what is recorded in the text will show that, in fact, he left him. at the right moment. We have seen that his first plan was to be gone before Weltden arrived at Mergui. By 14th June 1687 the *Resolution*, loaded with her cargo and provisioned for eighteen months, was ready to start. Weltden appeared on June 23rd. There followed the period of diplomacy in the harbour, June 26th to July 14th. It was impossible for White to leave then, short of forcing his way out, an action which he could never have explained away, no matter how otherwise in order were his papers. The massacre solved the problem of what he should do, for it obliged him and Weltden to leave together. From July 14th to August 31st they sailed in consort among the islands, That was the height of the monsoon and White could not have got out of the Bay of Bengal against the S. W. wind. On September 1st Weltden left him alone at Tenasserim Island and went to Negrais in Burma, promising to be back on October 20th, but not actually returning until November 2nd. White could have made for home before then, for the monsoon is over by October 15th, but he preferred to hang on in the hope of meeting with his merchantmen, the *Satisfaction* and the *Derrea Dowlat*. The two men met again at Achin on November 7th. In that port, where there were several other English ships, White was cleared of the charge of treason (the only dangerous charge), and the moment was approaching when he could take the first convenient opportunity of slipping away. He and Weltden left Achin early in December for the Indian coast, arriving at Madapollam, north of Madras, on December 11th. Why did White go as far as the Indian coast? Surely he was cutting it rather fine? The answer can only be that he had a chance of some exceptionally good business at Pulicat and Pondicherry, which it would have been faint-hearted to throw away. He could assume that the risk of being apprehended in either place was negligible, because Weltden could be relied on to give Yale a report that would keep him quiet for a few days. That White should have taken this risk and sailed right past Madras was entirely consistent with his daring character. He will also have calculated that this course, if his actions were called in question at home, would look more like an innocent man's than to flee from Weltden on the high seas. How right he was in his estimate the result shows.

PART THREE

The Fate, of the 'Pearl' (p. 261); This chapter is founded on Captain Perriman's letter to Madras dated 24th December 1687, in *Records and Relations*, vol. iv, p. 227.

Torture and Death of Phaulkon (p. 264): The curious fact that the French offered Phaulkon asylum in France is to be found in de Chaumont's *Relation Manuscrit* quoted by Lanier on p. 74 of his *Étude Historique*. That Phaulkon had taken the precaution of sending money to England is proved by a letter from Madras to London dated 20th November 1691 (*Records and Relations*, vol.v, p, 135). The description of Phaulkon's house and table is taken from Père Tachard's *Second Voyage*, pp. 195 and 213. For the details of his death I have consulted le Père d'Orléans, Kämpfer and Turpin. Bashpool's fate is related by Captain Hamilton, who met him later.

White In London (p. 271): The unpopularity of the East India Company about this time is evidenced, to cite one authority, by an entry in Evelyn's diary, dated 6th June 1689. 'The East India Company likely to be dissolved by Parliament for many arbitrary actions.'

Davenport's chart of the Hugli (p. 282): That Davenport continued to serve the Company as pilot is shown by the following note on p, 172 of the Hakluyt Society's edition of Thomas Bowrey. 'There exists at the Horse Guards a map No. Z/30/43 entitled the "Mouth of the River Ganges". Its date is 1694 and it was made by the pilot Davenport for Captain William Gyfford of the "Seymour". With the map are some interesting sailing directions for getting out of the Hugli initialled by Davenport.

The last of Weltden (p. 282): This chapter is founded on the researches of Mr. C.R.Wilson, incorporated in his book, *The Early Annals of the English in Bengal.* By the rime of Weltden's appointment, Fort William at Calcutta had displaced Hugli as the headquarters of the Company at the head of the Bay of Bengal, and it had become a charge independent of Madras.

The pertinacious reader may inquire the ultimate fate of Ayudhya. It was burnt to the ground by the Burmese in 1767.

And I have an interesting little item about the *Derrea Dowlat*, the ship which hits been mentioned so often in this narrative, first of all as an elephant ship and then as the merchantman for whose return White was so anxious. At the time of preparing the present edition I received a letter from Mr. R.C.Bainbridge of Bombay in which was enclosed a cutting from *The Times of India*, dated 8th March 1951 stating that the country craft "Daria Daulat"' had arrived from Aden and requesting consignees to present their documents to the shipping agents, on this notice first catching Mr. Bainbridge's eye, he remembered the *Denea Dowlat* of this book. The *Daria Daulnt*, he was told, was a sailing ship of 180 tons capacity. White's ship was probably of similar tonnage and as the difference in the names is to be attributed to the vagaries of seventeenth-century spelling (the words mean 'Wealth of the ocean'), one has the spectacle of a vessel of the same name and type entering Masulipatam on the 19th March 1680 and Bombay on the 8th March 1951. There are some very old ships on eastern runs and the belief that White's ship is still in the coast trade might pass as a permissible fancy, though I do not suggest that anyone should hold it. The truth is that in all parts of the world old names linger on. In 1933 the government launch at Mergui was Called the *Curtana*.

APPENDIX IV.
LETTER FROM WHITE FOUND IN BATH

Siamese White was published in February 1936. In July of that year I received a letter from Mr. Reginald Wright, the Director of the Victoria Art Gallery and Municipal Libraries, Bath, stating that a letter signed by Samuel White had been found inside the cover of a volume of Church architecture, one of several books which had been presented to the Library a few days before. In due course Mr. Wright forwarded a copy of the letter to me. He was unable to account for how it came to be where he found it. As so often is the case when old papers are brought to light, the letter has survived by pure chance. Without the key to its significance which

Siamese White now provides, it would have occurred to nobody that it was a document of importance in an extraordinary Story.

The name of the man to whom it was addressed is not given, but internal evidence shows that he was the uncle of Mary Povey, Samuel White's wife, for she is described in it as his niece. Beyond that, his identity is unknown; we cannot say whether he was her paternal or maternal uncle, and whether, therefore, lie bore the name of Povey or her mother's maiden name, whatever that may have been.

The letter is a long one and of particular interest because it reveals the domestic side of White's character in more intimate detail than any of the documents available to me when I was writing this book. Two other original letters from White are extant, the one dated 20th September 1686, written to his brother George, in which the Macassar rebellion is described (a copy of it is in the British Museum) and the other dated 24th December 1687, addressed to Elihu Yale, the President of Fort St. George, Madras (preserved among the India Office records). But these letters, both of which are quoted from in my text, have nothing to do with family matters. It is true that Davenport tells us a certain amount about White's private affairs, but this new letter found in Bath was written two and a half years before Davenport entered on his duties as secretary.

Its date is 20th November 1683 and the address at the top is Ayudhya. That was the very week when White was created by King Narai Shāhbandar of Mergui, an appointment that made his fortune. He wrote in answer to a letter which he had received from the uncle in January 1683, ten months previously. Mary White had died at Mergui in September 1682, but the uncle, who had sent off his letter in the January of that year, had addressed himself to both White and his wife. White therefore had to start his letter by saying that Mary was dead. 'She poore heart was not soe fortunate to receive your welcome tidings of your health,' he explains, 'which she so long and earnestly desired, providence being pleased otherwise to order it by taking her to himself the 6 of September 82, her distemper a violent flux and what hastened her end was miscarrying of a 3 months child in the height of her distemper in which condition an escape is rarely heard of.' In my account on page 61 I assumed that she died of some tropical disease. We now see that it was probably dysentery, complicated by a miscarriage.

In his letter, to which the present is a reply, the uncle had reproached the Whites for having written him only one short note all the six years they had been abroad. White now explains how that happened. it will be recalled that Mary Povey's sudden jilting of Mr. Jearsay in 1676 had so shocked opinion at Fort St. George that the Minister of the Fort refused to marry her to Samuel White and they had to get the French padre to do it. in a small place like Madras this will have caused a great scandal and been very unpleasant for the young couple. White now tells the uncle that, in fact, they both did write to him at length, explaining how they came to marry. Since these letters were not received, they must have been lost in transit, 'no new thing,' remarks White, in view of the unreliability of posts between India and England. on their getting no reply, White continues, they assumed that he was 'disgusted' with them. That made them afraid to write again, except for the little note saying they were well, the brevity of which had seemed to him wanting in respect. 'But pray let all this bee buried in oblivion,' White urges, 'for if she had bin liveing I am well assured twould exceedingly trouble her in any measure to disoblige so worthy, not only relation, but friend. . . . Be so kind and charitable to forgitt what amisse.'

It appears that in the course of the uncle's letter he had said that they must not think that he disapproved of the marriage, for in fact he thought White not unworthy of his niece.

White now thanks him for this saying: 'I am indeed as a strainger extremely obliged for your good opinion and that you were pleased to be soe well content with her unexpected change and believe me my best endeavours shall always be imployed to deserve your esteem.'

The letter then deals with the matter of White's two daughters, Susan and Mary. He gives the dates of their births, 3rd October 1676 and 29th May 1678, from which it follows that Susan will have been born at Madras and Mary at Mergui. After the death of their mother in September 1682, he goes on, he kept the little girls with hint for another year, sending them home shortly before writing the present letter in charge of Captain Alley of the *Lumley Castle*. On page 26 I have given a glimpse of Captain Alley when he went ashore at HugE on 26th September 1683, It may be that the two children, by then seven and five years old respectively, were on board at the time, for from a sentence later in the present letter it seems that White was on the Indian coast early in September, where no doubt he met Alley and handed the children over to him. on leaving Hugli, Alley will have sailed for England, for that was the season for the homeward voyage.

White then tells the uncle that Captain Alley has instructions to deliver his charges to George White. But here he sees the possibility of trouble. Though certain that George would be kind to them, he was not quite sure of Mrs. George White, since she had been 'ever averse to a freindly correspondence to me and mine'. Should there be any coldness in their reception, he went on, Captain Alley had orders to board them with some suitable family and have them sent to school. The family should be people fitted to bring them up in comfort and with propriety. And he adds: 'I have ordered him (Captain Alley) to provide them with a maide servant and for defraying theire charges have ordered him £200 in England and on his shipp have sent to the amount of £400 more, consigned to Brother George for their use and will yearly remitt such effects as shall provide them for a future happier state.'

After speaking of this very ample prevision, which should be multiplied by at least five or six to get modem equivalents, White says that though he has implicit trust in Captain Alley, he would count it 'an inexpressible favour' if the uncle 'at leizure hours' would pay them visits 'however and wherever they bee and inquire into the manner of their entertainment', and report the result in his next letter, so as to avoid any possibility of their being unhappy through 'the frownes or hard usage of unnaturall relations or unkind friends. If either of theise should happen,' he declares, 'I shall take care to remove them, for I neither desire nor designe they shall be troublesome or depend on the courtesie of any.'

Having thus explained tow the children stood and asked his correspondent to have an eye to them, he refers to a rather delicate matter. It appears that the uncle, in his letter to White, had complained that Mary's father had asked him to pay her passage from England to Madras in 1675, but had never repaid him, 'which, since he is able,' writes White, 'really is very unkinde both to yourself and her.' He then declares that he is disinclined to take up the matter with 'ffather Povey', because he does not know hint personally and besides does not want to risk unpleasantness with his late wife's family. Rather than that, he will pay for the passage himself. 'Since in her life rime she was earnestly desirous you should be satisfied, I owe soe great and deserved respect to her memory that am willing to make good that obligation (if not already done by ffather Povey as ought) of whose amount I am altogether ignorant. Therefore let me know it by your next and I will order the payment of it in England, or here which you shall best approve of.'

So ends the part of the letter which has to do with White's family. It shows him in a very favourable light, tender to the memory of his wife, careful, wise and liberal towards his little daughters, amiable and generous to the uncle. Davenport did not deny that he was high principled in family matters. It will be recalled that in October 1686, when White was leaving Ayudhya after emerging successfully from the inquiry into his conduct and obtaining greatly increased emoluments from Phaulkon, Davenport records how his thoughts were with the children in England and how he sent home two thousand pounds' worth of goods, the proceeds of which were to be laid out on the purchase of land, to be held in trust for them. The passage (page 139) shows that George White and Thomas Povey, who was Mary's brother, were the children's guardians and trustees. This is evidence that George White received the children kindly and that their mother's family also rallied to them. I must note here that Mr. Wright, the finder of the letter, kindly examined the Bath Abbey burial register and after coming upon the entry under the year 1689: 'April 27. Mr. Samuell White, a stranger, in ye church' (which suggests that White's grave is somewhere inside the Abbey), discovered under the year 1692 the further entry: 'Aug. 17. Mary White.' If this entry, as seems likely, refers to the second of Samuel White's daughters, she must have died at the age of fourteen.

To return now to the rest of the letter, in his next paragraph White thanks the uncle for informing him that Sir William Langhorne had given him a good character. This person was one of the senior members of the East India Company. That he should have spoken as he did is further proof that up till the date of the uncle's letter (1682) White, though he had been serving on Siamese ships for six years, was still well liked by the Company.

The remainder of the letter may be shortly reviewed. It contains the news of his splendid appointment as Shāhbandar of Mergui, so remarkable a sign of the King's favour, he explains, that it encourages him to think of a longer stay in the East than he had originally intended. There follow notes on the interloper trade, wherein he declares forcibly how damaging to British trade in general is the East India Company's monopoly. He relates how, in order to prevent competition in the home market, the Company was in the habit of bribing the native Governors of ports on the Indian littoral to refuse cargoes to interlopers, a course which led the more wily governors to invite them, in order to frighten the Company and induce it to pay larger bribes. 'It is no strange thing here to ruine a country to serve some particular interest,' he concludes, and argues that the Company must open its books and admit new members or else the unregulated traffic will lead to overbuying in India with a resultant rise of prices, and at the same time to a flooding of the home market and so to a lowering of the selling price. White was always an anti-monopoly man and no admirer of the Stuarts. As the events of 1694 and 1708 (see page 280) were to prove, his views were a shrewd anticipation of what was to follow. Finally, it is amusing to note that he refers to the tricky Governor of Masulipatam, Ali Beague, as 'a mouster'.

This letter evidently satisfied the uncle and interested him too, for we find in its margin, entered in his neat clear handwriting, a concise summary of each paragraph, Indeed, he is so meticulous that even against the postscript, which stated that the bearer would deliver to him 'a gould headed Japan cane', he duly notes: 'A Goldheaded Staff.' The letter is not in White's hand, but in the regular and rather ornate hand of a clerk trained to engross documents. The signature, however, is White's, and here it is:

INDEX

Printed in Great Britain
by Amazon